Rest

(SERACETINOL)

written by:
Mark Powers

line art by:
Shawn McManus, Marco Castiello
and Abhishek Malsuni

colors by:
Lizzy John, William Farmer
Carlos Lopez and Michael Atiyeh

letters by:
Ed Dukeshire and Troy Peteri

created by:
Michael O'Sullivan

TOP COW PRODUCTIONS, INC.®

Rest℞™

(SERACETINOL)

special thanks to:

Steven Selikoff, Jeff Frankel
and The William Morris Agency

• • • • •

Josh Blaylock, Stephen Christy
and Sam Wells

• • • • •

Nelson Blake II

MATURE AUDIENCE
GRAPHIC CONTENT
SOME MATERIAL MAY NOT BE SUITABLE FOR CHILDREN

For Top Cow Productions, Inc.:
Marc Silvestri - Chief Executive Officer
Matt Hawkins - President and Chief Operating Officer
Filip Sablik - Publisher
Phil Smith - Managing Editor
Bryan Rountree - Assistant to the Publisher
Christine Dinh - Marketing Assistant
Mark Haynes - Webmaster
Atom Freeman - Direct-Market Liaison
Anthony McAfee and **Ernesto Gomez** - Interns

For DiVide Pictures:
Milo Ventimiglia and **Russ Cundiff**

for *image* comics
publisher:
Eric Stephenson

to find the comic shop nearest you call:
1-888-COMICBOOK

Want more info? check out:
www.topcow.com and ***www.thetopcowstore.com***
for news and exclusive Top Cow merchandise!

For this edition
Cover Art by:
Phil Jimenez & Lizzy John

For this edition
Book Design and Layout by:
Phil Smith

Original editions edited by:
Cody DeMatteis, Stephen Christy, Filip Sabilk & Phil Smith
Original editions Book Design and Layout by:
Sean K. Dove with Stephen Christy

REST volume 1 Trade Paperback, October 2010. FIRST PRINTING.
Softcover ISBN: 978-1-60706-192-2, Hardcover New York Comic-Con Exclusive ISBN: 978-1-60706-210-3
Published by Image Comics Inc. Office of Publication: 2134 Allston Way, 2nd Floor Berkeley, CA 94704. Softcover $14.99 U.S.D.. Convention Exclusive Hardcover $30.00 U.S.D.. Originally published in single magazine form as REST volume 1 issue #0-5.

PRINTED IN KOREA.

TABLE of CONTENTS

INTRODUCTION — PG.4

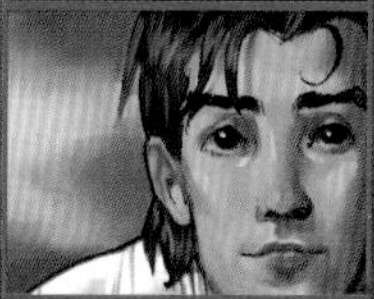

REST #0 — PG.6

REST #1 — PG.16

REST #2 — PG.40

REST #3 — PG.66

REST #4 — PG.90

REST #5 — PG.112

BONUS MATERIALS — PG.133

DIVIDE

Introduction

What if there was a drug that you could take that would keep you awake 24 hours a day, 7 days a week? What if you would never get drowsy or tired? What if that drug kept you at your sharpest, constantly?

What if the drug had NO side effects?

Would you take it?

That's REST, or what it's boiling down to. We have both lived with this story for a few years and this comic is only a window into a much larger world. In making this book, we both realized that working in independent publishing is fucking hard. We have so much respect for any publisher that puts out books consistently. Our hats are off to you. Over the past few months, our goal was to make sure REST got into a trade and finish the graphic novel - no matter what the cost.

There are so many people that made this book possible. The list is incredibly long and distinguished. We would like to thank Michael O' Sullivan for his amazing idea, Devil's Due Publishing for giving us entrée in the world and Stephen Christy who shared in our vision. Our genuine thanks goes out to Top Cow, Matt Hawkins, Filip Sablik and Philip Smith for finishing out the series. A special thank you goes to Mark Powers for being patient and 'hanging in there' with us.

We would also like to thank all the people that showed interest in this project. It's truly inspiring meeting all the different people involved with one comic. A heartfelt thank you to all the fans and to those who walked up to us individually and asked, "What about REST?" That question was always painful, but it drove us to the end goal which you are reading now.

Milo Ventimiglia & **Russ Cundiff**

26th Street
Santa Monica

We are DIVIDE™

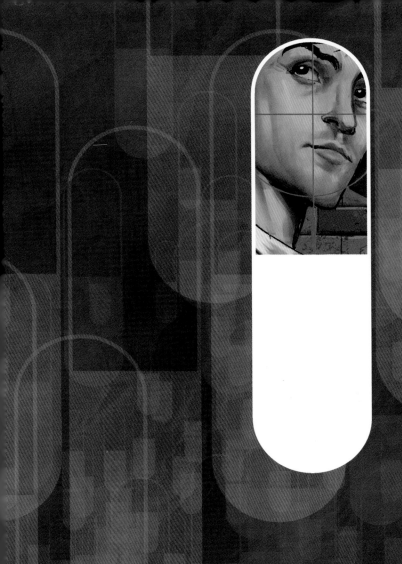

Rest #0

written by: **Mark Powers**
line art by: **Shawn McManus**
colors by: **Lizzy John**
letters by: **Ed Dukeshire**
• • • • •
original edition edited by: **Cody DeMatteis**
& Stephen Christy
original edition designed by: **Sean K. Dove**
with **Stephen Christy**

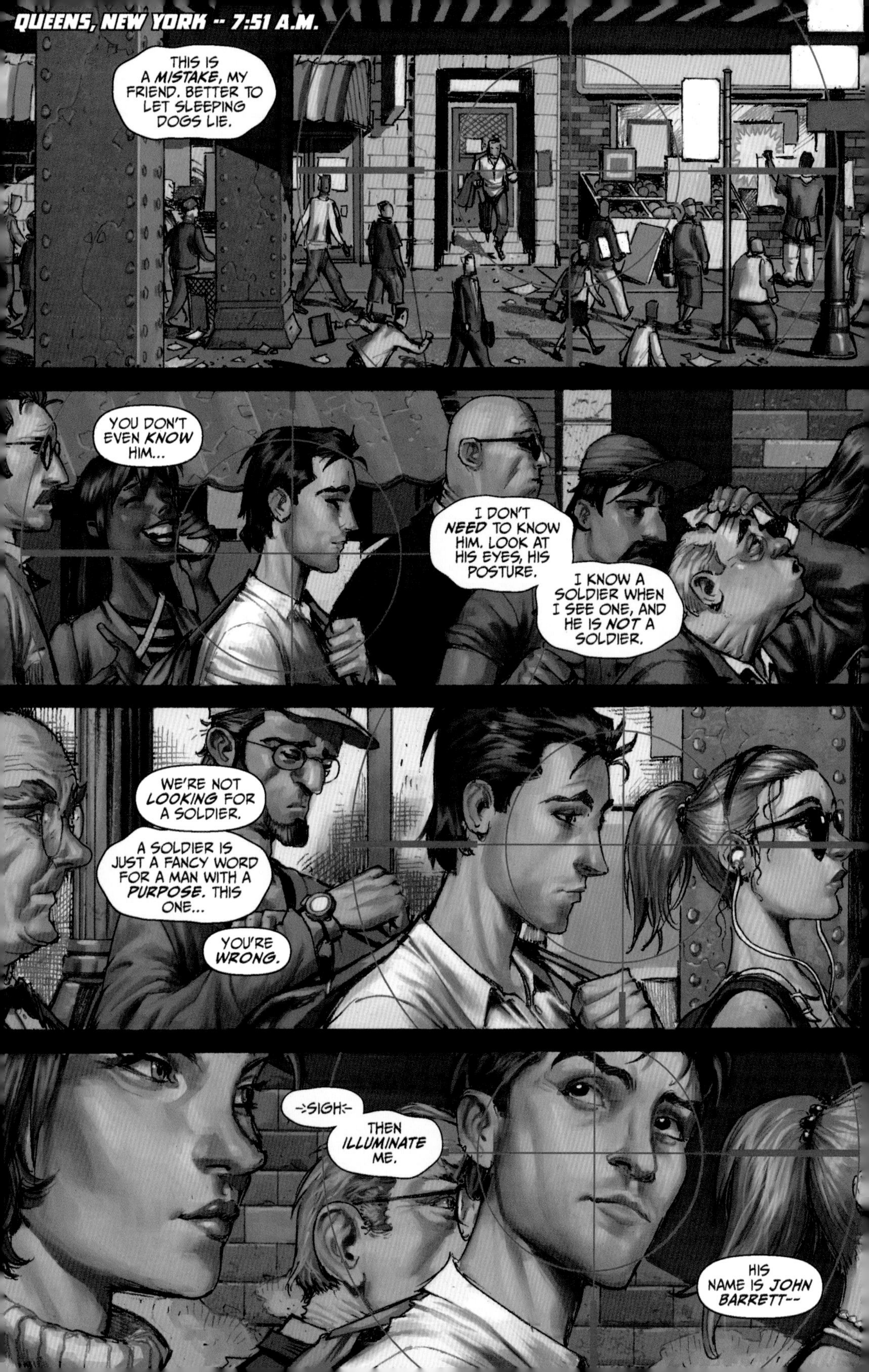
QUEENS, NEW YORK -- 7:51 A.M.
THIS IS A MISTAKE, MY FRIEND. BETTER TO LET SLEEPING DOGS LIE.
YOU DON'T EVEN KNOW HIM...
I DON'T NEED TO KNOW HIM. LOOK AT HIS EYES, HIS POSTURE.
I KNOW A SOLDIER WHEN I SEE ONE, AND HE IS NOT A SOLDIER.
WE'RE NOT LOOKING FOR A SOLDIER.
A SOLDIER IS JUST A FANCY WORD FOR A MAN WITH A PURPOSE. THIS ONE...
YOU'RE WRONG.
-SIGH-
THEN ILLUMINATE ME.
HIS NAME IS JOHN BARRETT--

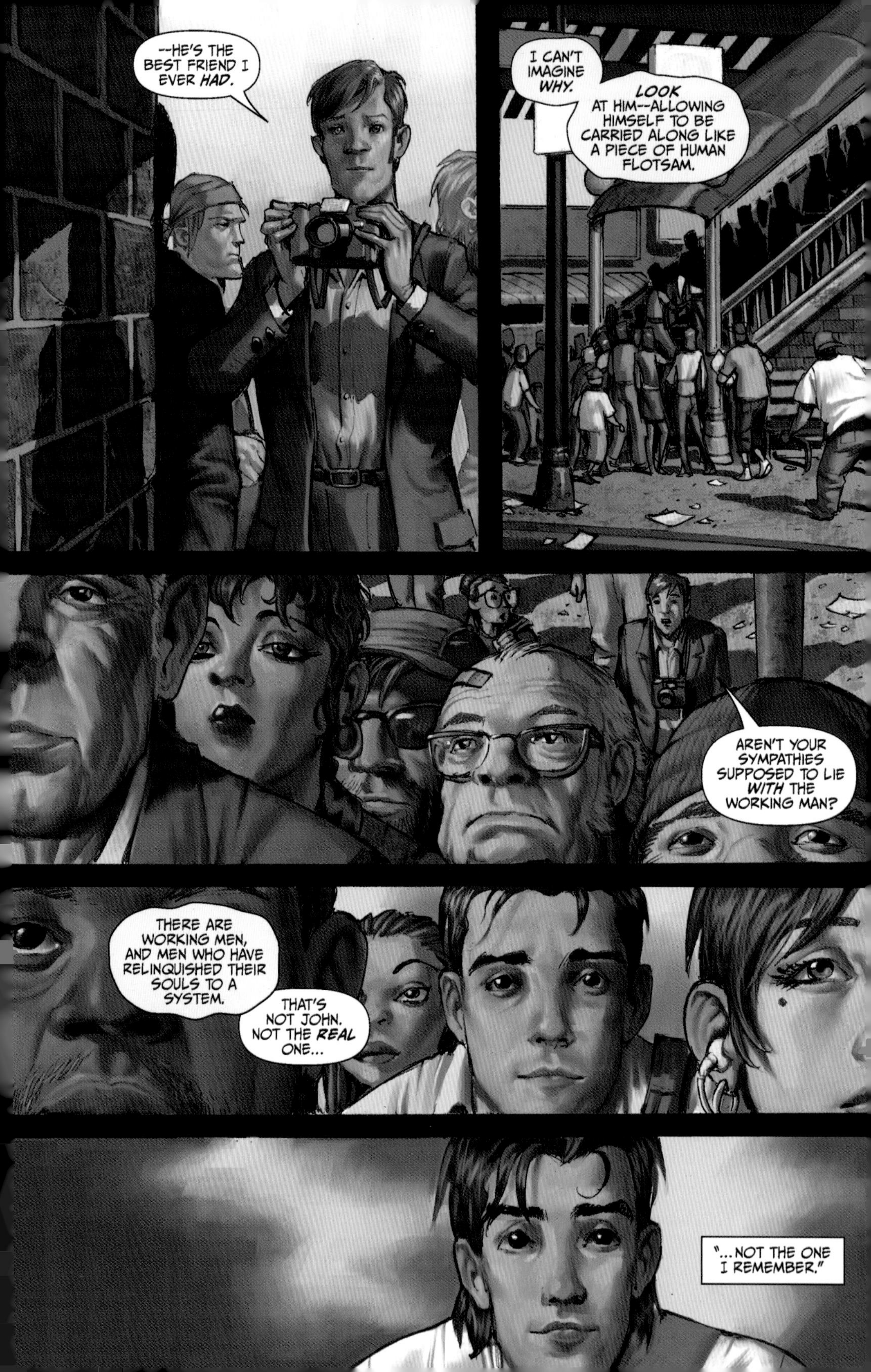
--HE'S THE BEST FRIEND I EVER *HAD*.
I CAN'T IMAGINE *WHY*.
LOOK AT HIM--ALLOWING HIMSELF TO BE CARRIED ALONG LIKE A PIECE OF HUMAN FLOTSAM.
AREN'T YOUR SYMPATHIES SUPPOSED TO LIE *WITH* THE WORKING MAN?
THERE ARE WORKING MEN, AND MEN WHO HAVE RELINQUISHED THEIR SOULS TO A SYSTEM.
THAT'S NOT JOHN. NOT THE *REAL* ONE...
"...NOT THE ONE I REMEMBER."

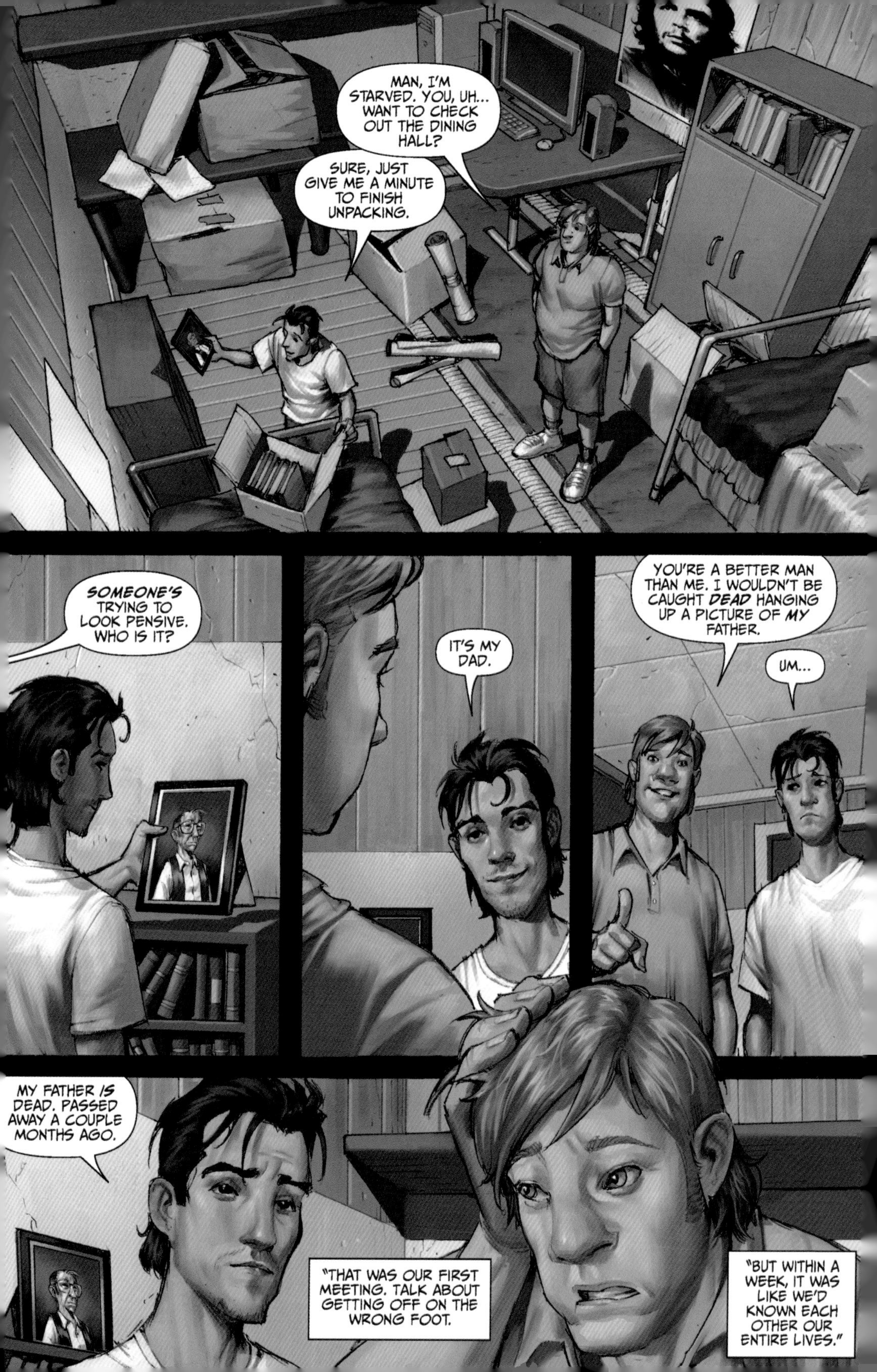
MAN, I'M STARVED. YOU, UH... WANT TO CHECK OUT THE DINING HALL?
SURE, JUST GIVE ME A MINUTE TO FINISH UNPACKING.
SOMEONE'S TRYING TO LOOK PENSIVE. WHO IS IT?
IT'S MY DAD.
YOU'RE A BETTER MAN THAN ME. I WOULDN'T BE CAUGHT DEAD HANGING UP A PICTURE OF MY FATHER.
UM...
MY FATHER IS DEAD. PASSED AWAY A COUPLE MONTHS AGO.
"THAT WAS OUR FIRST MEETING. TALK ABOUT GETTING OFF ON THE WRONG FOOT.
"BUT WITHIN A WEEK, IT WAS LIKE WE'D KNOWN EACH OTHER OUR ENTIRE LIVES."

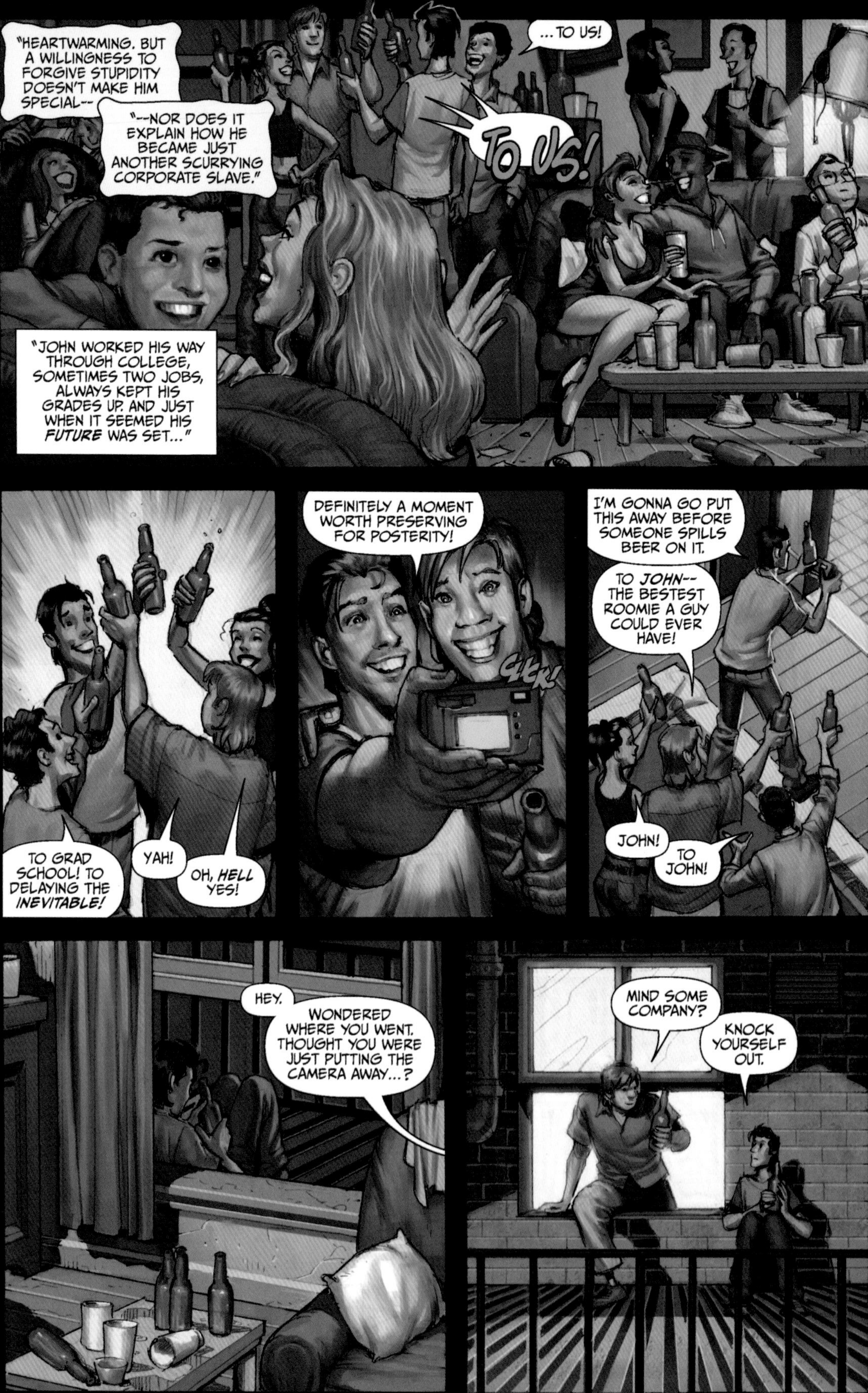
"HEARTWARMING. BUT A WILLINGNESS TO FORGIVE STUPIDITY DOESN'T MAKE HIM SPECIAL--
"--NOR DOES IT EXPLAIN HOW HE BECAME JUST ANOTHER SCURRYING CORPORATE SLAVE."
...TO US!
TO US!
"JOHN WORKED HIS WAY THROUGH COLLEGE, SOMETIMES TWO JOBS, ALWAYS KEPT HIS GRADES UP. AND JUST WHEN IT SEEMED HIS *FUTURE* WAS SET..."
TO GRAD SCHOOL! TO DELAYING THE *INEVITABLE!*
YAH!
OH, *HELL* YES!
DEFINITELY A MOMENT WORTH PRESERVING FOR POSTERITY!
CLICK!
I'M GONNA GO PUT THIS AWAY BEFORE SOMEONE SPILLS BEER ON IT.
TO *JOHN*-- THE BESTEST ROOMIE A GUY COULD EVER HAVE!
JOHN!
TO JOHN!
HEY.
WONDERED WHERE YOU WENT. THOUGHT YOU WERE JUST PUTTING THE CAMERA AWAY...?
MIND SOME COMPANY?
KNOCK YOURSELF OUT.

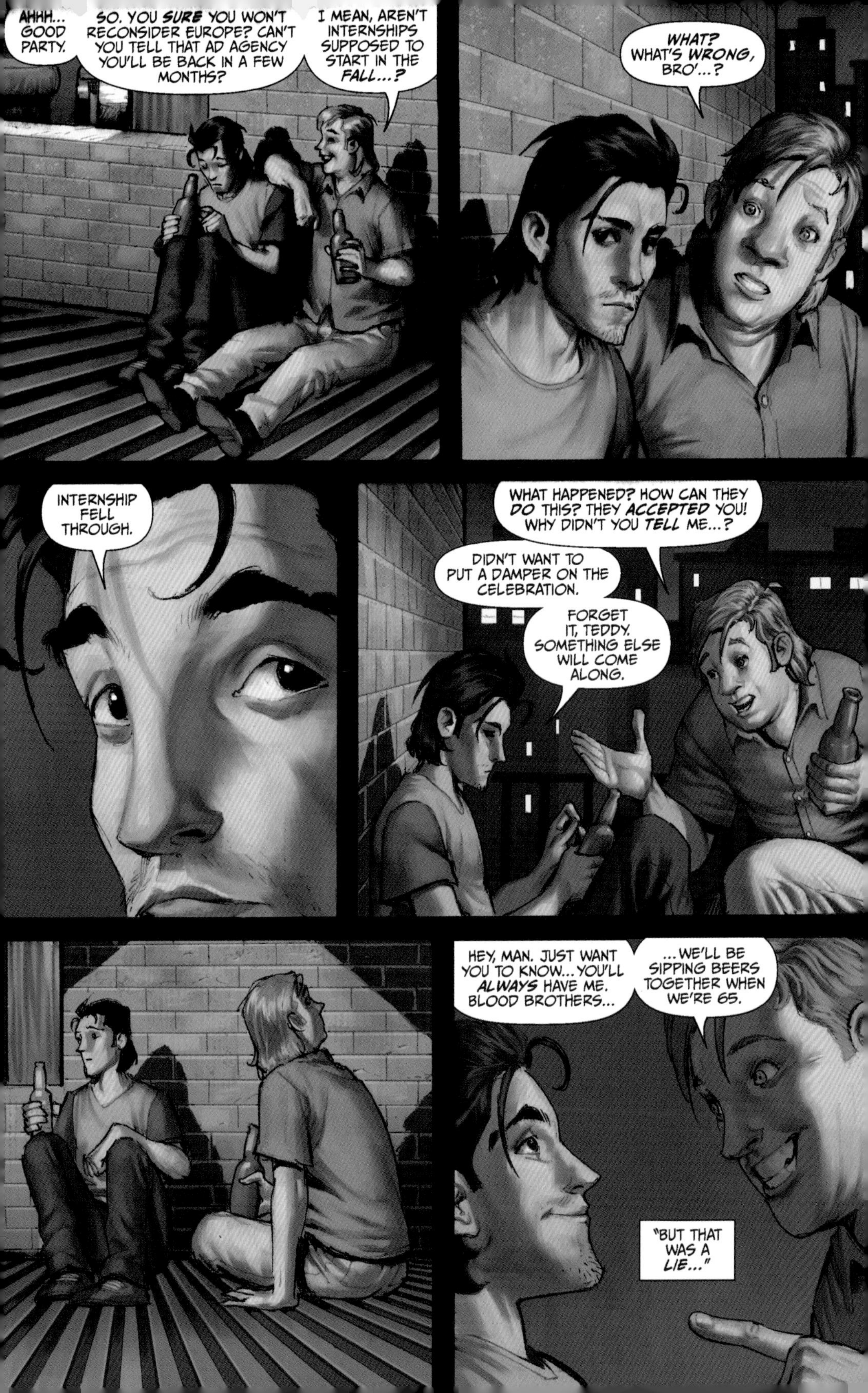
AHHH... GOOD PARTY.
SO. YOU *SURE* YOU WON'T RECONSIDER EUROPE? CAN'T YOU TELL THAT AD AGENCY YOU'LL BE BACK IN A FEW MONTHS?
I MEAN, AREN'T INTERNSHIPS SUPPOSED TO START IN THE *FALL...?*
WHAT? WHAT'S *WRONG,* BRO'...?
INTERNSHIP FELL THROUGH.
WHAT HAPPENED? HOW CAN THEY *DO* THIS? THEY *ACCEPTED* YOU! WHY DIDN'T YOU *TELL* ME...?
DIDN'T WANT TO PUT A DAMPER ON THE CELEBRATION.
FORGET IT, TEDDY. SOMETHING ELSE WILL COME ALONG.
HEY, MAN. JUST WANT YOU TO KNOW...YOU'LL *ALWAYS* HAVE ME. BLOOD BROTHERS...
...WE'LL BE SIPPING BEERS TOGETHER WHEN WE'RE 65.
"BUT THAT WAS A *LIE...*"

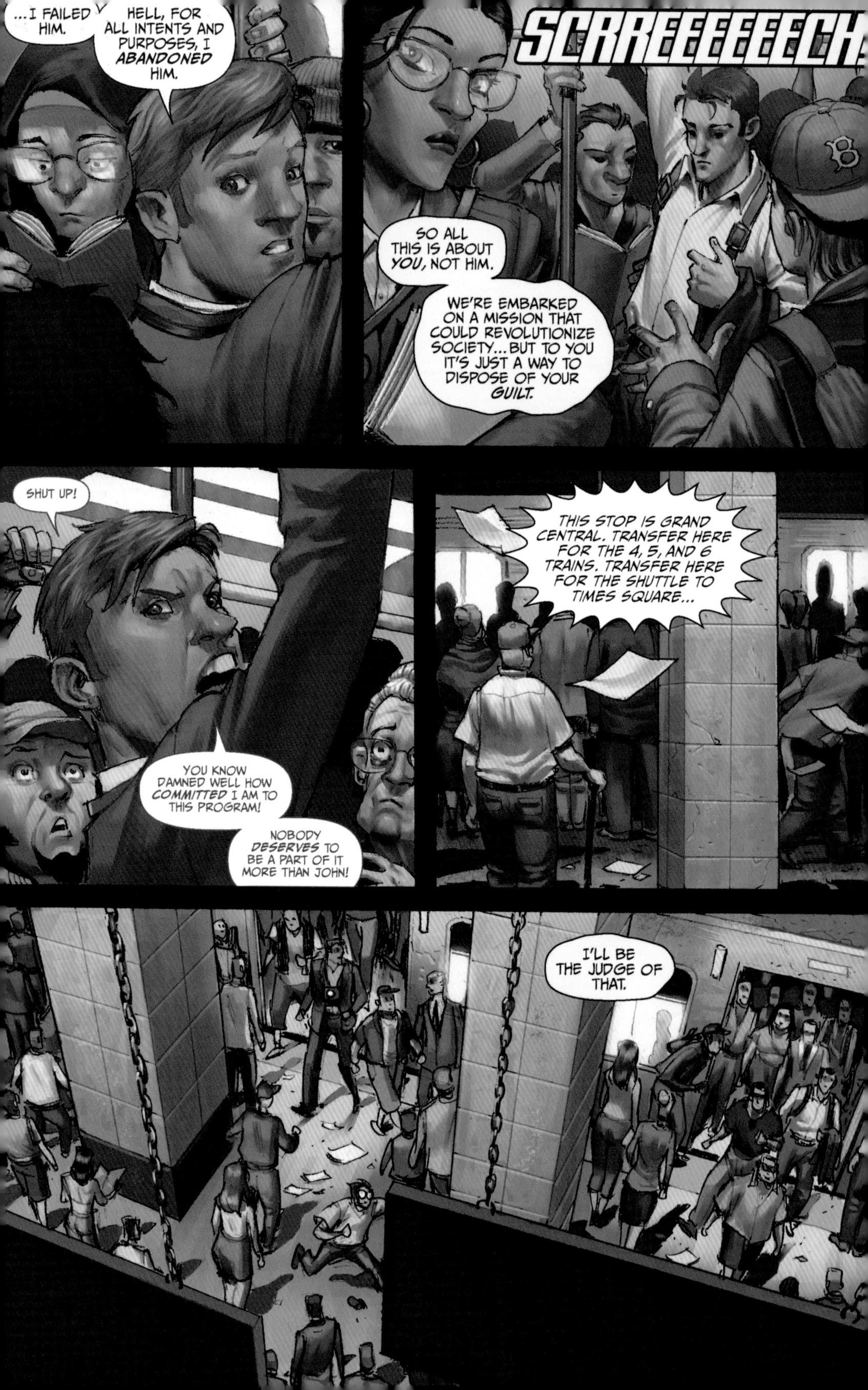
...I FAILED HIM.
HELL, FOR ALL INTENTS AND PURPOSES, I *ABANDONED* HIM.
SCRREEEEEEECH!
SO ALL THIS IS ABOUT *YOU*, NOT HIM.
WE'RE EMBARKED ON A MISSION THAT COULD REVOLUTIONIZE SOCIETY...BUT TO YOU IT'S JUST A WAY TO DISPOSE OF YOUR *GUILT.*
SHUT UP!
YOU KNOW DAMNED WELL HOW *COMMITTED* I AM TO THIS PROGRAM!
NOBODY *DESERVES* TO BE A PART OF IT MORE THAN JOHN!
THIS STOP IS GRAND CENTRAL. TRANSFER HERE FOR THE 4, 5, AND 6 TRAINS. TRANSFER HERE FOR THE SHUTTLE TO TIMES SQUARE...
I'LL BE THE JUDGE OF THAT.

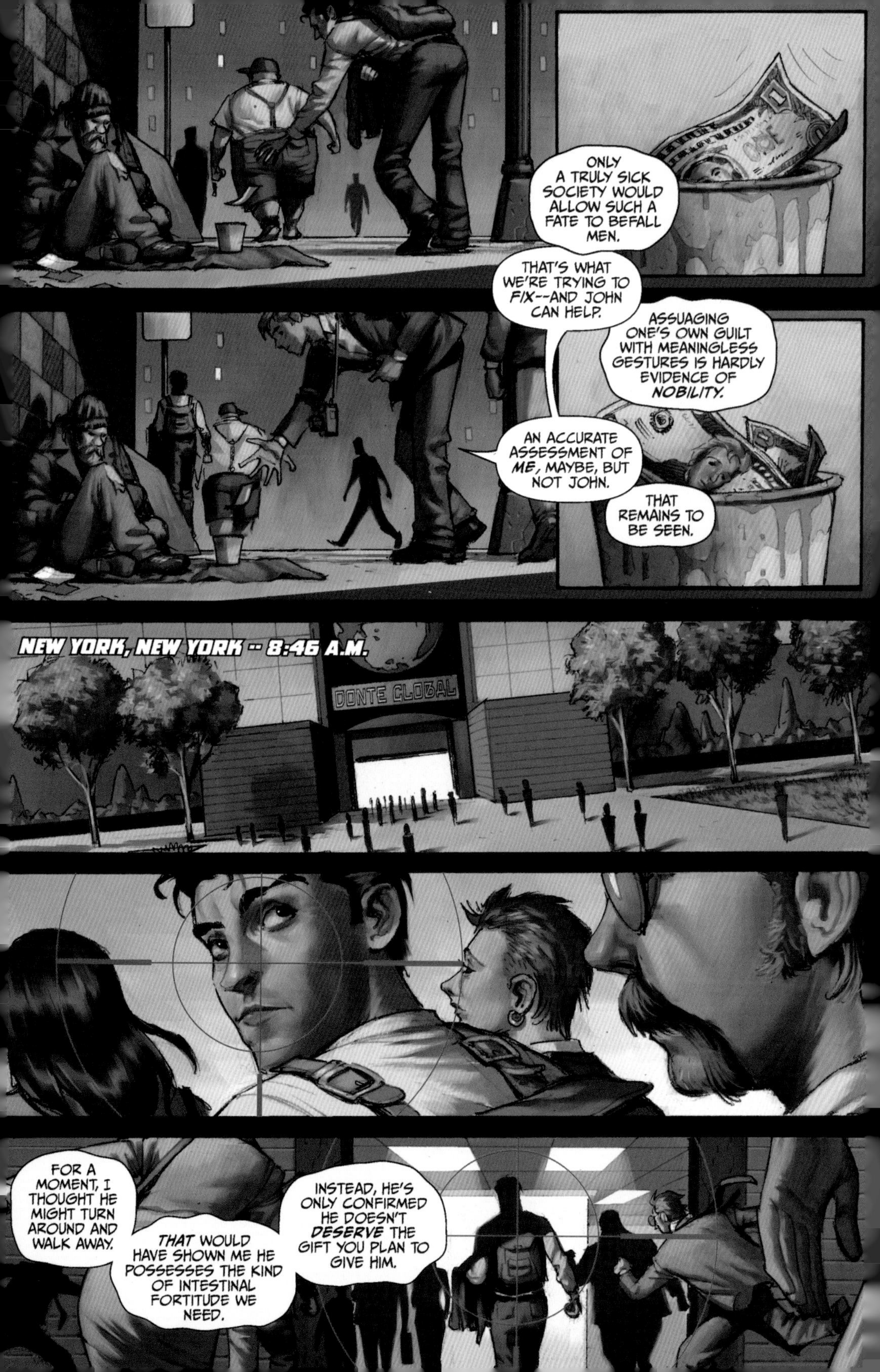
ONLY A TRULY SICK SOCIETY WOULD ALLOW SUCH A FATE TO BEFALL MEN.
THAT'S WHAT WE'RE TRYING TO FIX--AND JOHN CAN HELP.
ASSUAGING ONE'S OWN GUILT WITH MEANINGLESS GESTURES IS HARDLY EVIDENCE OF NOBILITY.
AN ACCURATE ASSESSMENT OF ME, MAYBE, BUT NOT JOHN.
THAT REMAINS TO BE SEEN.
NEW YORK, NEW YORK -- 8:46 A.M.
DONTE GLOBAL
FOR A MOMENT, I THOUGHT HE MIGHT TURN AROUND AND WALK AWAY.
THAT WOULD HAVE SHOWN ME HE POSSESSES THE KIND OF INTESTINAL FORTITUDE WE NEED.
INSTEAD, HE'S ONLY CONFIRMED HE DOESN'T DESERVE THE GIFT YOU PLAN TO GIVE HIM.

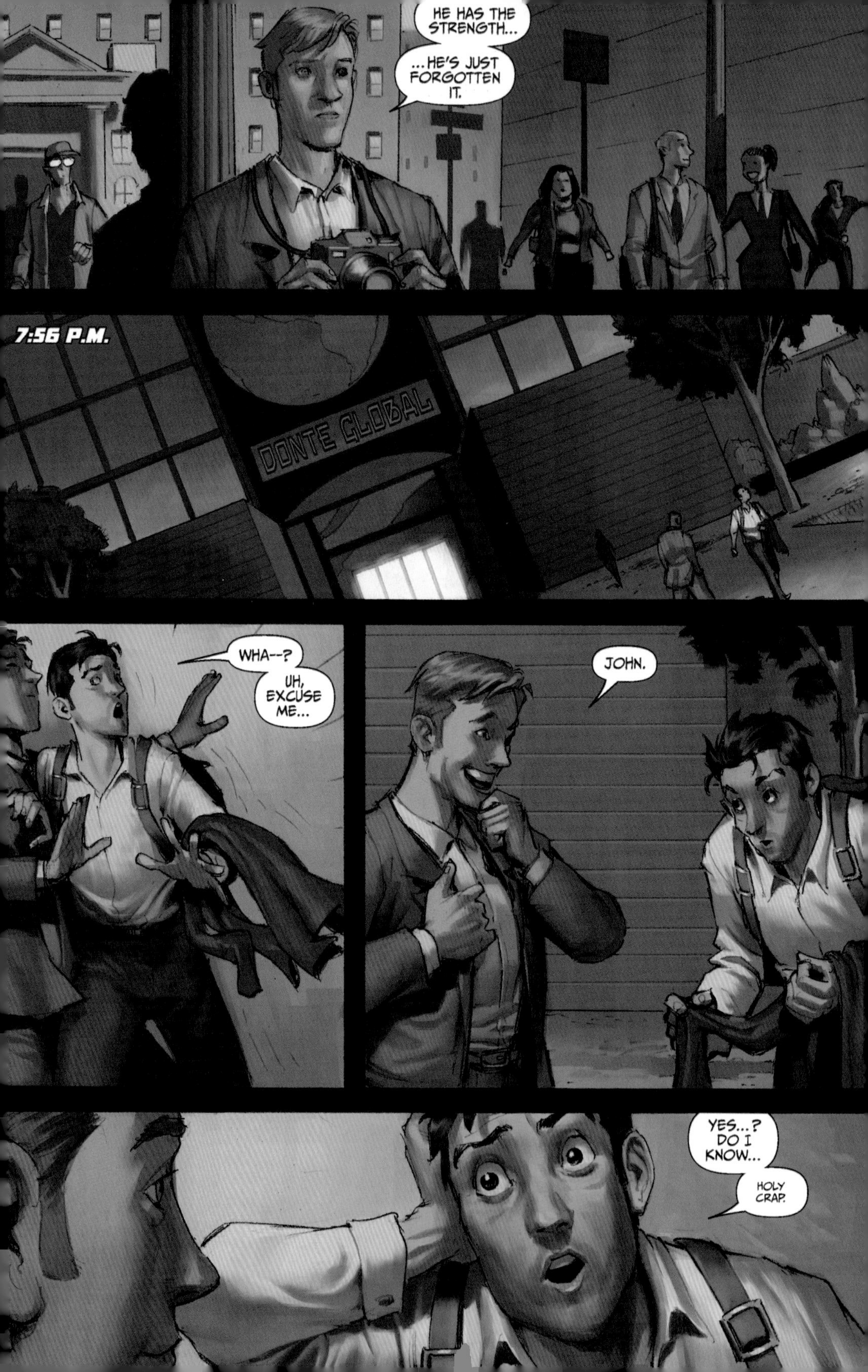
HE HAS THE STRENGTH...
...HE'S JUST FORGOTTEN IT.
7:56 P.M.
DONTE GLOBAL
WHA--?
UH, EXCUSE ME...
JOHN.
YES...? DO I KNOW...
HOLY CRAP.

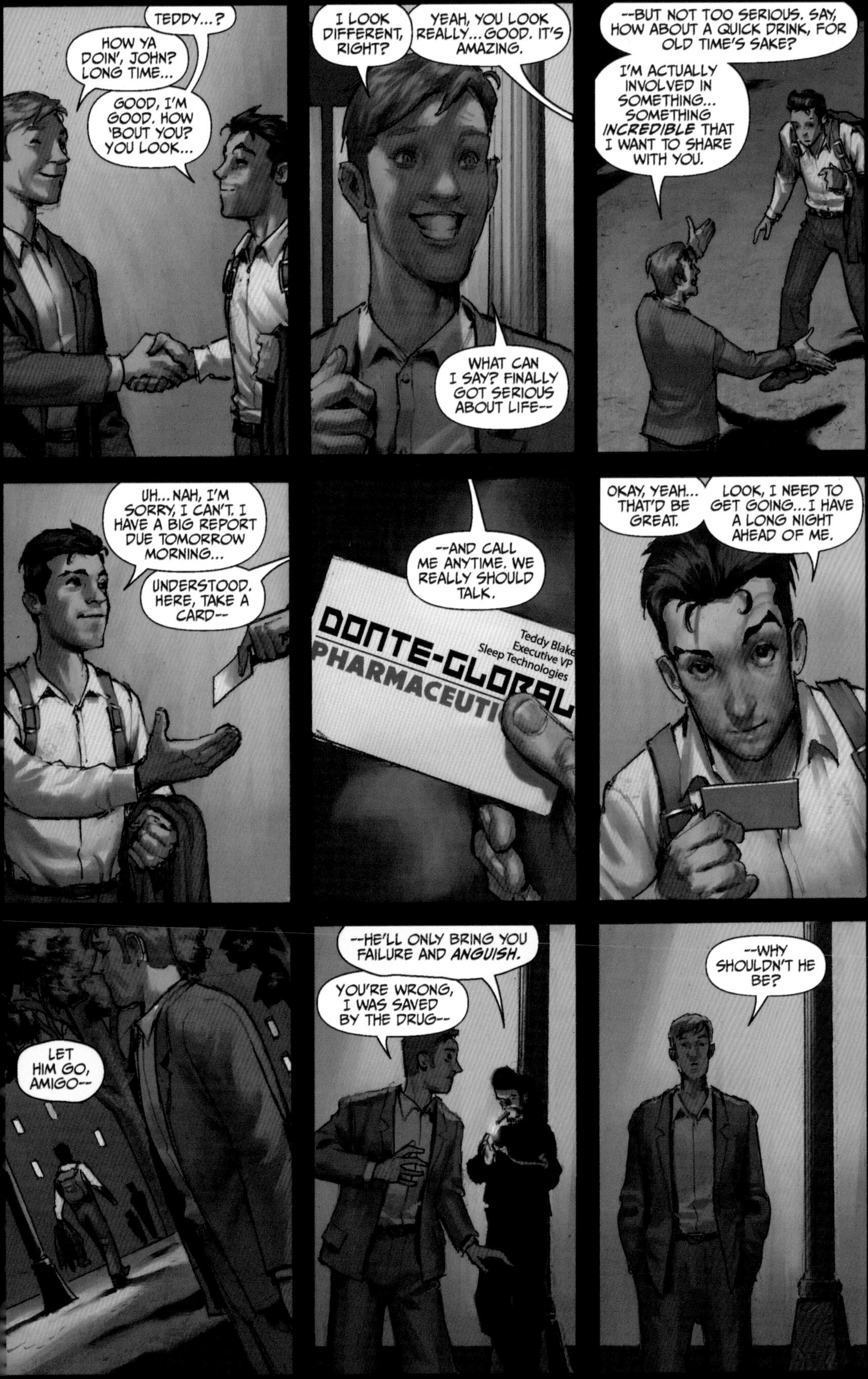
TEDDY...?
HOW YA DOIN', JOHN? LONG TIME...
GOOD, I'M GOOD. HOW 'BOUT YOU? YOU LOOK...
I LOOK DIFFERENT, RIGHT?
YEAH, YOU LOOK REALLY... GOOD. IT'S AMAZING.
WHAT CAN I SAY? FINALLY GOT SERIOUS ABOUT LIFE--
--BUT NOT TOO SERIOUS. SAY, HOW ABOUT A QUICK DRINK, FOR OLD TIME'S SAKE?
I'M ACTUALLY INVOLVED IN SOMETHING... SOMETHING INCREDIBLE THAT I WANT TO SHARE WITH YOU.
UH... NAH, I'M SORRY, I CAN'T. I HAVE A BIG REPORT DUE TOMORROW MORNING...
UNDERSTOOD. HERE, TAKE A CARD--
--AND CALL ME ANYTIME. WE REALLY SHOULD TALK.
Teddy Blake
Executive VP
Sleep Technologies
OKAY, YEAH... THAT'D BE GREAT.
LOOK, I NEED TO GET GOING... I HAVE A LONG NIGHT AHEAD OF ME.
LET HIM GO, AMIGO--
--HE'LL ONLY BRING YOU FAILURE AND ANGUISH.
YOU'RE WRONG, I WAS SAVED BY THE DRUG--
--WHY SHOULDN'T HE BE?

Rest #1

written by: **Mark Powers**
line art by: **Shawn McManus**
colors by: **Lizzy John**
letters by: **Ed Dukeshire**
• • • • •
original edition edited by: **Cody DeMatteis**
& Stephen Christy
original edition designed by: **Sean K. Dove**
with **Stephen Christy**

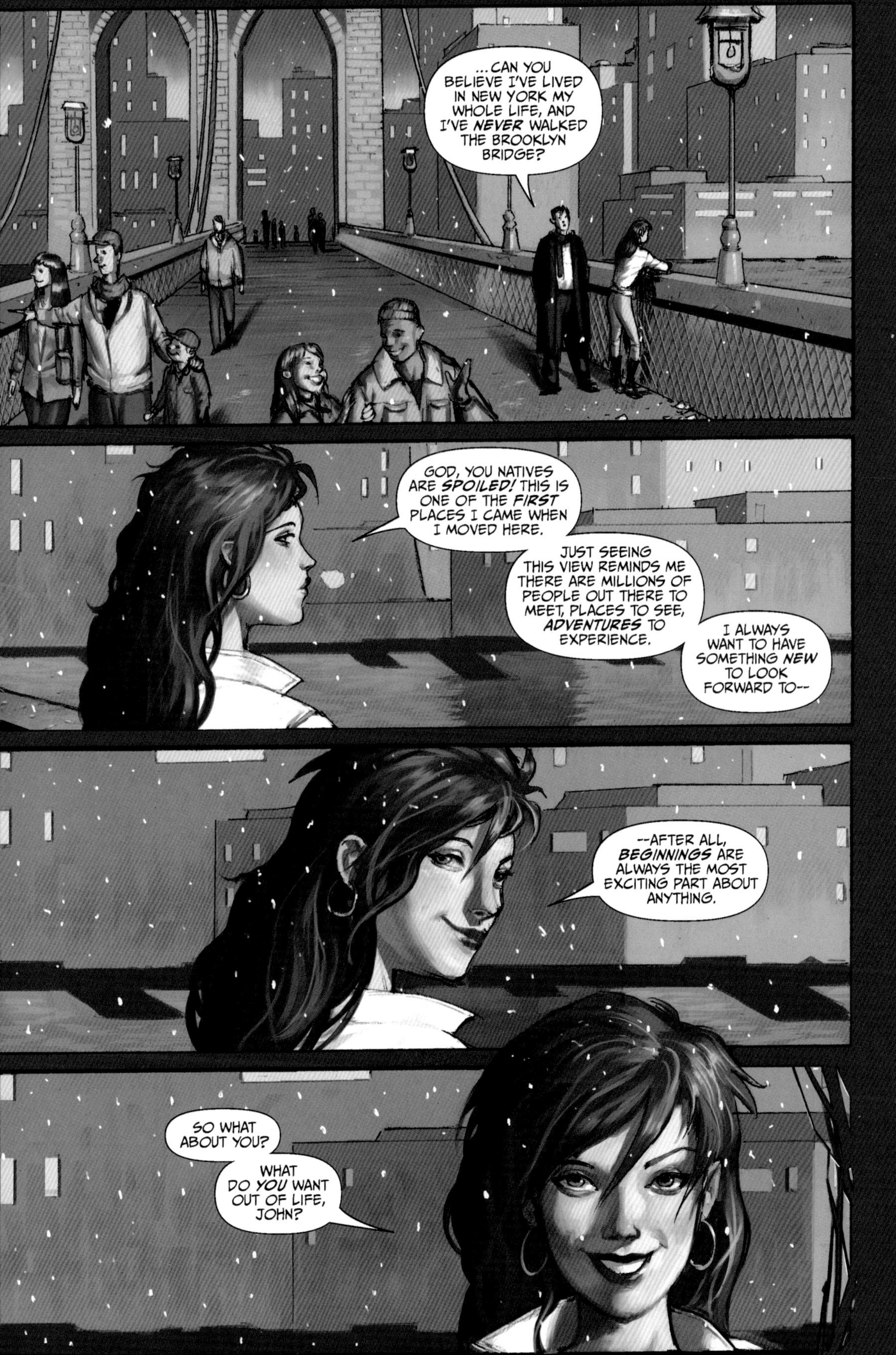
...CAN YOU BELIEVE I'VE LIVED IN NEW YORK MY WHOLE LIFE, AND I'VE *NEVER* WALKED THE BROOKLYN BRIDGE?
GOD, YOU NATIVES ARE *SPOILED!* THIS IS ONE OF THE *FIRST* PLACES I CAME WHEN I MOVED HERE.
JUST SEEING THIS VIEW REMINDS ME THERE ARE MILLIONS OF PEOPLE OUT THERE TO MEET, PLACES TO SEE, *ADVENTURES* TO EXPERIENCE.
I ALWAYS WANT TO HAVE SOMETHING *NEW* TO LOOK FORWARD TO--
--AFTER ALL, *BEGINNINGS* ARE ALWAYS THE MOST EXCITING PART ABOUT ANYTHING.
SO WHAT ABOUT YOU?
WHAT DO *YOU* WANT OUT OF LIFE, JOHN?

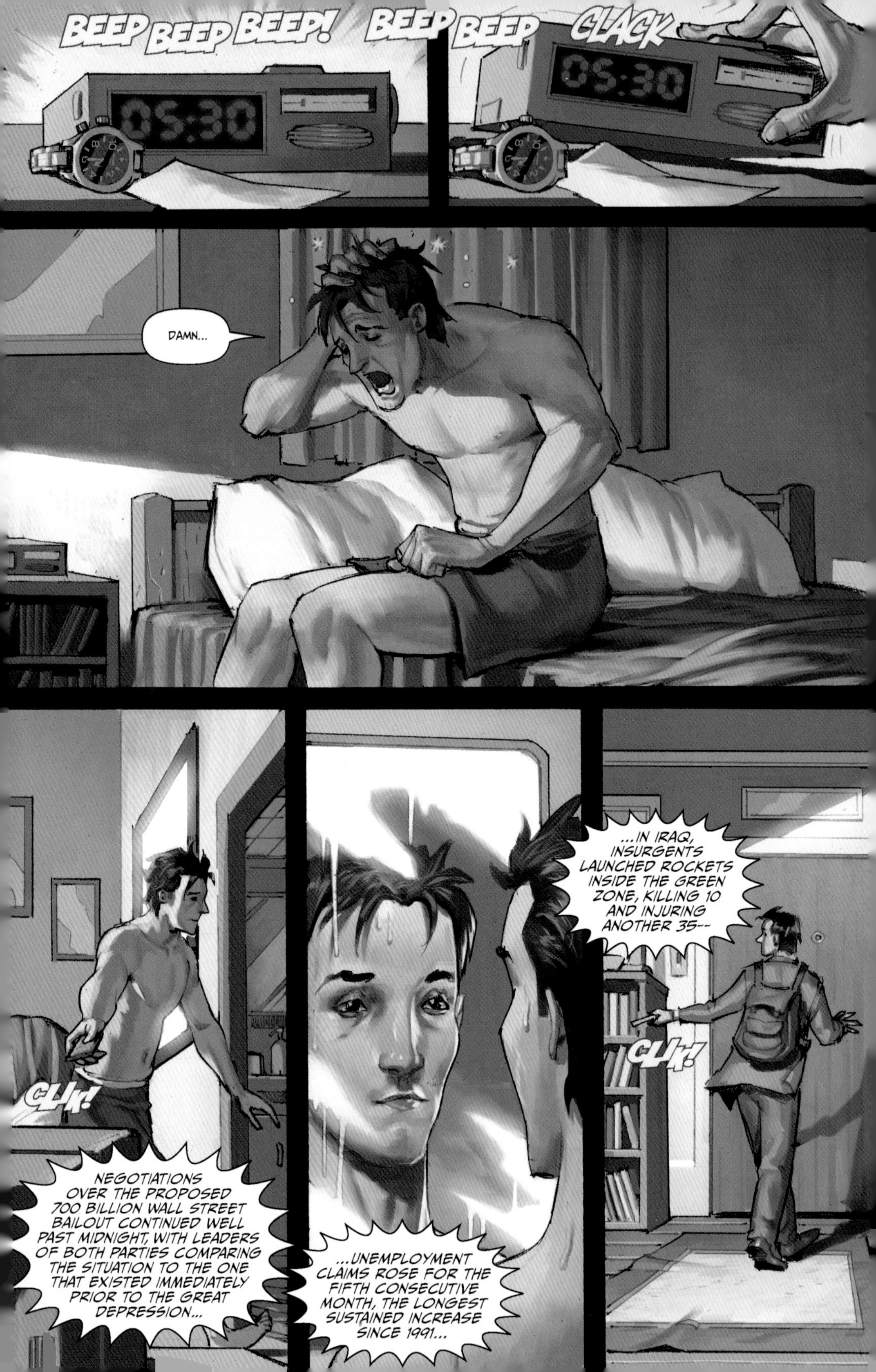
BEEP BEEP BEEP!
BEEP BEEP
CLACK
DAMN...
CLIK!
NEGOTIATIONS OVER THE PROPOSED 700 BILLION WALL STREET BAILOUT CONTINUED WELL PAST MIDNIGHT, WITH LEADERS OF BOTH PARTIES COMPARING THE SITUATION TO THE ONE THAT EXISTED IMMEDIATELY PRIOR TO THE GREAT DEPRESSION...
...UNEMPLOYMENT CLAIMS ROSE FOR THE FIFTH CONSECUTIVE MONTH, THE LONGEST SUSTAINED INCREASE SINCE 1991...
...IN IRAQ, INSURGENTS LAUNCHED ROCKETS INSIDE THE GREEN ZONE, KILLING 10 AND INJURING ANOTHER 35--
CLIK!

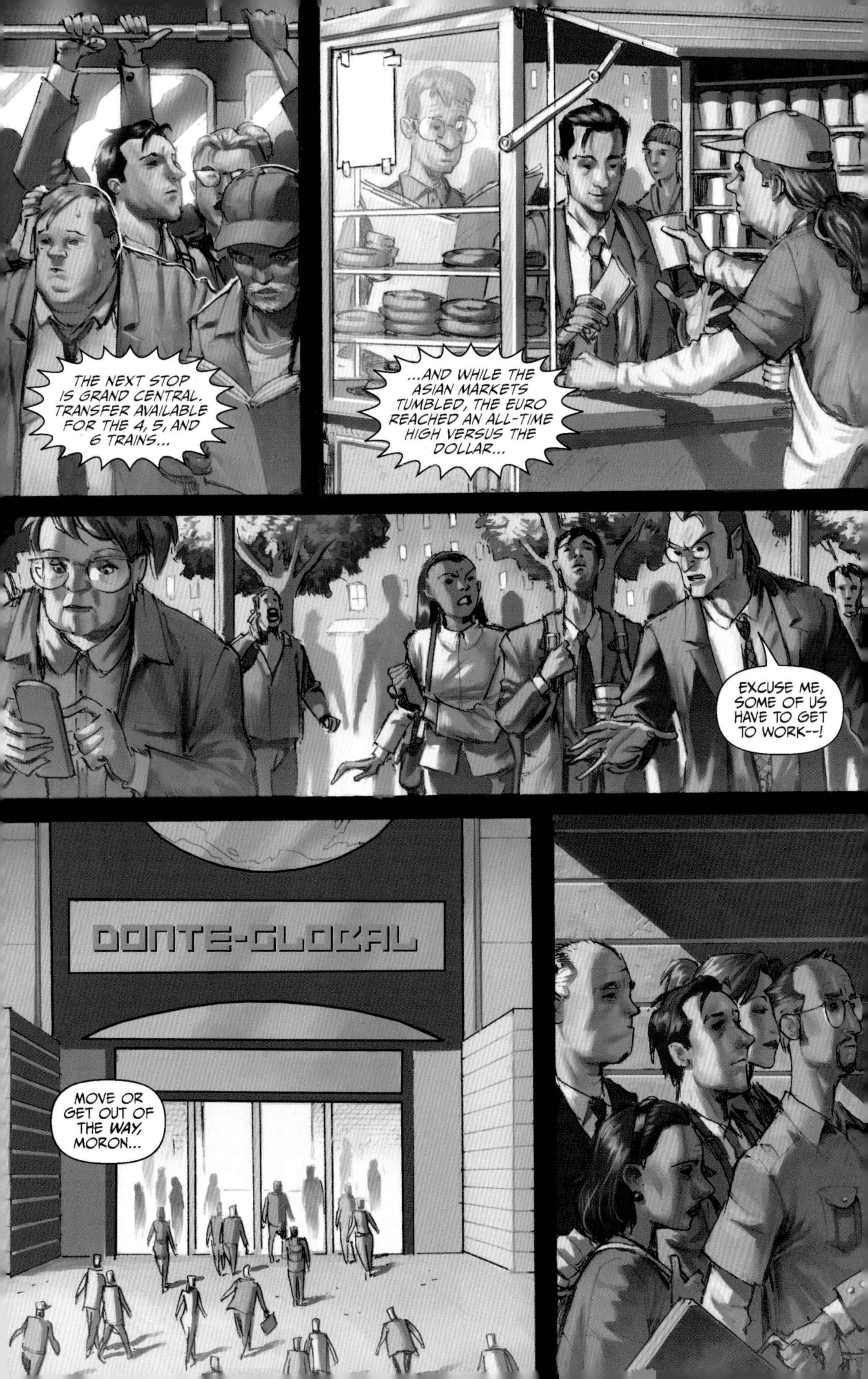
THE NEXT STOP IS GRAND CENTRAL. TRANSFER AVAILABLE FOR THE 4, 5, AND 6 TRAINS...
...AND WHILE THE ASIAN MARKETS TUMBLED, THE EURO REACHED AN ALL-TIME HIGH VERSUS THE DOLLAR...
EXCUSE ME, SOME OF US HAVE TO GET TO WORK--!
DONTE-GLOBAL
MOVE OR GET OUT OF THE WAY, MORON...

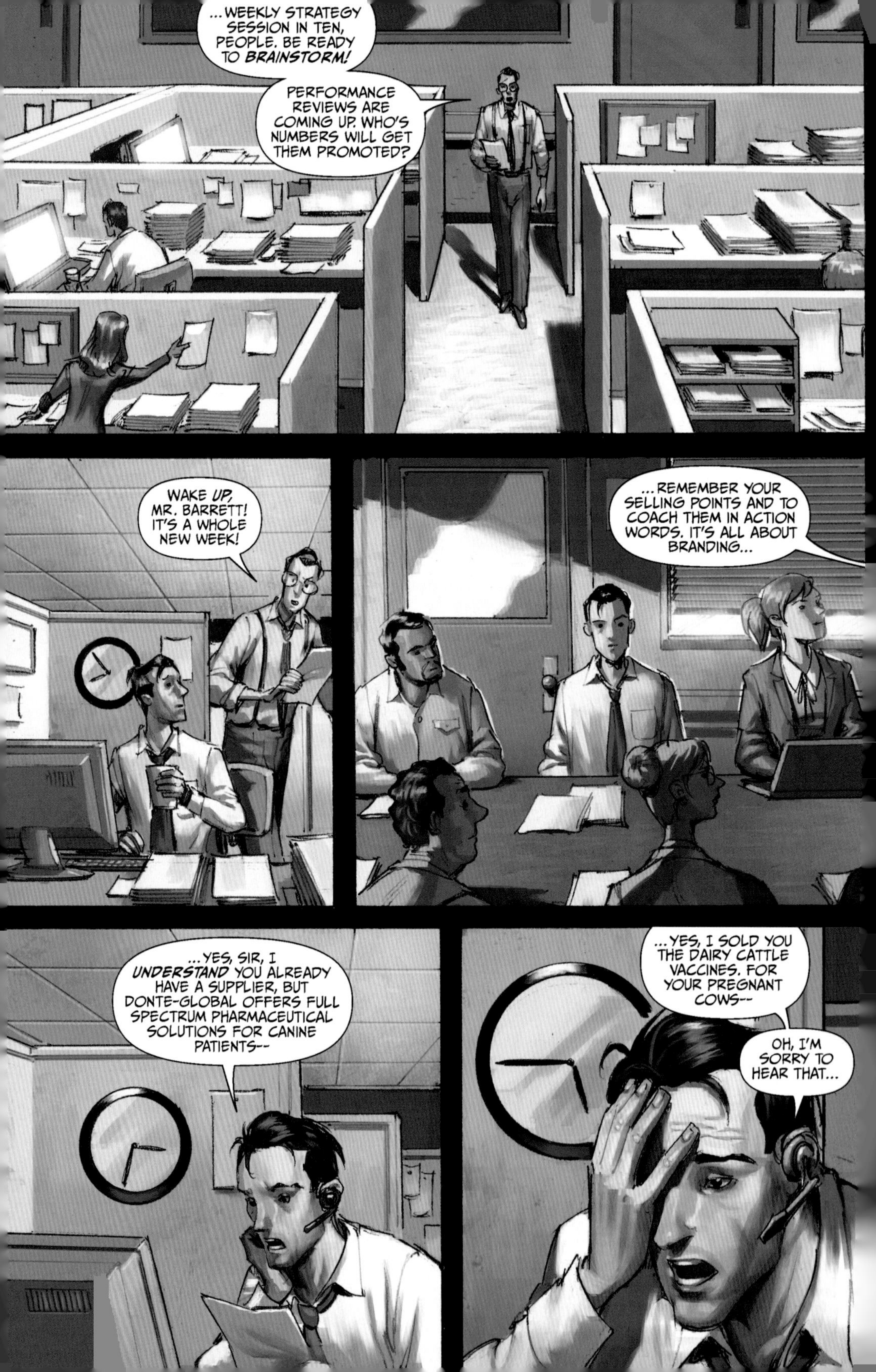
...WEEKLY STRATEGY SESSION IN TEN, PEOPLE. BE READY TO *BRAINSTORM!*
PERFORMANCE REVIEWS ARE COMING UP. WHO'S NUMBERS WILL GET THEM PROMOTED?
WAKE *UP,* MR. BARRETT! IT'S A WHOLE NEW WEEK!
...REMEMBER YOUR SELLING POINTS AND TO COACH THEM IN ACTION WORDS. IT'S ALL ABOUT BRANDING...
...YES, SIR, I *UNDERSTAND* YOU ALREADY HAVE A SUPPLIER, BUT DONTE-GLOBAL OFFERS FULL SPECTRUM PHARMACEUTICAL SOLUTIONS FOR CANINE PATIENTS--
...YES, I SOLD YOU THE DAIRY CATTLE VACCINES. FOR YOUR PREGNANT COWS--
OH, I'M SORRY TO HEAR THAT...

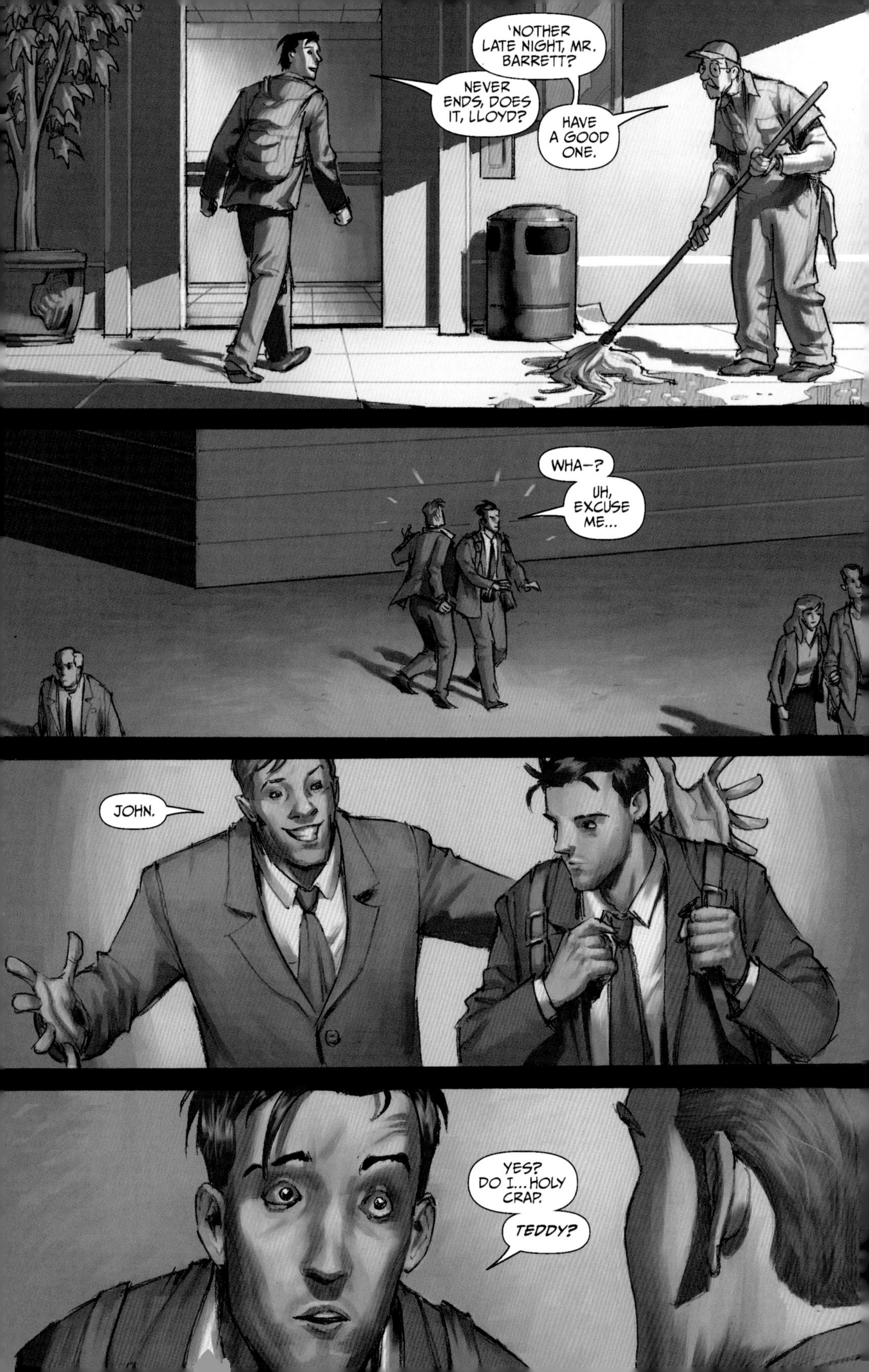
'NOTHER LATE NIGHT, MR. BARRETT?
NEVER ENDS, DOES IT, LLOYD?
HAVE A GOOD ONE.
WHA–?
UH, EXCUSE ME...
JOHN.
YES? DO I...HOLY CRAP.
TEDDY?

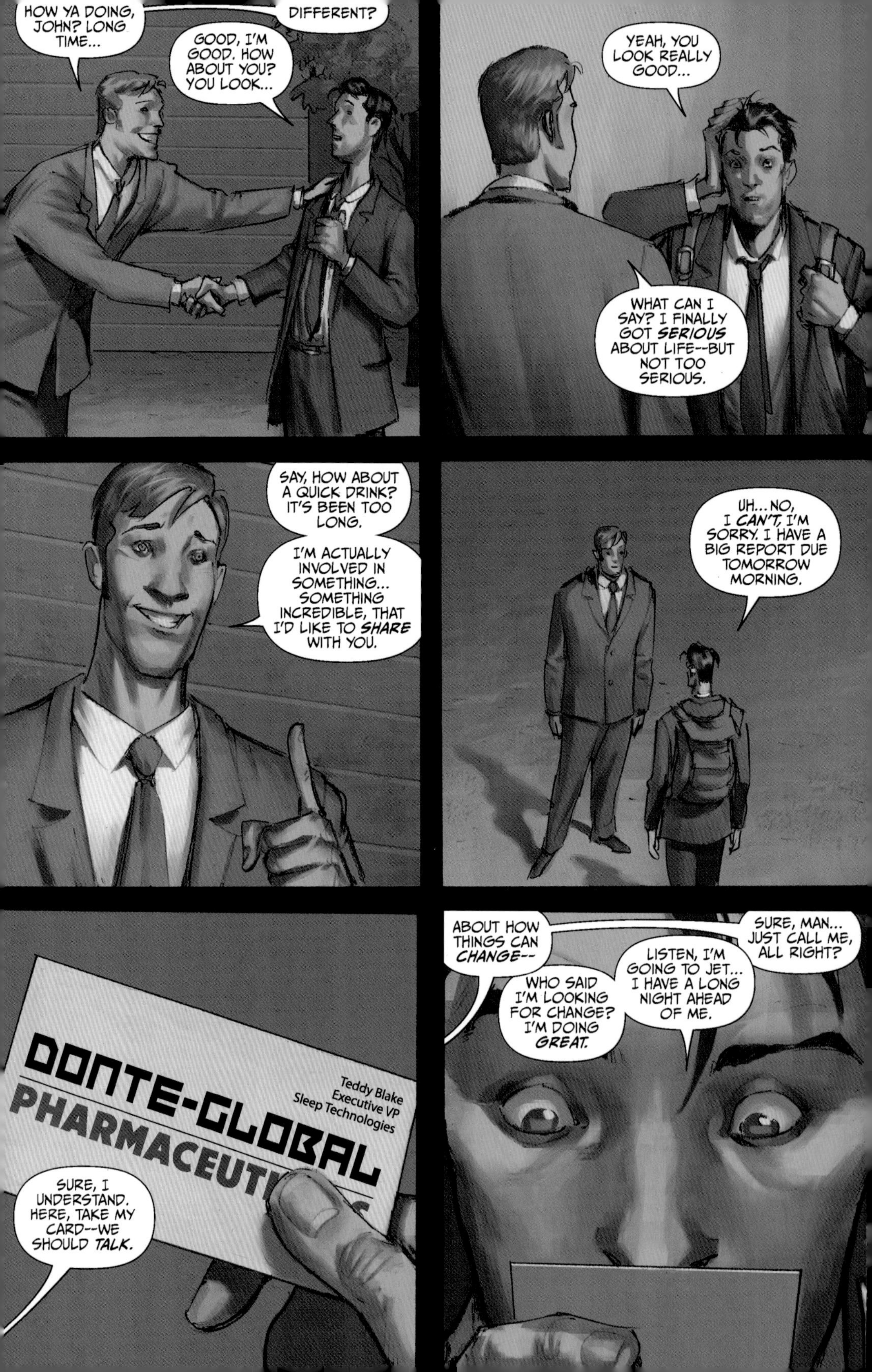
HOW YA DOING, JOHN? LONG TIME...
GOOD, I'M GOOD. HOW ABOUT YOU? YOU LOOK...
DIFFERENT?
YEAH, YOU LOOK REALLY GOOD...
WHAT CAN I SAY? I FINALLY GOT SERIOUS ABOUT LIFE--BUT NOT TOO SERIOUS.
SAY, HOW ABOUT A QUICK DRINK? IT'S BEEN TOO LONG.
I'M ACTUALLY INVOLVED IN SOMETHING... SOMETHING INCREDIBLE, THAT I'D LIKE TO SHARE WITH YOU.
UH... NO, I CAN'T, I'M SORRY. I HAVE A BIG REPORT DUE TOMORROW MORNING.
DONTE-GLOBAL
PHARMACEUTI
Teddy Blake
Executive VP
Sleep Technologies
SURE, I UNDERSTAND. HERE, TAKE MY CARD--WE SHOULD TALK.
ABOUT HOW THINGS CAN CHANGE--
WHO SAID I'M LOOKING FOR CHANGE? I'M DOING GREAT.
LISTEN, I'M GOING TO JET... I HAVE A LONG NIGHT AHEAD OF ME.
SURE, MAN... JUST CALL ME, ALL RIGHT?

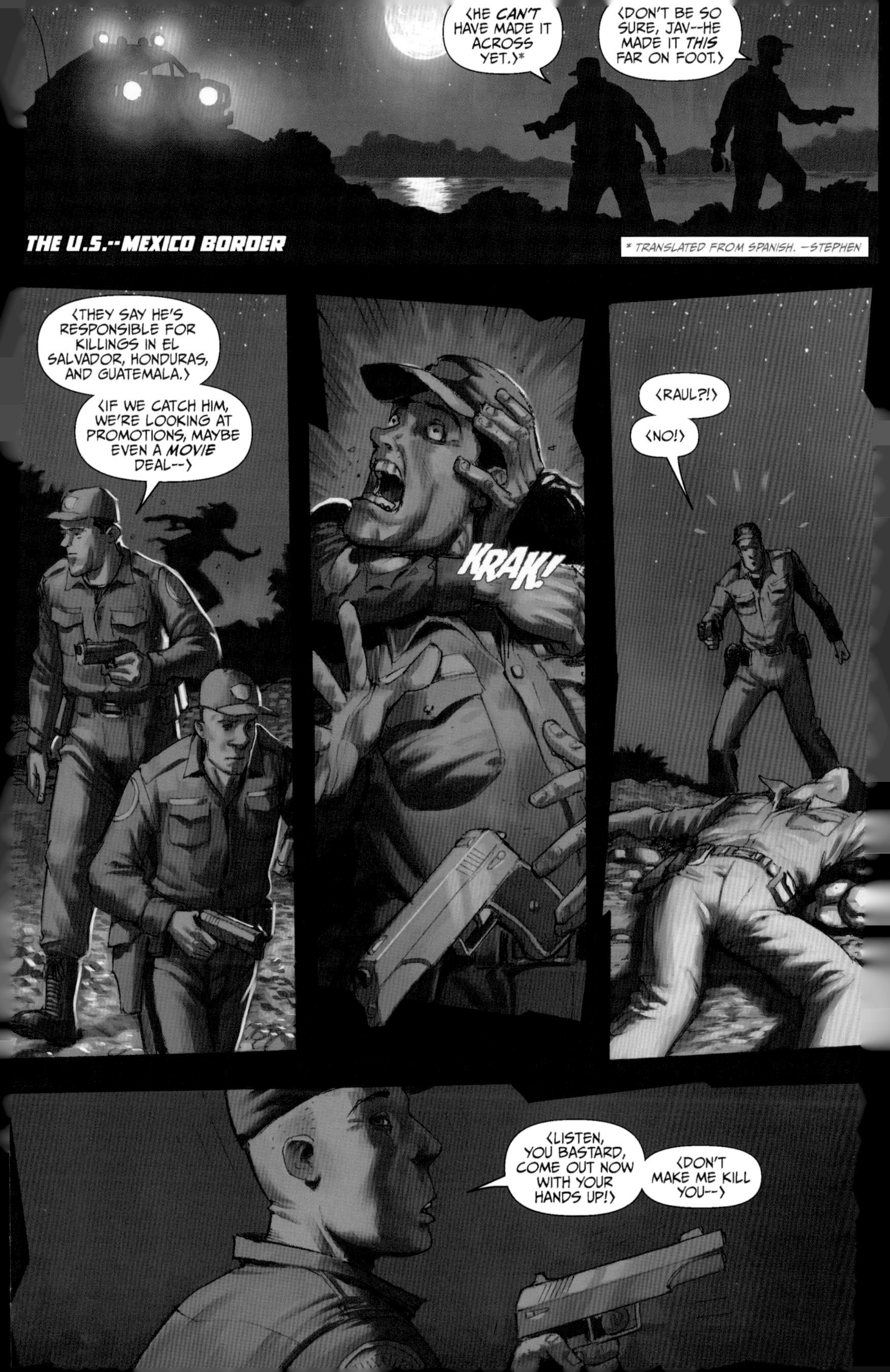
THE U.S.--MEXICO BORDER
⟨HE CAN'T HAVE MADE IT ACROSS YET.⟩*
⟨DON'T BE SO SURE, JAV--HE MADE IT THIS FAR ON FOOT.⟩
* TRANSLATED FROM SPANISH. —STEPHEN
⟨THEY SAY HE'S RESPONSIBLE FOR KILLINGS IN EL SALVADOR, HONDURAS, AND GUATEMALA.⟩
⟨IF WE CATCH HIM, WE'RE LOOKING AT PROMOTIONS, MAYBE EVEN A MOVIE DEAL--⟩
KRAK!
⟨RAUL?!⟩
⟨NO!⟩
⟨LISTEN, YOU BASTARD, COME OUT NOW WITH YOUR HANDS UP!⟩
⟨DON'T MAKE ME KILL YOU--⟩

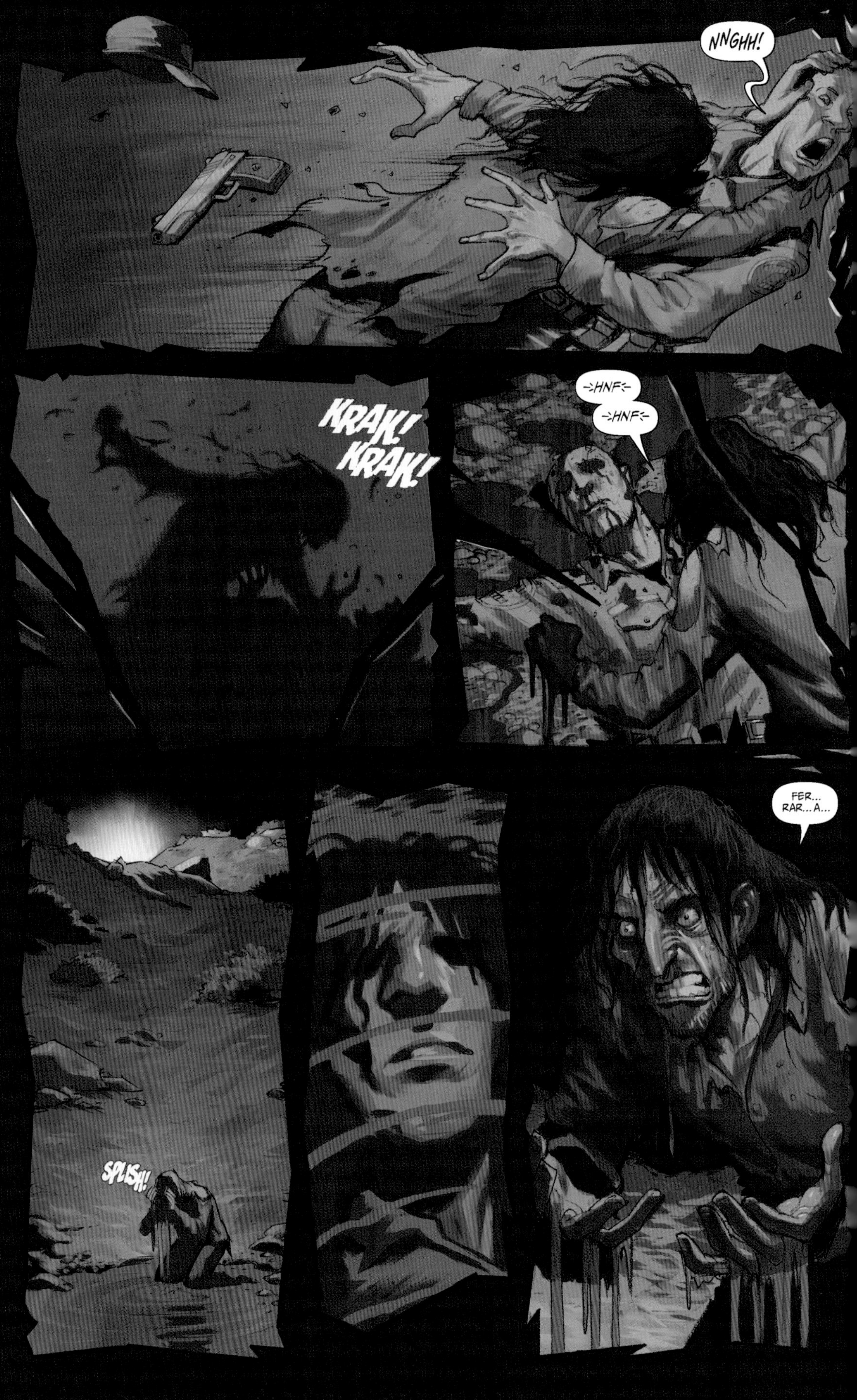
NNGHH!
KRAK! KRAK!
HNF
HNF
SPLISH!
FER... RAR... A...

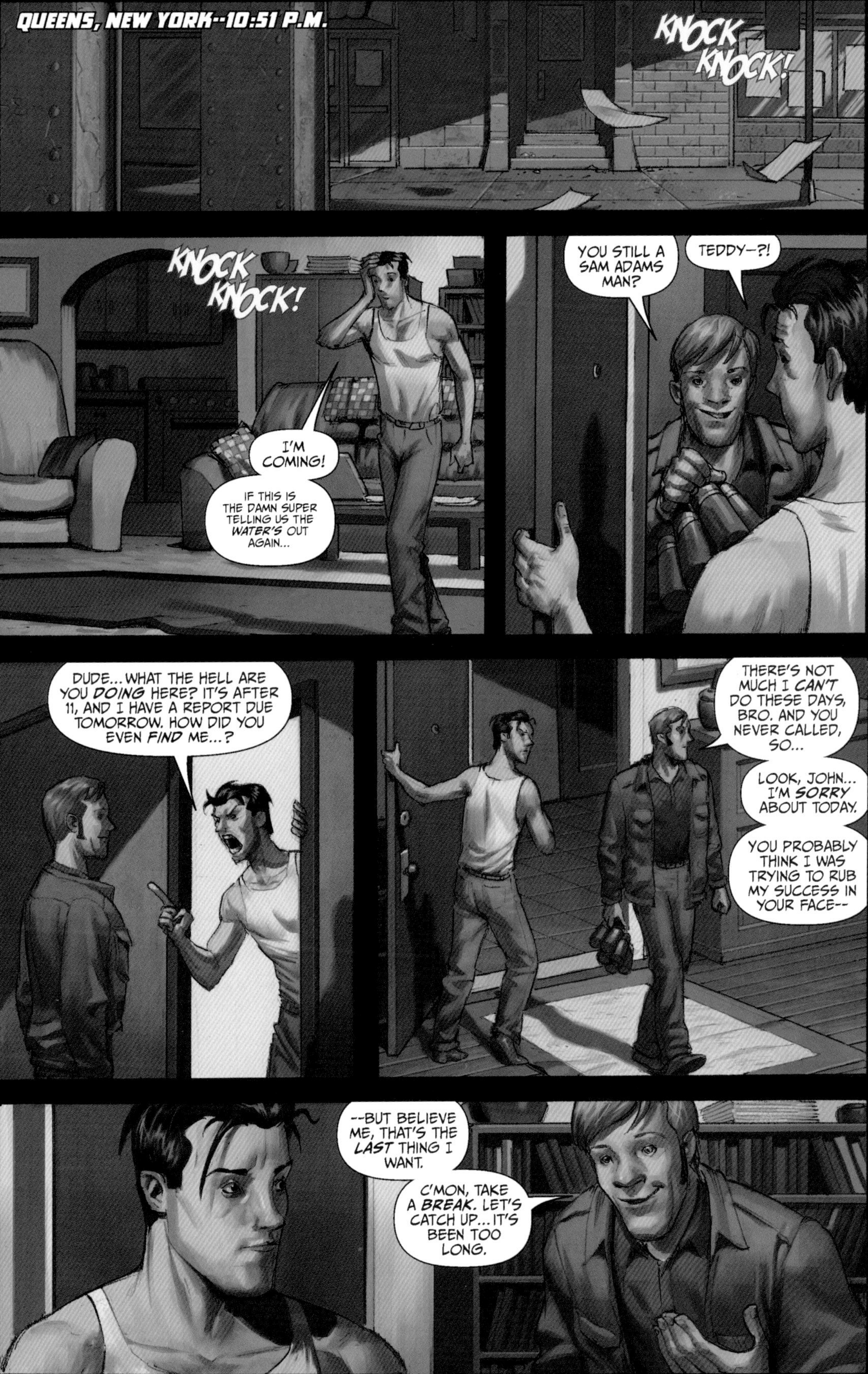
QUEENS, NEW YORK--10:51 P.M.
KNOCK KNOCK!
KNOCK KNOCK!
I'M COMING!
IF THIS IS THE DAMN SUPER TELLING US THE WATER'S OUT AGAIN...
YOU STILL A SAM ADAMS MAN?
TEDDY--?!
DUDE... WHAT THE HELL ARE YOU DOING HERE? IT'S AFTER 11, AND I HAVE A REPORT DUE TOMORROW. HOW DID YOU EVEN FIND ME...?
THERE'S NOT MUCH I CAN'T DO THESE DAYS, BRO. AND YOU NEVER CALLED, SO...
LOOK, JOHN... I'M SORRY ABOUT TODAY.
YOU PROBABLY THINK I WAS TRYING TO RUB MY SUCCESS IN YOUR FACE--
--BUT BELIEVE ME, THAT'S THE LAST THING I WANT.
C'MON, TAKE A BREAK. LET'S CATCH UP... IT'S BEEN TOO LONG.

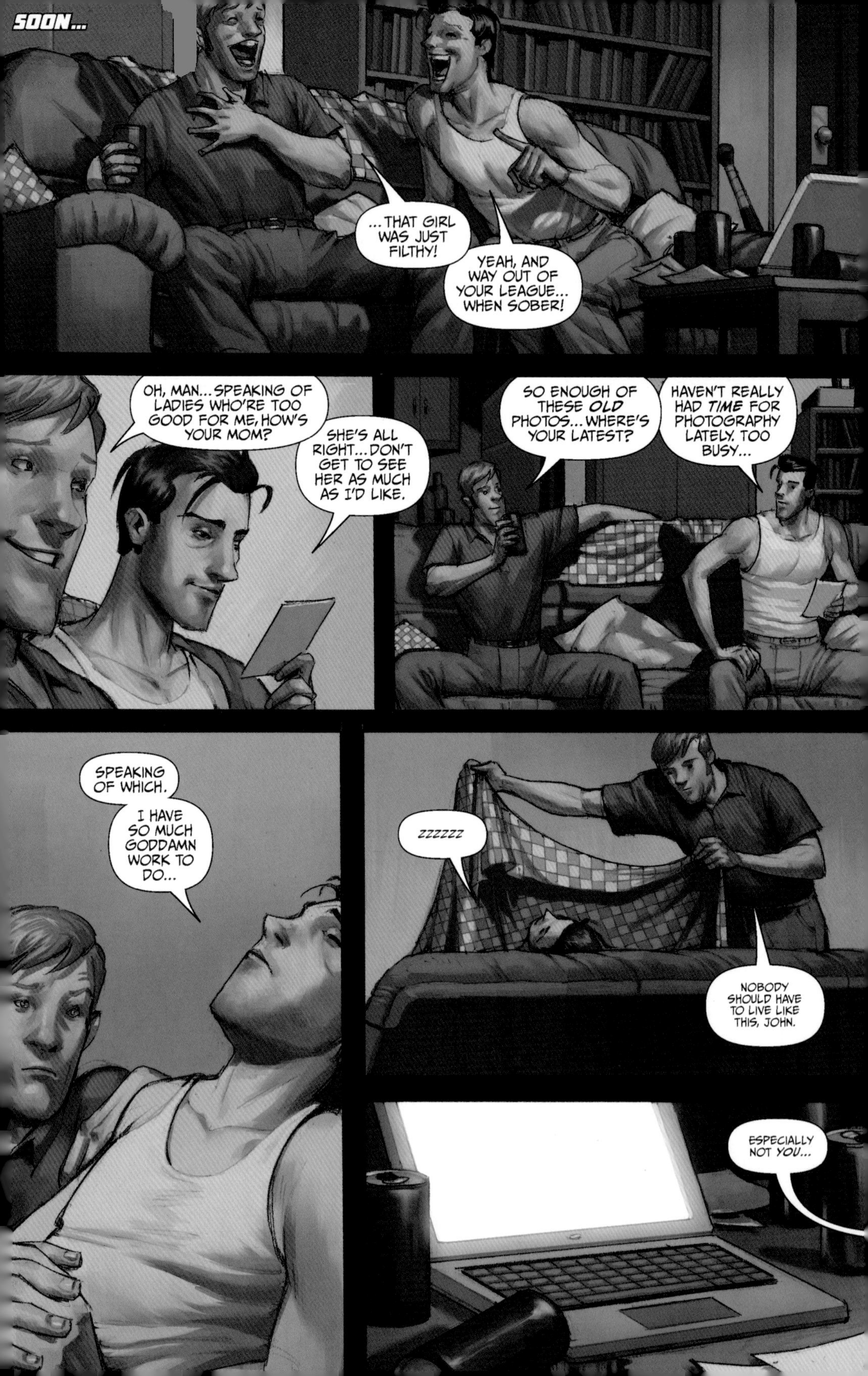
SOON...
...THAT GIRL WAS JUST FILTHY!
YEAH, AND WAY OUT OF YOUR LEAGUE... WHEN SOBER!
OH, MAN... SPEAKING OF LADIES WHO'RE TOO GOOD FOR ME, HOW'S YOUR MOM?
SHE'S ALL RIGHT... DON'T GET TO SEE HER AS MUCH AS I'D LIKE.
SO ENOUGH OF THESE OLD PHOTOS... WHERE'S YOUR LATEST?
HAVEN'T REALLY HAD TIME FOR PHOTOGRAPHY LATELY. TOO BUSY...
SPEAKING OF WHICH.
I HAVE SO MUCH GODDAMN WORK TO DO...
ZZZZZZ
NOBODY SHOULD HAVE TO LIVE LIKE THIS, JOHN.
ESPECIALLY NOT YOU...

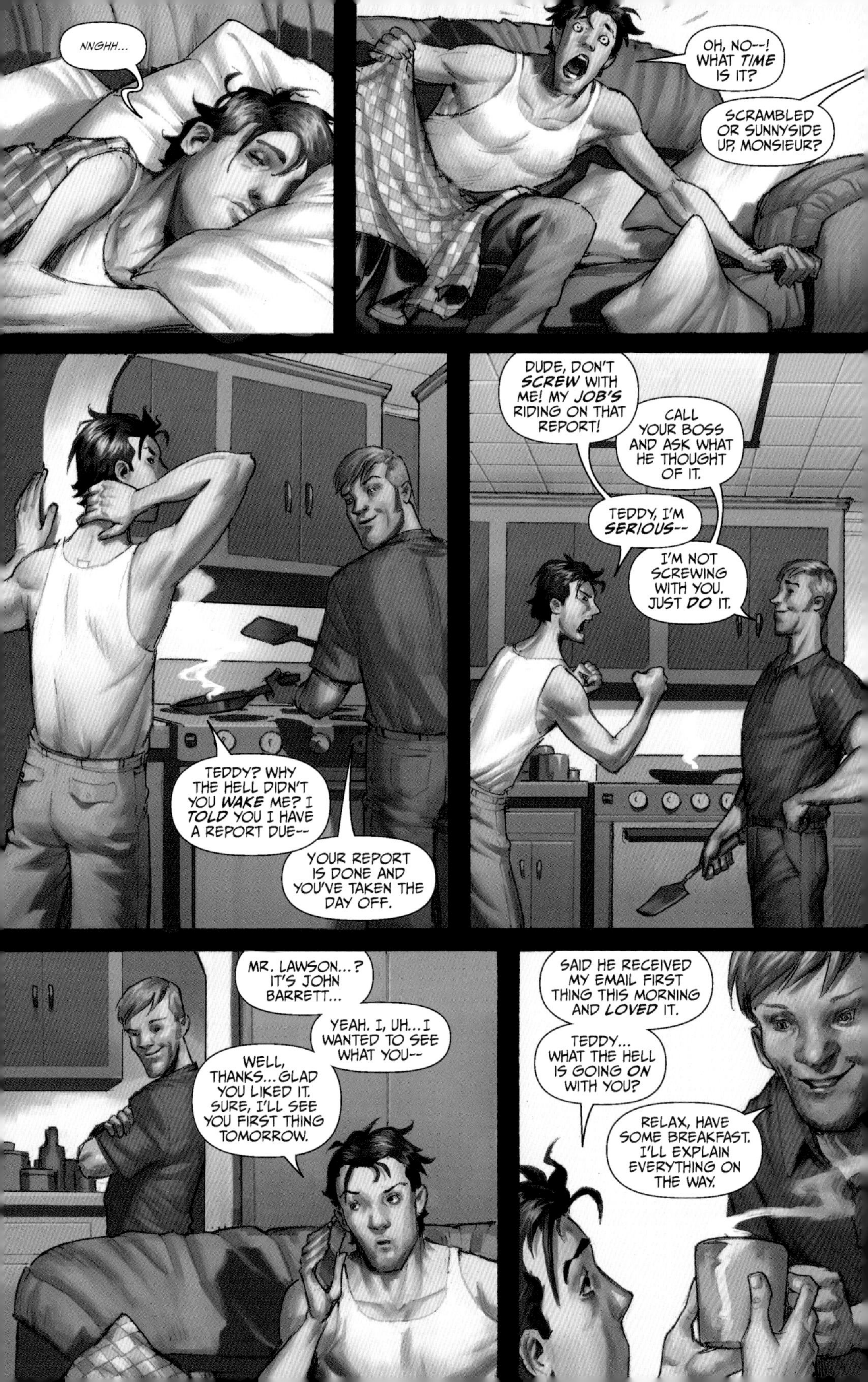
NNGHH...
OH, NO--! WHAT TIME IS IT?
SCRAMBLED OR SUNNYSIDE UP, MONSIEUR?
TEDDY? WHY THE HELL DIDN'T YOU WAKE ME? I TOLD YOU I HAVE A REPORT DUE--
YOUR REPORT IS DONE AND YOU'VE TAKEN THE DAY OFF.
DUDE, DON'T SCREW WITH ME! MY JOB'S RIDING ON THAT REPORT!
CALL YOUR BOSS AND ASK WHAT HE THOUGHT OF IT.
TEDDY, I'M SERIOUS--
I'M NOT SCREWING WITH YOU. JUST DO IT.
MR. LAWSON...? IT'S JOHN BARRETT...
YEAH. I, UH...I WANTED TO SEE WHAT YOU--
WELL, THANKS...GLAD YOU LIKED IT. SURE, I'LL SEE YOU FIRST THING TOMORROW.
SAID HE RECEIVED MY EMAIL FIRST THING THIS MORNING AND LOVED IT.
TEDDY... WHAT THE HELL IS GOING ON WITH YOU?
RELAX, HAVE SOME BREAKFAST. I'LL EXPLAIN EVERYTHING ON THE WAY.

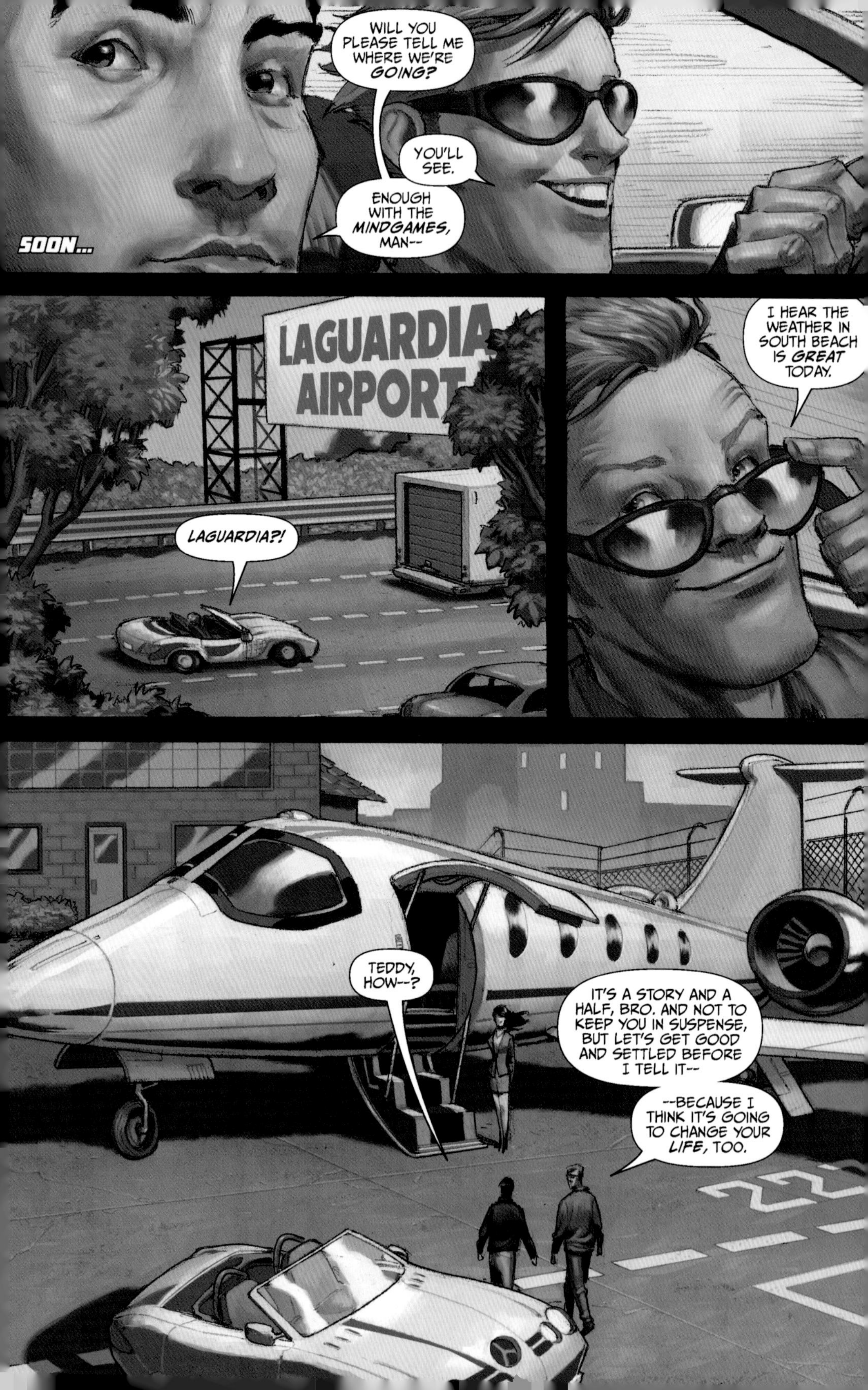
SOON...
WILL YOU PLEASE TELL ME WHERE WE'RE GOING?
YOU'LL SEE.
ENOUGH WITH THE MINDGAMES, MAN--
LAGUARDIA AIRPORT
LAGUARDIA?!
I HEAR THE WEATHER IN SOUTH BEACH IS GREAT TODAY.
TEDDY, HOW--?
IT'S A STORY AND A HALF, BRO. AND NOT TO KEEP YOU IN SUSPENSE, BUT LET'S GET GOOD AND SETTLED BEFORE I TELL IT--
--BECAUSE I THINK IT'S GOING TO CHANGE YOUR LIFE, TOO.

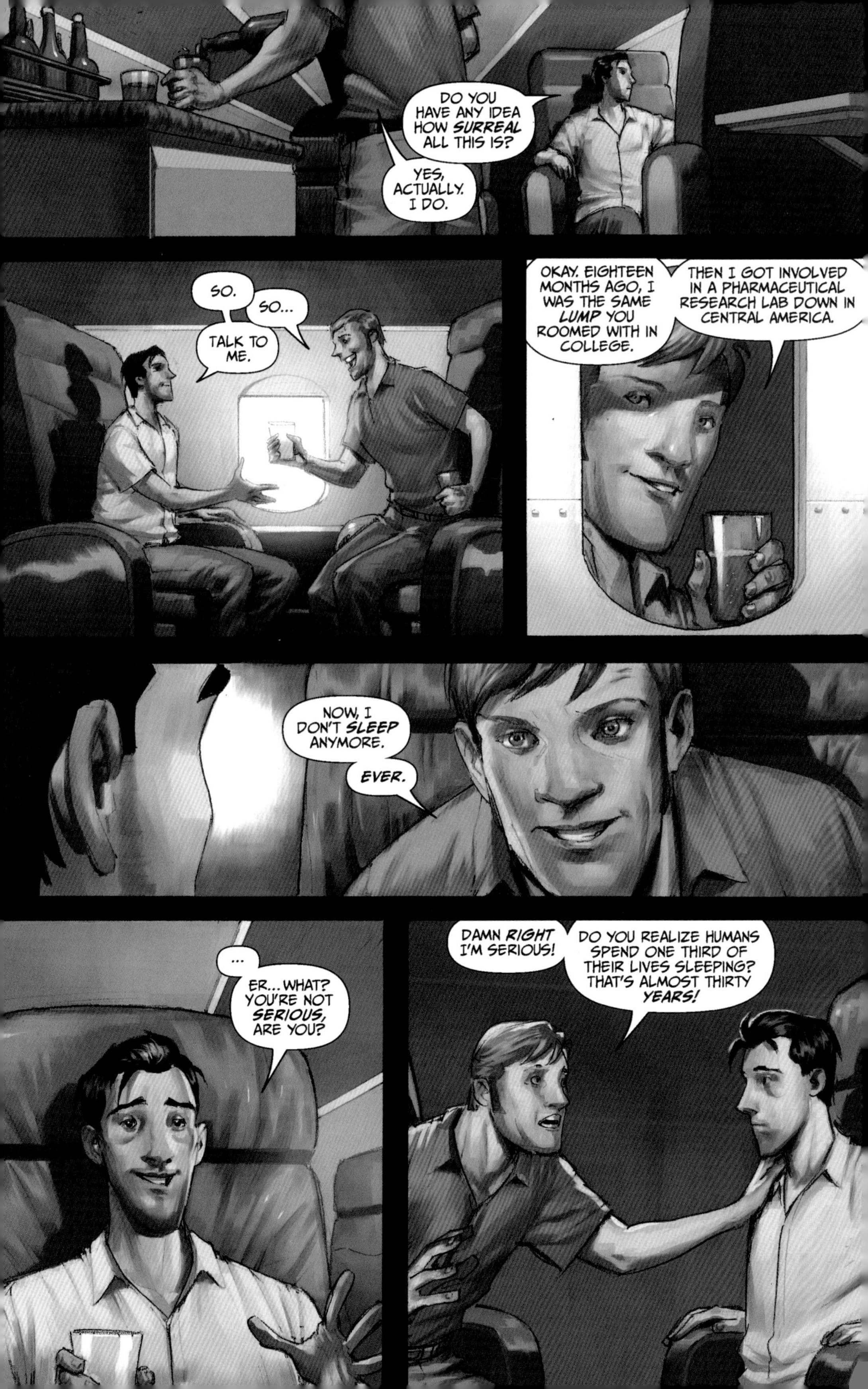
DO YOU HAVE ANY IDEA HOW SURREAL ALL THIS IS?
YES, ACTUALLY. I DO.
SO.
SO...
TALK TO ME.
OKAY. EIGHTEEN MONTHS AGO, I WAS THE SAME LUMP YOU ROOMED WITH IN COLLEGE.
THEN I GOT INVOLVED IN A PHARMACEUTICAL RESEARCH LAB DOWN IN CENTRAL AMERICA.
NOW, I DON'T SLEEP ANYMORE.
EVER.
...
ER... WHAT? YOU'RE NOT SERIOUS, ARE YOU?
DAMN RIGHT I'M SERIOUS!
DO YOU REALIZE HUMANS SPEND ONE THIRD OF THEIR LIVES SLEEPING? THAT'S ALMOST THIRTY YEARS!

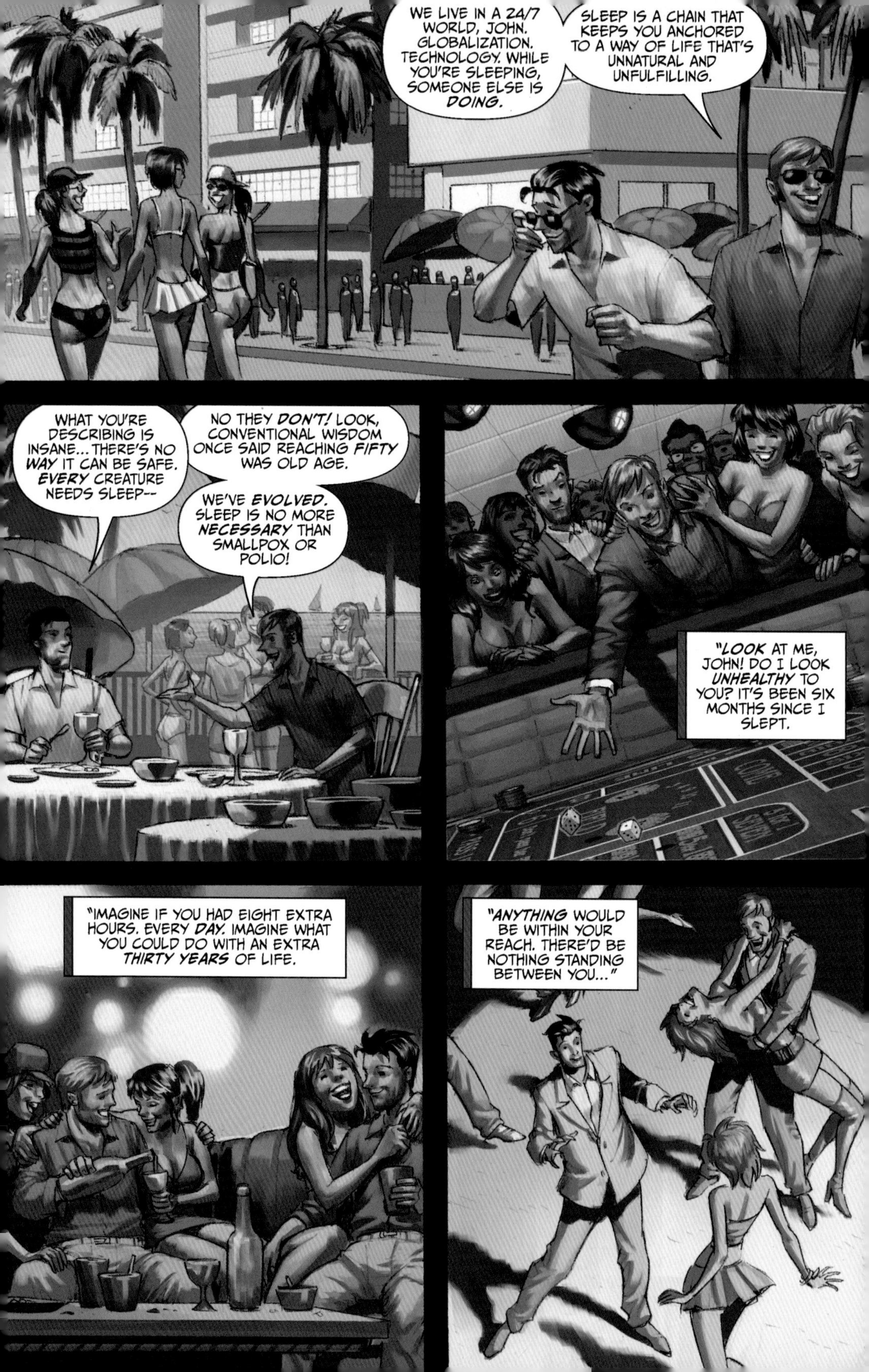
WE LIVE IN A 24/7 WORLD, JOHN. GLOBALIZATION. TECHNOLOGY. WHILE YOU'RE SLEEPING, SOMEONE ELSE IS *DOING.*
SLEEP IS A CHAIN THAT KEEPS YOU ANCHORED TO A WAY OF LIFE THAT'S UNNATURAL AND UNFULFILLING.
WHAT YOU'RE DESCRIBING IS INSANE... THERE'S NO *WAY* IT CAN BE SAFE. *EVERY* CREATURE NEEDS SLEEP--
NO THEY *DON'T!* LOOK, CONVENTIONAL WISDOM ONCE SAID REACHING *FIFTY* WAS OLD AGE.
WE'VE *EVOLVED.* SLEEP IS NO MORE *NECESSARY* THAN SMALLPOX OR POLIO!
"*LOOK* AT ME, JOHN! DO I LOOK *UNHEALTHY* TO YOU? IT'S BEEN SIX MONTHS SINCE I SLEPT.
"IMAGINE IF YOU HAD EIGHT EXTRA HOURS. EVERY *DAY.* IMAGINE WHAT YOU COULD DO WITH AN EXTRA *THIRTY YEARS* OF LIFE.
"*ANYTHING* WOULD BE WITHIN YOUR REACH. THERE'D BE NOTHING STANDING BETWEEN YOU..."

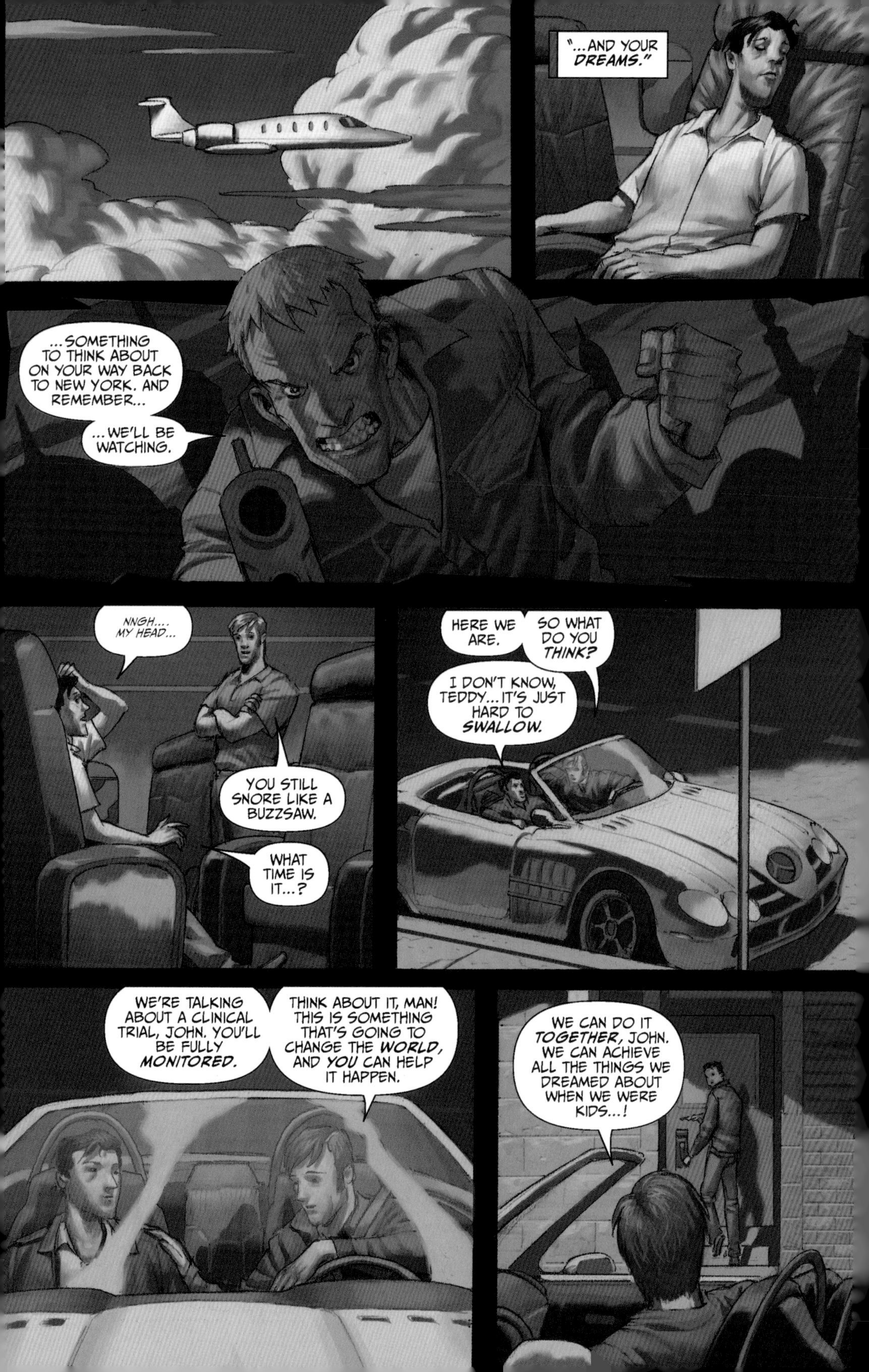
"...AND YOUR DREAMS."
...SOMETHING TO THINK ABOUT ON YOUR WAY BACK TO NEW YORK. AND REMEMBER...
...WE'LL BE WATCHING.
NNGH.... MY HEAD...
YOU STILL SNORE LIKE A BUZZSAW.
WHAT TIME IS IT...?
HERE WE ARE.
SO WHAT DO YOU THINK?
I DON'T KNOW, TEDDY... IT'S JUST HARD TO SWALLOW.
WE'RE TALKING ABOUT A CLINICAL TRIAL, JOHN. YOU'LL BE FULLY MONITORED.
THINK ABOUT IT, MAN! THIS IS SOMETHING THAT'S GOING TO CHANGE THE WORLD, AND YOU CAN HELP IT HAPPEN.
WE CAN DO IT TOGETHER, JOHN. WE CAN ACHIEVE ALL THE THINGS WE DREAMED ABOUT WHEN WE WERE KIDS...!

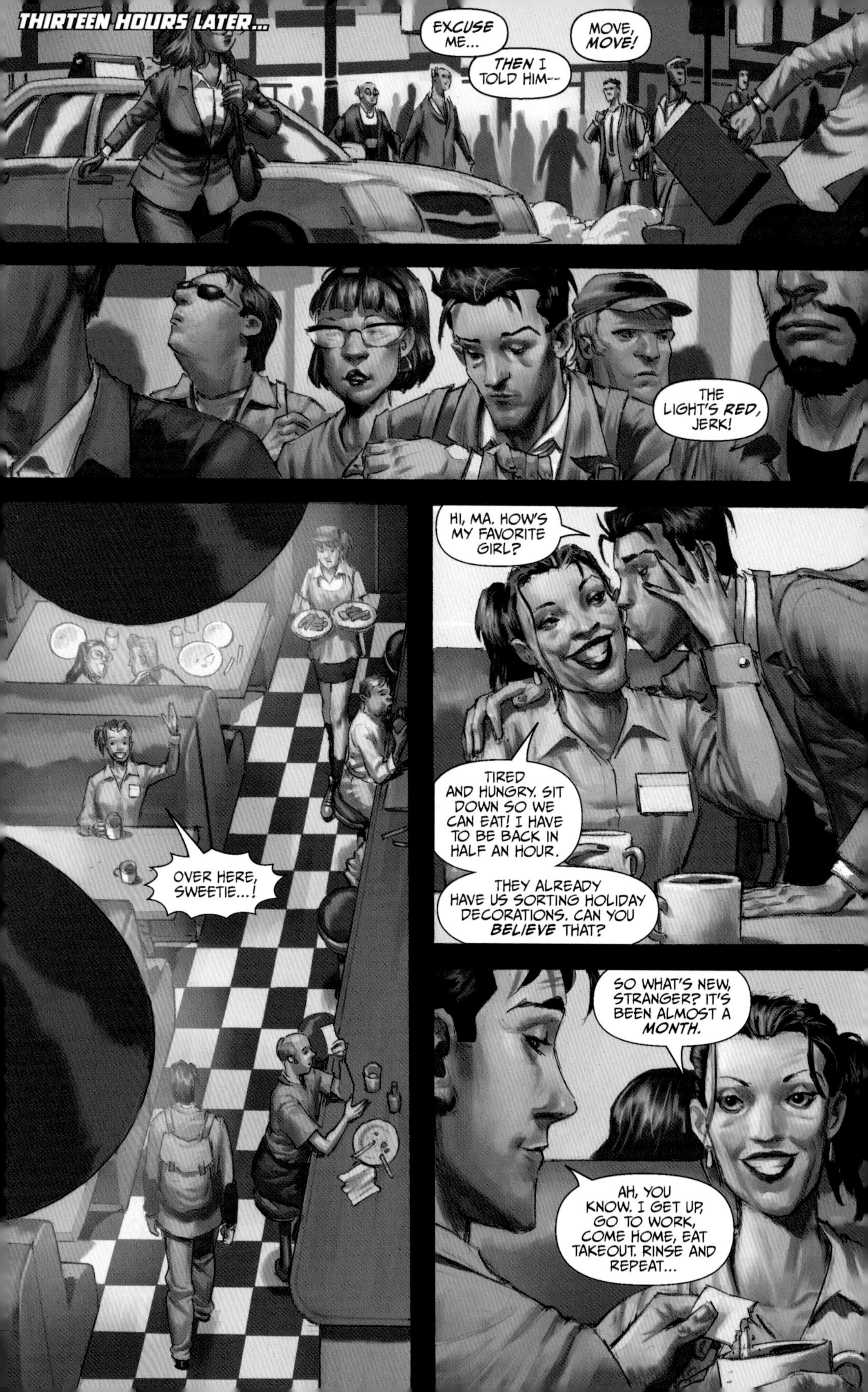
THIRTEEN HOURS LATER...
EXCUSE ME...
THEN I TOLD HIM--
MOVE, MOVE!
THE LIGHT'S RED, JERK!
OVER HERE, SWEETIE...!
HI, MA. HOW'S MY FAVORITE GIRL?
TIRED AND HUNGRY. SIT DOWN SO WE CAN EAT! I HAVE TO BE BACK IN HALF AN HOUR.
THEY ALREADY HAVE US SORTING HOLIDAY DECORATIONS. CAN YOU BELIEVE THAT?
SO WHAT'S NEW, STRANGER? IT'S BEEN ALMOST A MONTH.
AH, YOU KNOW. I GET UP, GO TO WORK, COME HOME, EAT TAKEOUT. RINSE AND REPEAT...

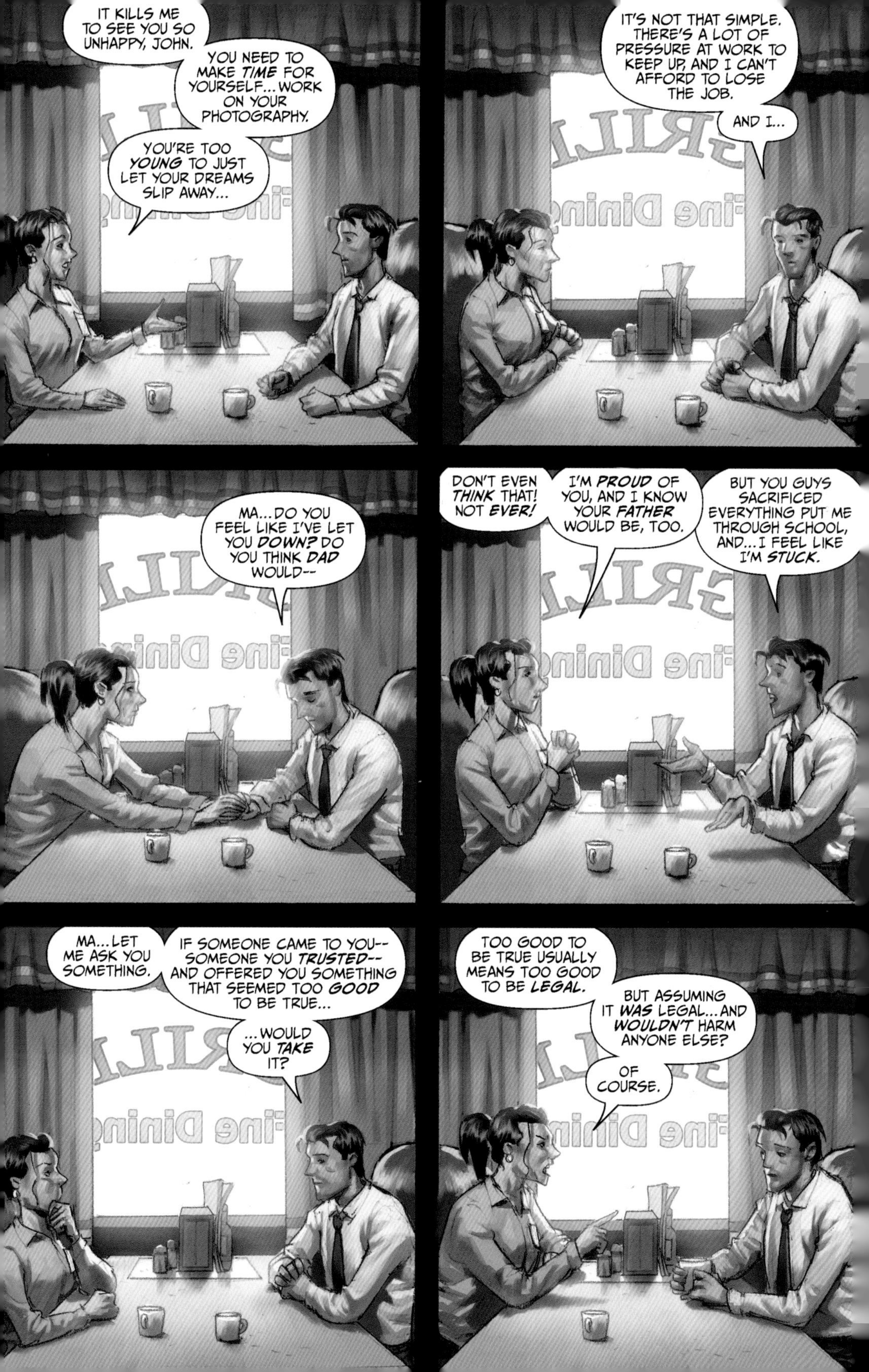

IT KILLS ME TO SEE YOU SO UNHAPPY, JOHN.
YOU NEED TO MAKE *TIME* FOR YOURSELF... WORK ON YOUR PHOTOGRAPHY.
YOU'RE TOO *YOUNG* TO JUST LET YOUR DREAMS SLIP AWAY...
IT'S NOT THAT SIMPLE. THERE'S A LOT OF PRESSURE AT WORK TO KEEP UP, AND I CAN'T AFFORD TO LOSE THE JOB.
AND I...
MA...DO YOU FEEL LIKE I'VE LET YOU *DOWN?* DO YOU THINK *DAD* WOULD--
DON'T EVEN *THINK* THAT! NOT *EVER!*
I'M *PROUD* OF YOU, AND I KNOW YOUR *FATHER* WOULD BE, TOO.
BUT YOU GUYS SACRIFICED EVERYTHING PUT ME THROUGH SCHOOL, AND...I FEEL LIKE I'M *STUCK.*
MA...LET ME ASK YOU SOMETHING.
IF SOMEONE CAME TO YOU-- SOMEONE YOU *TRUSTED*-- AND OFFERED YOU SOMETHING THAT SEEMED TOO *GOOD* TO BE TRUE...
...WOULD YOU *TAKE* IT?
TOO GOOD TO BE TRUE USUALLY MEANS TOO GOOD TO BE *LEGAL.*
BUT ASSUMING IT *WAS* LEGAL...AND *WOULDN'T* HARM ANYONE ELSE?
OF COURSE.

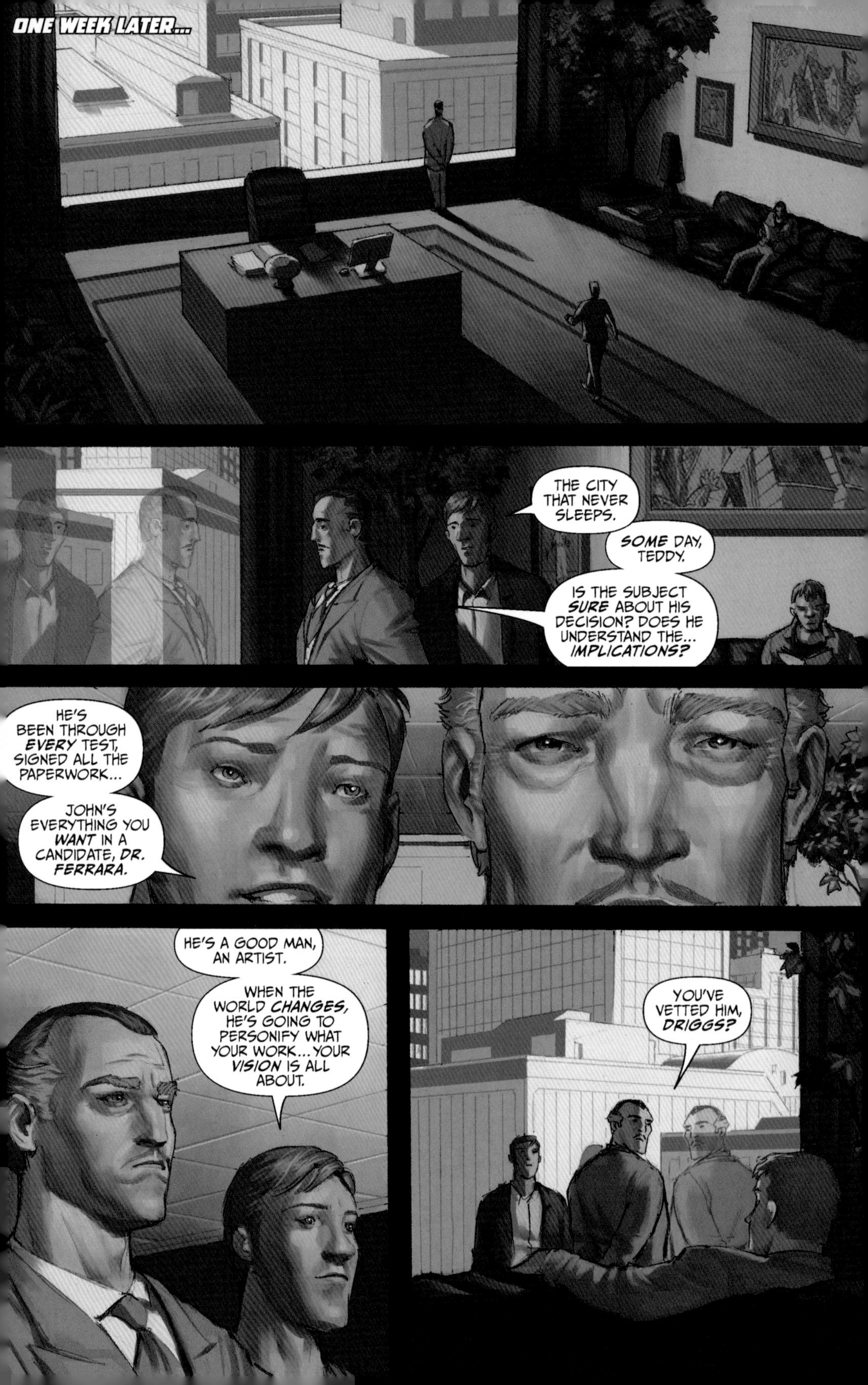
ONE WEEK LATER...
THE CITY THAT NEVER SLEEPS.
SOME DAY, TEDDY.
IS THE SUBJECT SURE ABOUT HIS DECISION? DOES HE UNDERSTAND THE... IMPLICATIONS?
HE'S BEEN THROUGH EVERY TEST, SIGNED ALL THE PAPERWORK...
JOHN'S EVERYTHING YOU WANT IN A CANDIDATE, DR. FERRARA.
HE'S A GOOD MAN, AN ARTIST.
WHEN THE WORLD CHANGES, HE'S GOING TO PERSONIFY WHAT YOUR WORK... YOUR VISION IS ALL ABOUT.
YOU'VE VETTED HIM, DRIGGS?

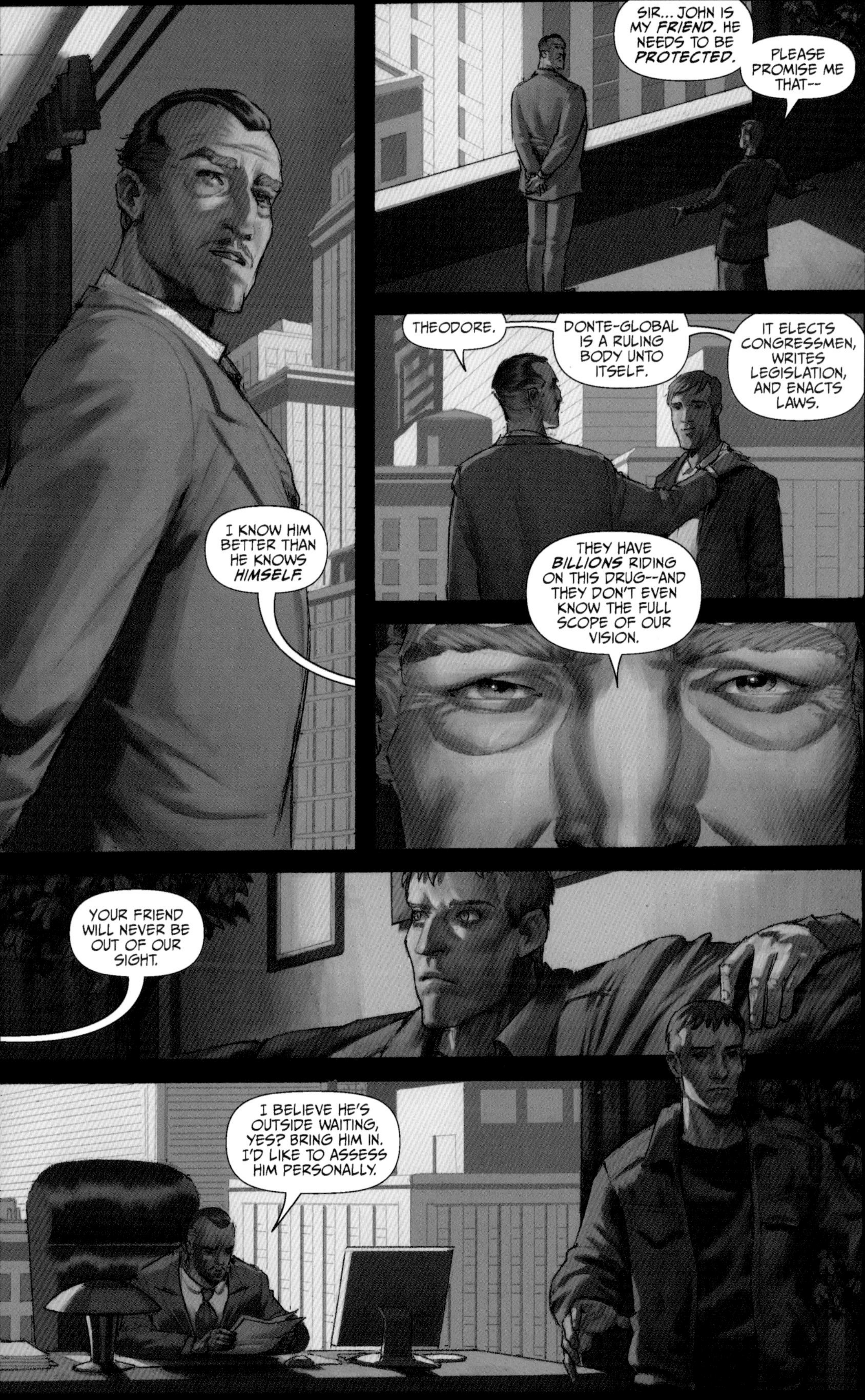
SIR... JOHN IS MY FRIEND. HE NEEDS TO BE PROTECTED.
PLEASE PROMISE ME THAT--
THEODORE.
DONTE-GLOBAL IS A RULING BODY UNTO ITSELF.
IT ELECTS CONGRESSMEN, WRITES LEGISLATION, AND ENACTS LAWS.
I KNOW HIM BETTER THAN HE KNOWS HIMSELF.
THEY HAVE BILLIONS RIDING ON THIS DRUG--AND THEY DON'T EVEN KNOW THE FULL SCOPE OF OUR VISION.
YOUR FRIEND WILL NEVER BE OUT OF OUR SIGHT.
I BELIEVE HE'S OUTSIDE WAITING, YES? BRING HIM IN. I'D LIKE TO ASSESS HIM PERSONALLY.

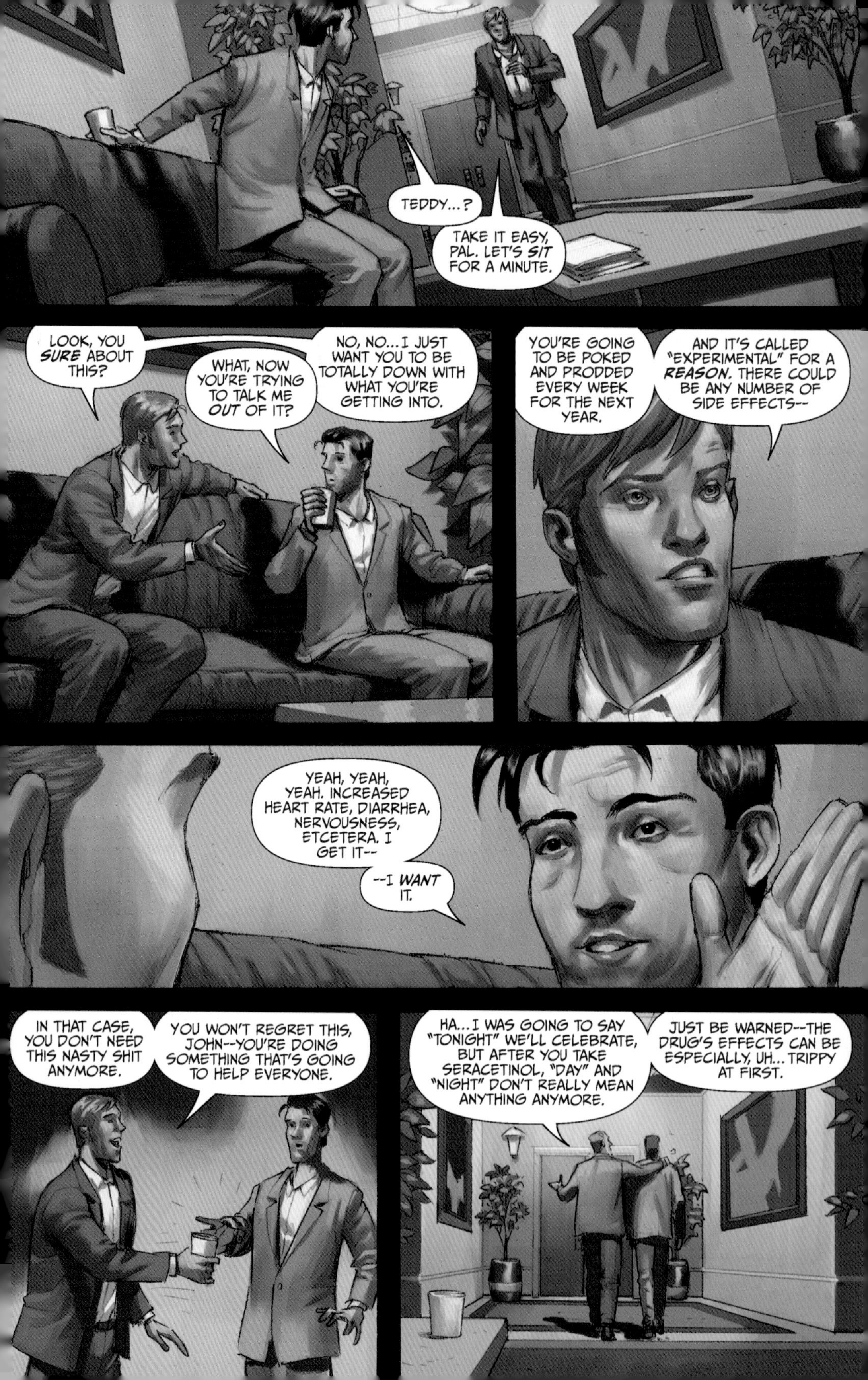
TEDDY...?
TAKE IT EASY, PAL. LET'S SIT FOR A MINUTE.
LOOK, YOU SURE ABOUT THIS?
NO, NO... I JUST WANT YOU TO BE TOTALLY DOWN WITH WHAT YOU'RE GETTING INTO.
WHAT, NOW YOU'RE TRYING TO TALK ME OUT OF IT?
YOU'RE GOING TO BE POKED AND PRODDED EVERY WEEK FOR THE NEXT YEAR.
AND IT'S CALLED "EXPERIMENTAL" FOR A REASON. THERE COULD BE ANY NUMBER OF SIDE EFFECTS--
YEAH, YEAH, YEAH. INCREASED HEART RATE, DIARRHEA, NERVOUSNESS, ETCETERA. I GET IT--
--I WANT IT.
IN THAT CASE, YOU DON'T NEED THIS NASTY SHIT ANYMORE.
YOU WON'T REGRET THIS, JOHN--YOU'RE DOING SOMETHING THAT'S GOING TO HELP EVERYONE.
HA... I WAS GOING TO SAY "TONIGHT" WE'LL CELEBRATE, BUT AFTER YOU TAKE SERACETINOL, "DAY" AND "NIGHT" DON'T REALLY MEAN ANYTHING ANYMORE.
JUST BE WARNED--THE DRUG'S EFFECTS CAN BE ESPECIALLY, UH... TRIPPY AT FIRST.

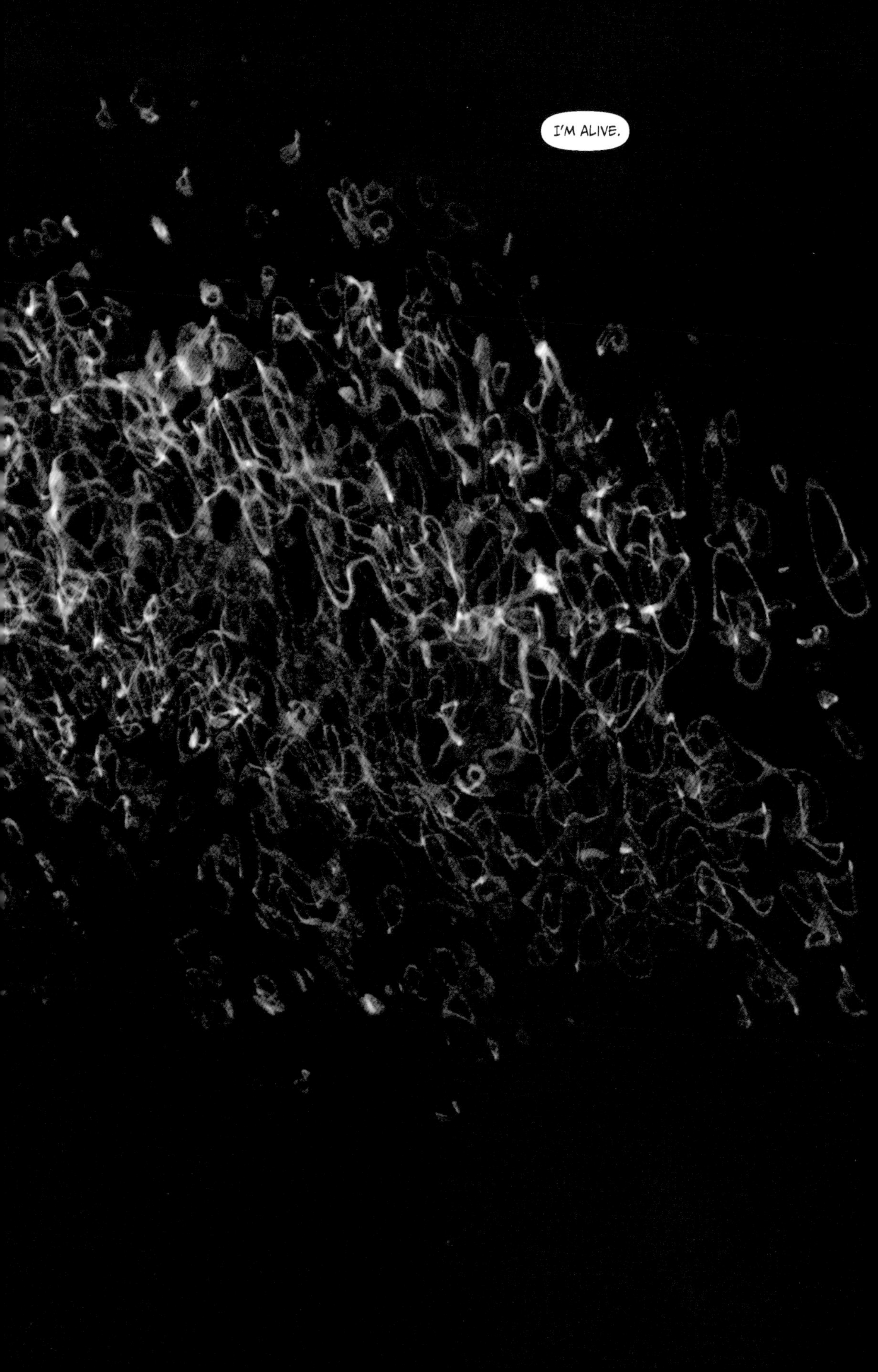
I'M ALIVE.

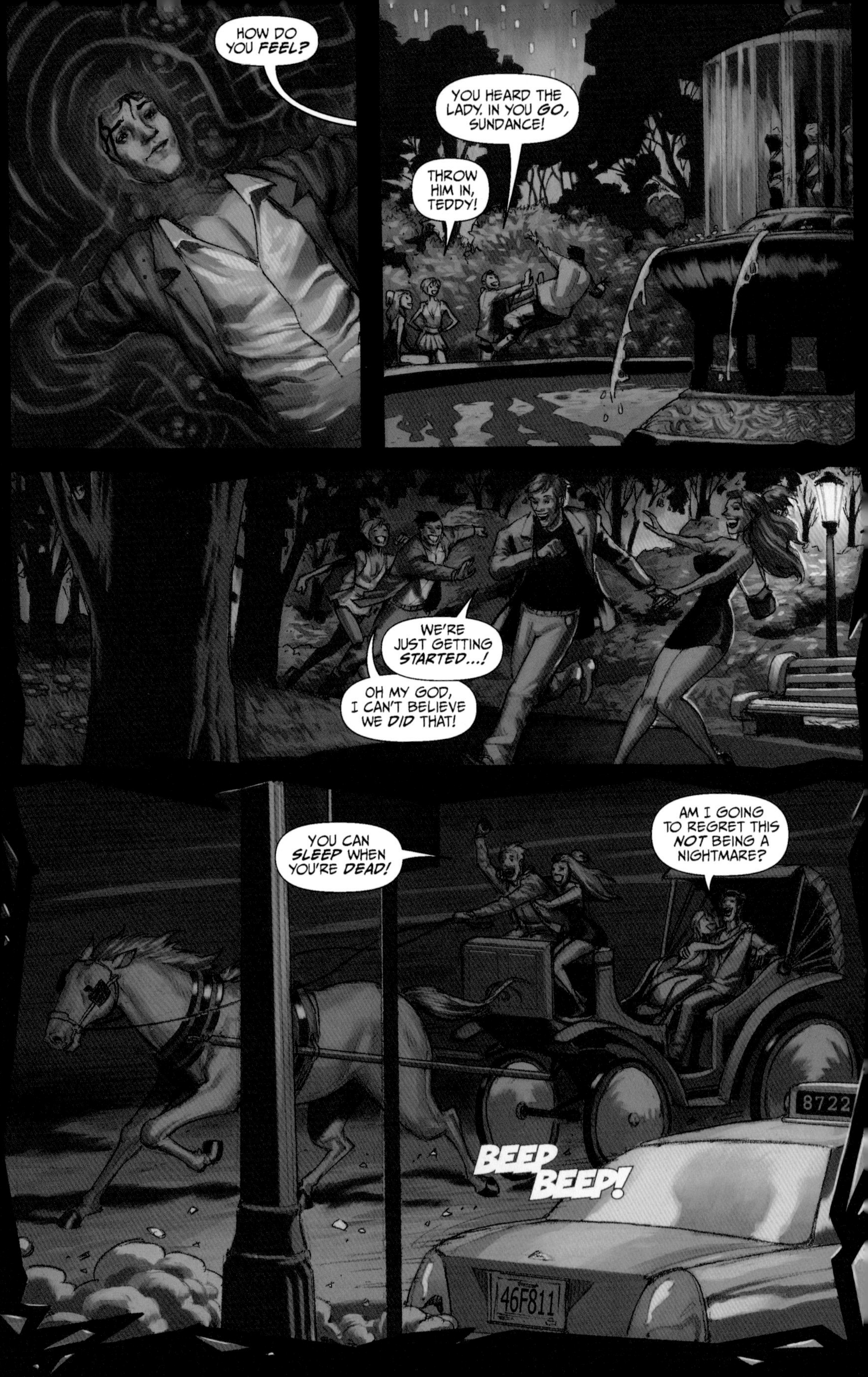
HOW DO YOU FEEL?
YOU HEARD THE LADY. IN YOU GO, SUNDANCE!
THROW HIM IN, TEDDY!
WE'RE JUST GETTING STARTED...!
OH MY GOD, I CAN'T BELIEVE WE DID THAT!
YOU CAN SLEEP WHEN YOU'RE DEAD!
AM I GOING TO REGRET THIS NOT BEING A NIGHTMARE?
8722
BEEP BEEP!
46F811

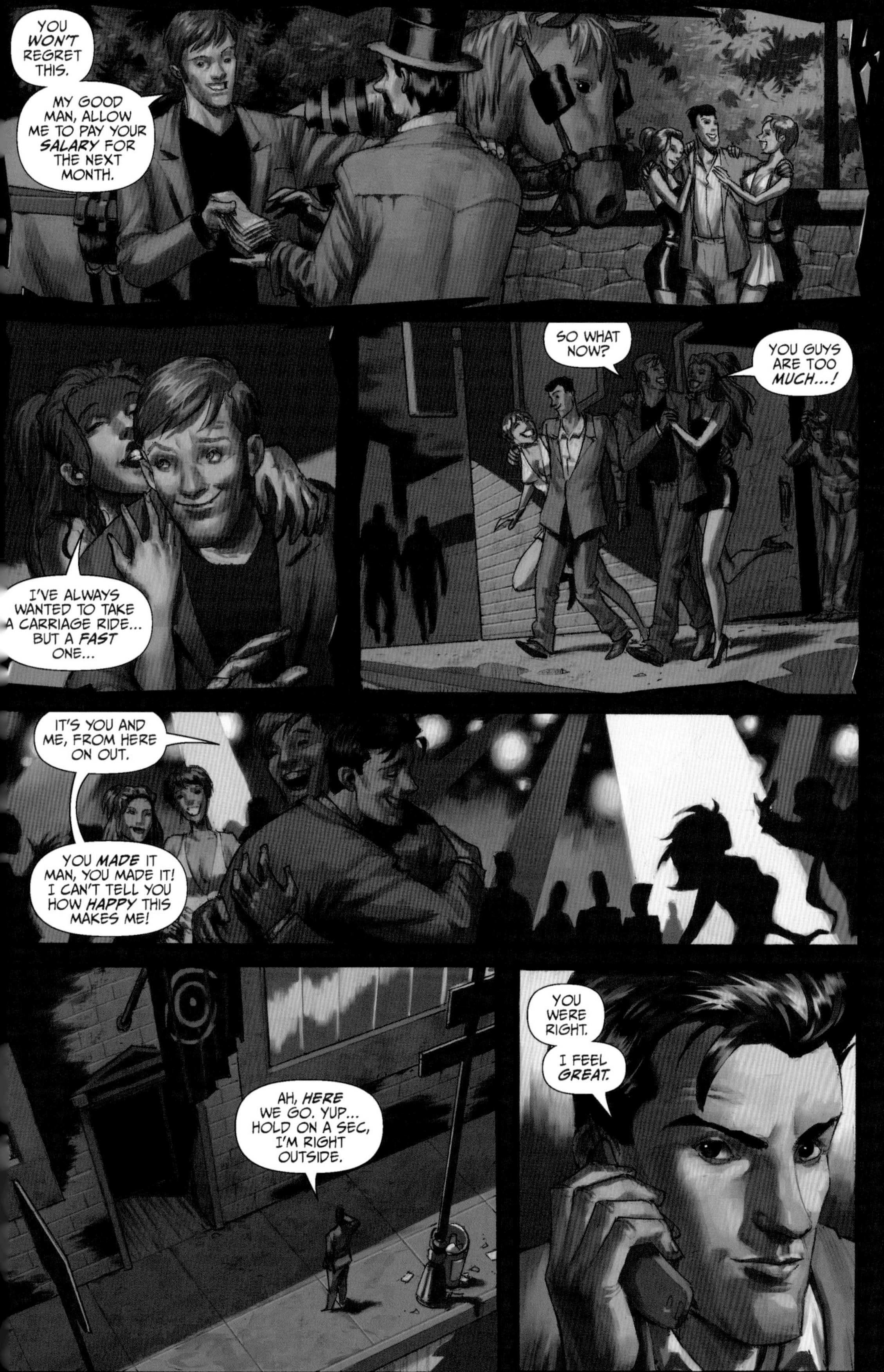
YOU WON'T REGRET THIS.
MY GOOD MAN, ALLOW ME TO PAY YOUR SALARY FOR THE NEXT MONTH.
I'VE ALWAYS WANTED TO TAKE A CARRIAGE RIDE... BUT A FAST ONE...
SO WHAT NOW?
YOU GUYS ARE TOO MUCH...!
IT'S YOU AND ME, FROM HERE ON OUT.
YOU MADE IT MAN, YOU MADE IT! I CAN'T TELL YOU HOW HAPPY THIS MAKES ME!
AH, HERE WE GO. YUP... HOLD ON A SEC, I'M RIGHT OUTSIDE.
YOU WERE RIGHT.
I FEEL GREAT.

Rest #2

written by: **Mark Powers**
line art by: **Shawn McManus**
colors by: **Lizzy John**
letters by: **Ed Dukeshire**
· · · · ·
original edition edited by: **Cody DeMatteis**
& Stephen Christy
original edition designed by: **Sean K. Dove**
with **Stephen Christy**

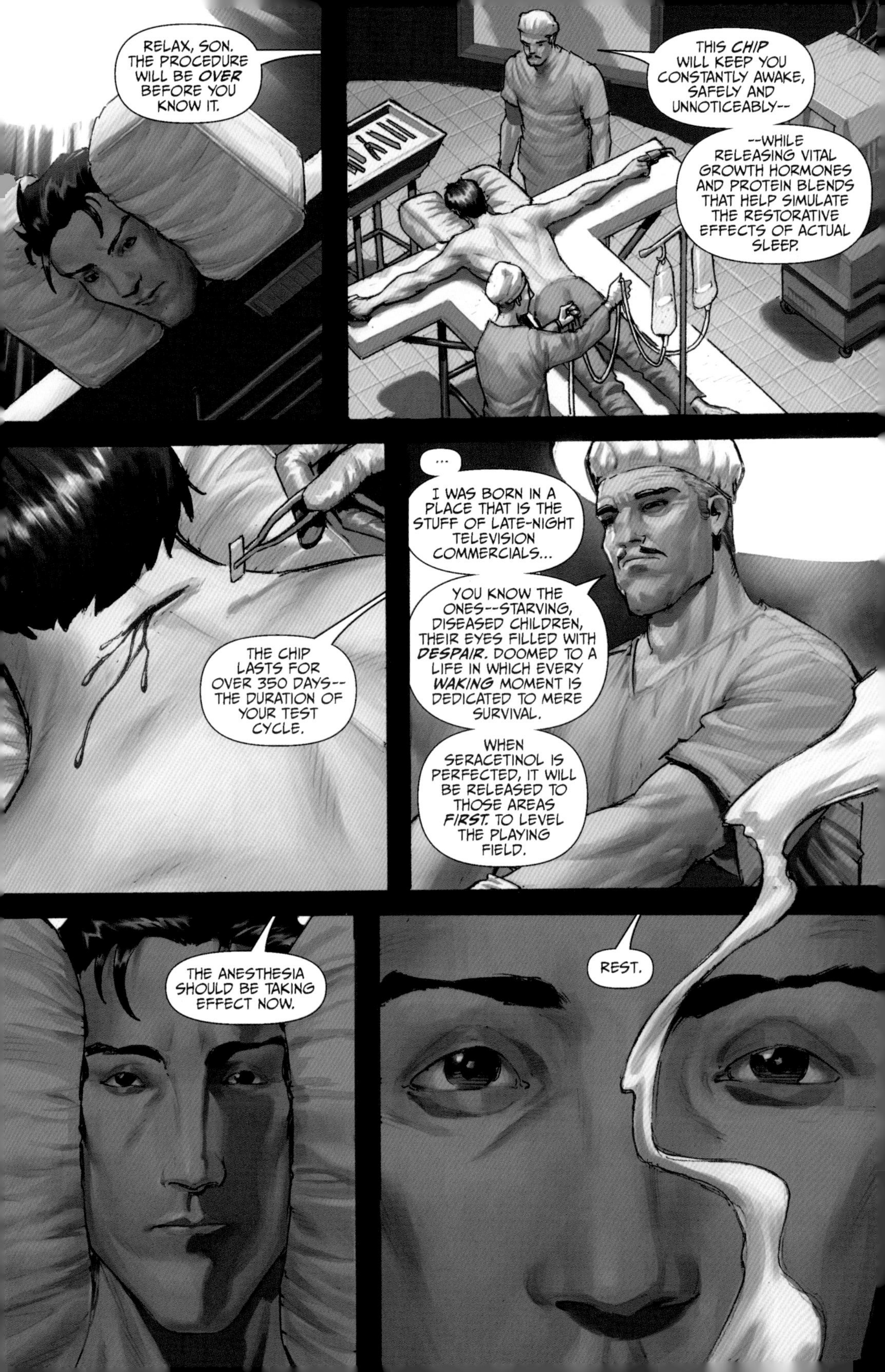
RELAX, SON. THE PROCEDURE WILL BE OVER BEFORE YOU KNOW IT.
THIS CHIP WILL KEEP YOU CONSTANTLY AWAKE, SAFELY AND UNNOTICEABLY--
--WHILE RELEASING VITAL GROWTH HORMONES AND PROTEIN BLENDS THAT HELP SIMULATE THE RESTORATIVE EFFECTS OF ACTUAL SLEEP.
THE CHIP LASTS FOR OVER 350 DAYS-- THE DURATION OF YOUR TEST CYCLE.
...
I WAS BORN IN A PLACE THAT IS THE STUFF OF LATE-NIGHT TELEVISION COMMERCIALS...
YOU KNOW THE ONES--STARVING, DISEASED CHILDREN, THEIR EYES FILLED WITH DESPAIR. DOOMED TO A LIFE IN WHICH EVERY WAKING MOMENT IS DEDICATED TO MERE SURVIVAL.
WHEN SERACETINOL IS PERFECTED, IT WILL BE RELEASED TO THOSE AREAS FIRST. TO LEVEL THE PLAYING FIELD.
THE ANESTHESIA SHOULD BE TAKING EFFECT NOW.
REST.

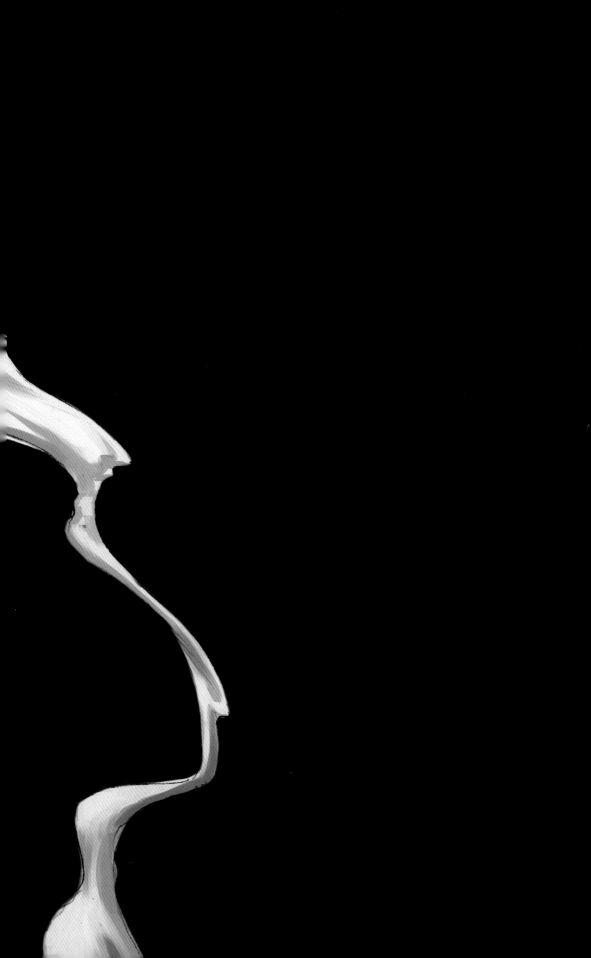

NEW YORK CITY, 4:54 AM

SIX MONTHS WITHOUT SLEEP

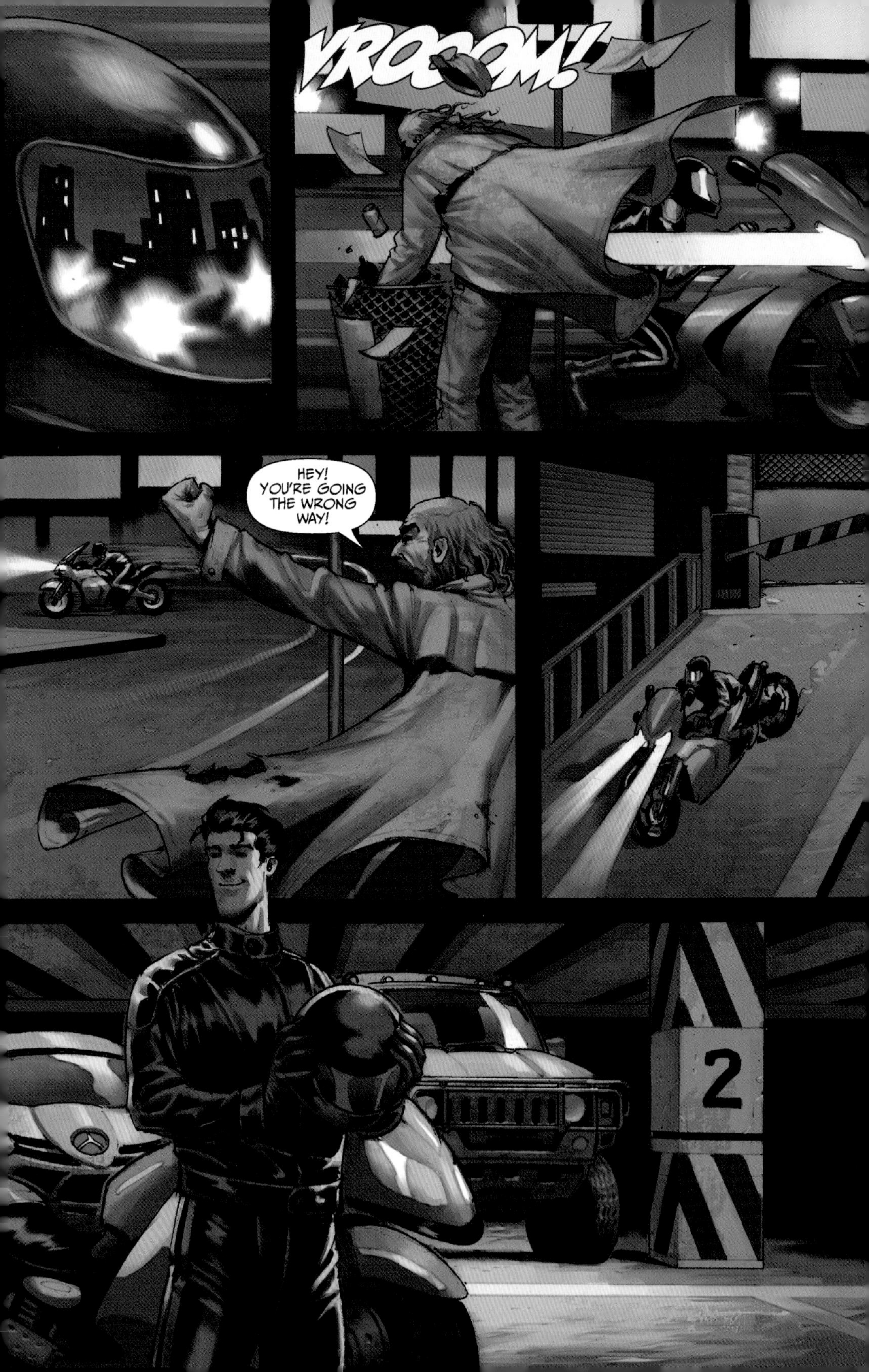
VROOOM!
HEY! YOU'RE GOING THE WRONG WAY!
2

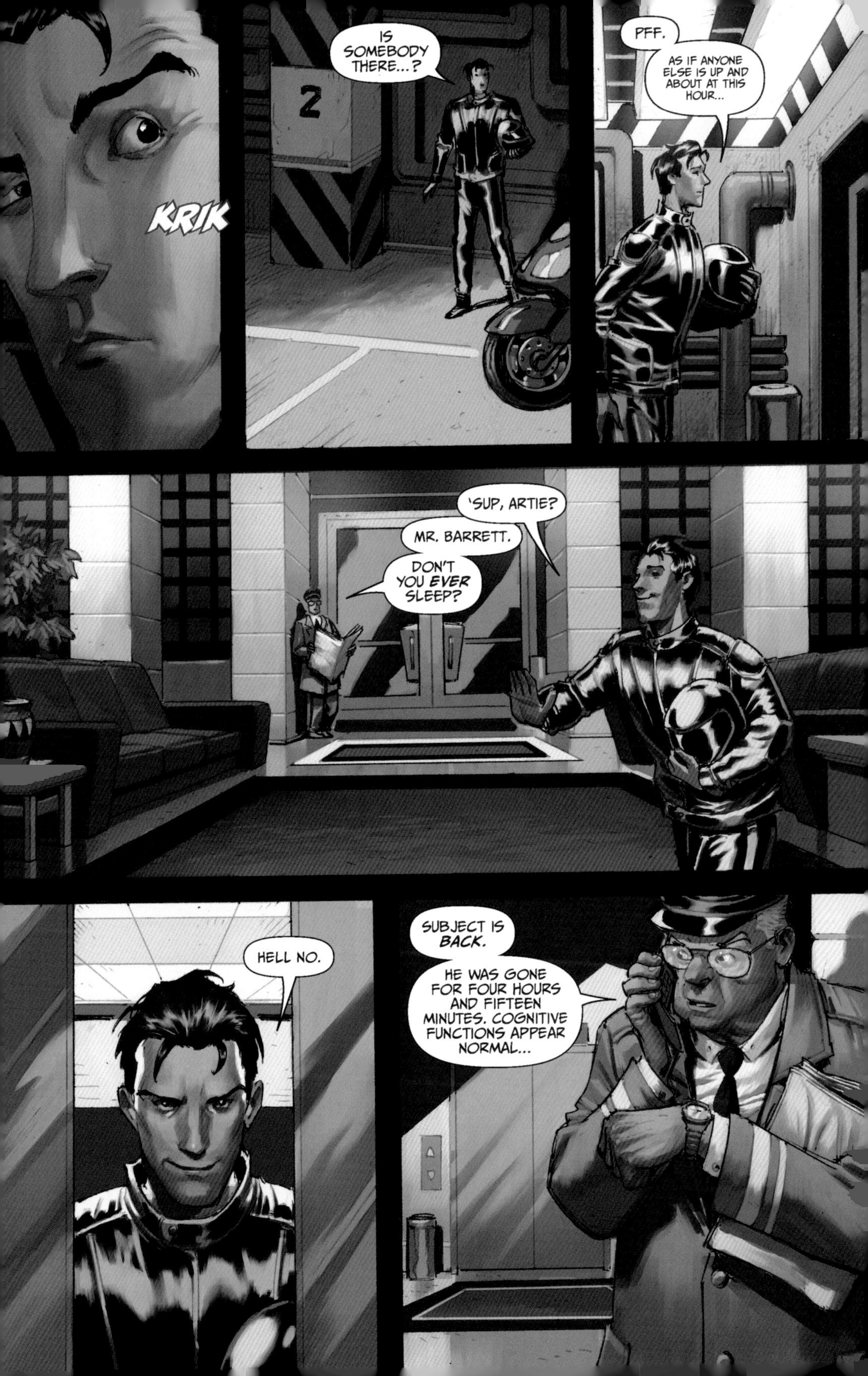

KRIK
IS SOMEBODY THERE...?
PFF.
AS IF ANYONE ELSE IS UP AND ABOUT AT THIS HOUR...
'SUP, ARTIE?
MR. BARRETT.
DON'T YOU *EVER* SLEEP?
HELL NO.
SUBJECT IS *BACK.*
HE WAS GONE FOR FOUR HOURS AND FIFTEEN MINUTES. COGNITIVE FUNCTIONS APPEAR NORMAL...

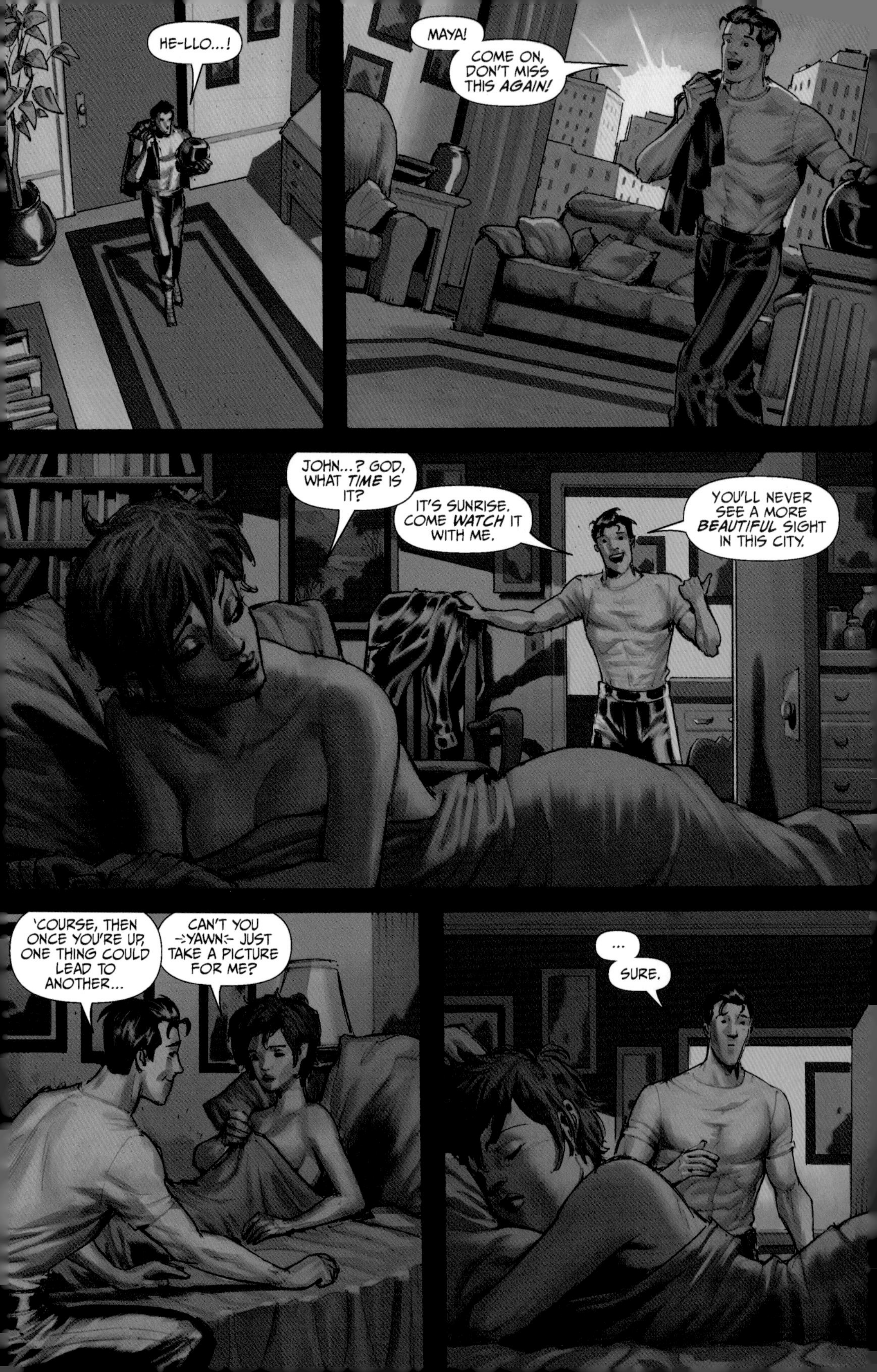
HE-LLO...!
MAYA!
COME ON, DON'T MISS THIS AGAIN!
JOHN...? GOD, WHAT TIME IS IT?
IT'S SUNRISE. COME WATCH IT WITH ME.
YOU'LL NEVER SEE A MORE BEAUTIFUL SIGHT IN THIS CITY.
'COURSE, THEN ONCE YOU'RE UP, ONE THING COULD LEAD TO ANOTHER...
CAN'T YOU -YAWN- JUST TAKE A PICTURE FOR ME?
...
SURE.

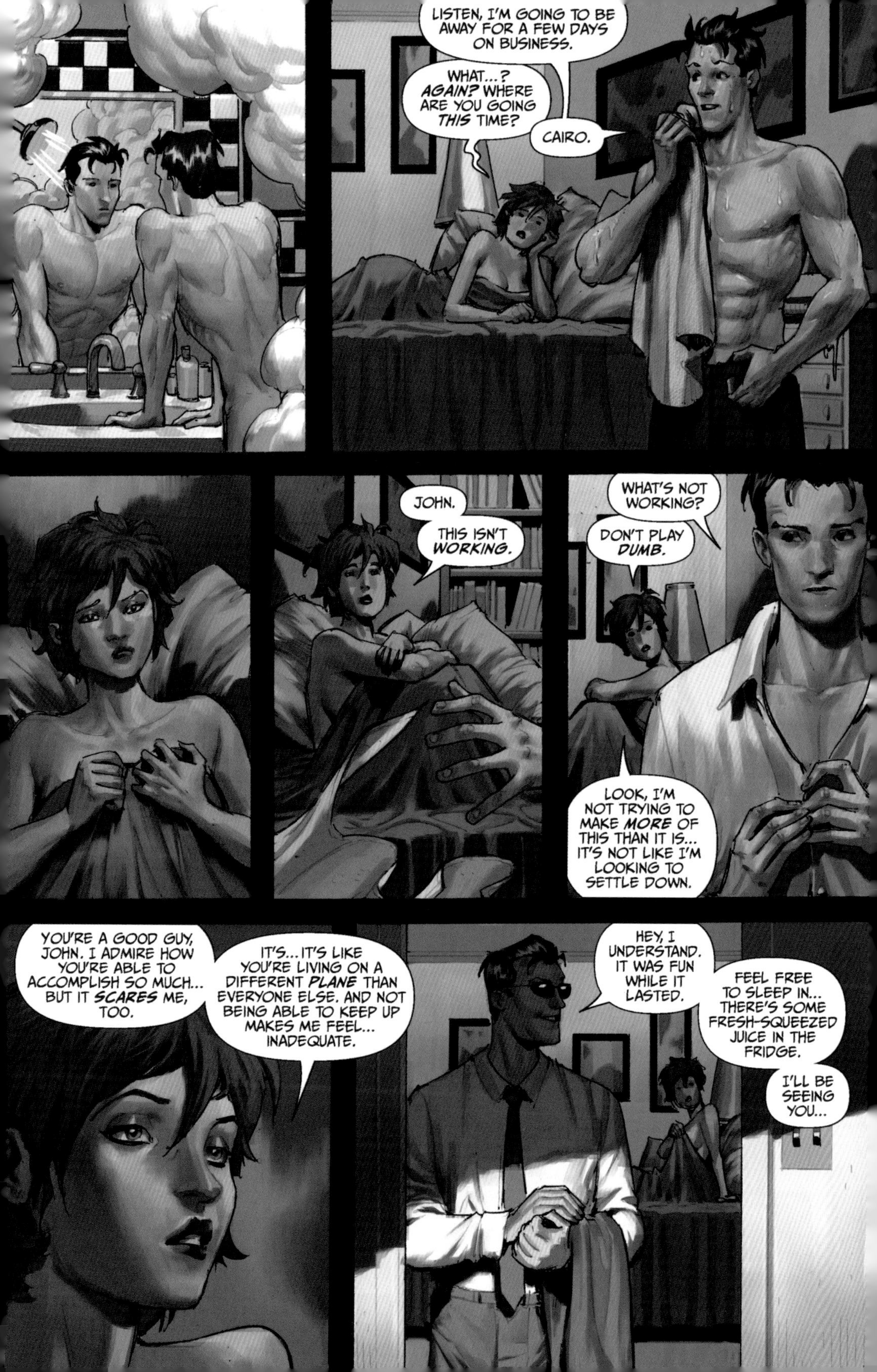
LISTEN, I'M GOING TO BE AWAY FOR A FEW DAYS ON BUSINESS.
WHAT...? AGAIN? WHERE ARE YOU GOING THIS TIME?
CAIRO.
JOHN.
THIS ISN'T WORKING.
WHAT'S NOT WORKING?
DON'T PLAY DUMB.
LOOK, I'M NOT TRYING TO MAKE MORE OF THIS THAN IT IS... IT'S NOT LIKE I'M LOOKING TO SETTLE DOWN.
YOU'RE A GOOD GUY, JOHN. I ADMIRE HOW YOU'RE ABLE TO ACCOMPLISH SO MUCH... BUT IT SCARES ME, TOO.
IT'S... IT'S LIKE YOU'RE LIVING ON A DIFFERENT PLANE THAN EVERYONE ELSE. AND NOT BEING ABLE TO KEEP UP MAKES ME FEEL... INADEQUATE.
HEY, I UNDERSTAND. IT WAS FUN WHILE IT LASTED.
FEEL FREE TO SLEEP IN... THERE'S SOME FRESH-SQUEEZED JUICE IN THE FRIDGE.
I'LL BE SEEING YOU...

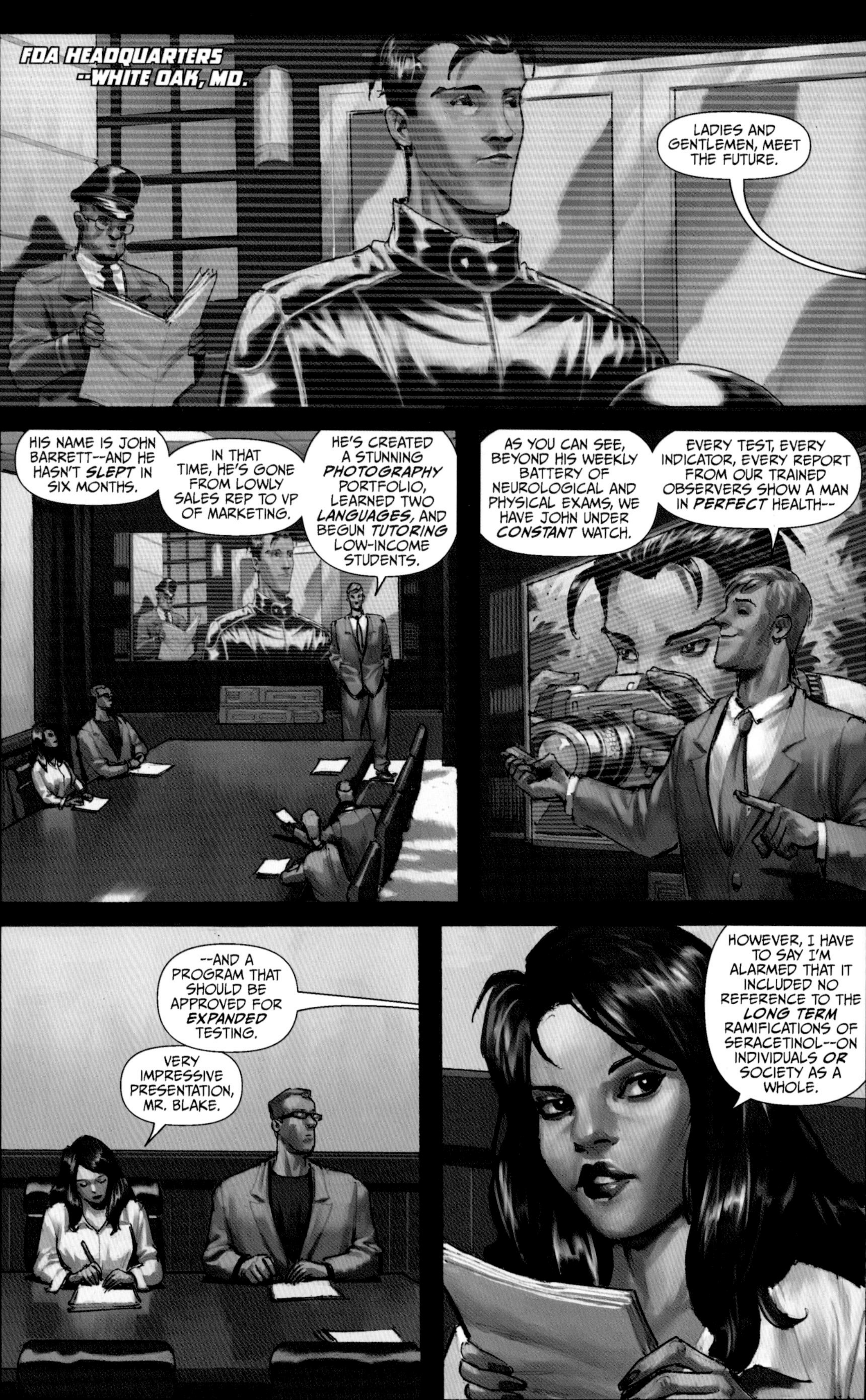
FDA HEADQUARTERS --WHITE OAK, MD.
LADIES AND GENTLEMEN, MEET THE FUTURE.
HIS NAME IS JOHN BARRETT--AND HE HASN'T SLEPT IN SIX MONTHS.
IN THAT TIME, HE'S GONE FROM LOWLY SALES REP TO VP OF MARKETING.
HE'S CREATED A STUNNING PHOTOGRAPHY PORTFOLIO, LEARNED TWO LANGUAGES, AND BEGUN TUTORING LOW-INCOME STUDENTS.
AS YOU CAN SEE, BEYOND HIS WEEKLY BATTERY OF NEUROLOGICAL AND PHYSICAL EXAMS, WE HAVE JOHN UNDER CONSTANT WATCH.
EVERY TEST, EVERY INDICATOR, EVERY REPORT FROM OUR TRAINED OBSERVERS SHOW A MAN IN PERFECT HEALTH--
--AND A PROGRAM THAT SHOULD BE APPROVED FOR EXPANDED TESTING.
VERY IMPRESSIVE PRESENTATION, MR. BLAKE.
HOWEVER, I HAVE TO SAY I'M ALARMED THAT IT INCLUDED NO REFERENCE TO THE LONG TERM RAMIFICATIONS OF SERACETINOL--ON INDIVIDUALS OR SOCIETY AS A WHOLE.

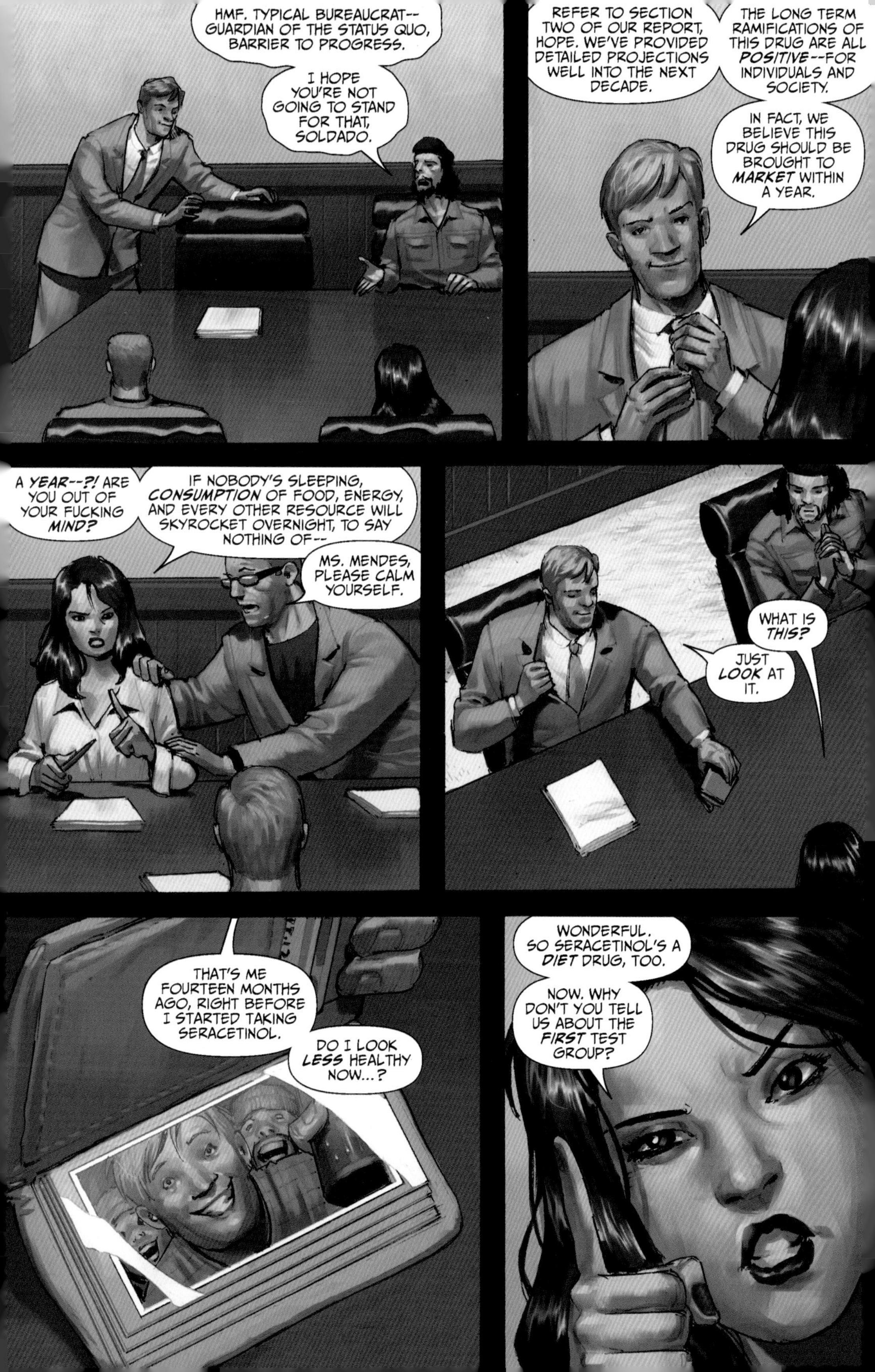

HMF. TYPICAL BUREAUCRAT--GUARDIAN OF THE STATUS QUO, BARRIER TO PROGRESS.
I HOPE YOU'RE NOT GOING TO STAND FOR THAT, SOLDADO.
REFER TO SECTION TWO OF OUR REPORT, HOPE. WE'VE PROVIDED DETAILED PROJECTIONS WELL INTO THE NEXT DECADE.
THE LONG TERM RAMIFICATIONS OF THIS DRUG ARE ALL *POSITIVE*--FOR INDIVIDUALS AND SOCIETY.
IN FACT, WE BELIEVE THIS DRUG SHOULD BE BROUGHT TO *MARKET* WITHIN A YEAR.
A *YEAR--?!* ARE YOU OUT OF YOUR FUCKING *MIND?*
IF NOBODY'S SLEEPING, *CONSUMPTION* OF FOOD, ENERGY, AND EVERY OTHER RESOURCE WILL SKYROCKET OVERNIGHT, TO SAY NOTHING OF--
MS. MENDES, PLEASE CALM YOURSELF.
WHAT IS *THIS?*
JUST *LOOK* AT IT.
THAT'S ME FOURTEEN MONTHS AGO, RIGHT BEFORE I STARTED TAKING SERACETINOL.
DO I LOOK *LESS* HEALTHY NOW...?
WONDERFUL. SO SERACETINOL'S A *DIET* DRUG, TOO.
NOW. WHY DON'T YOU TELL US ABOUT THE *FIRST* TEST GROUP?

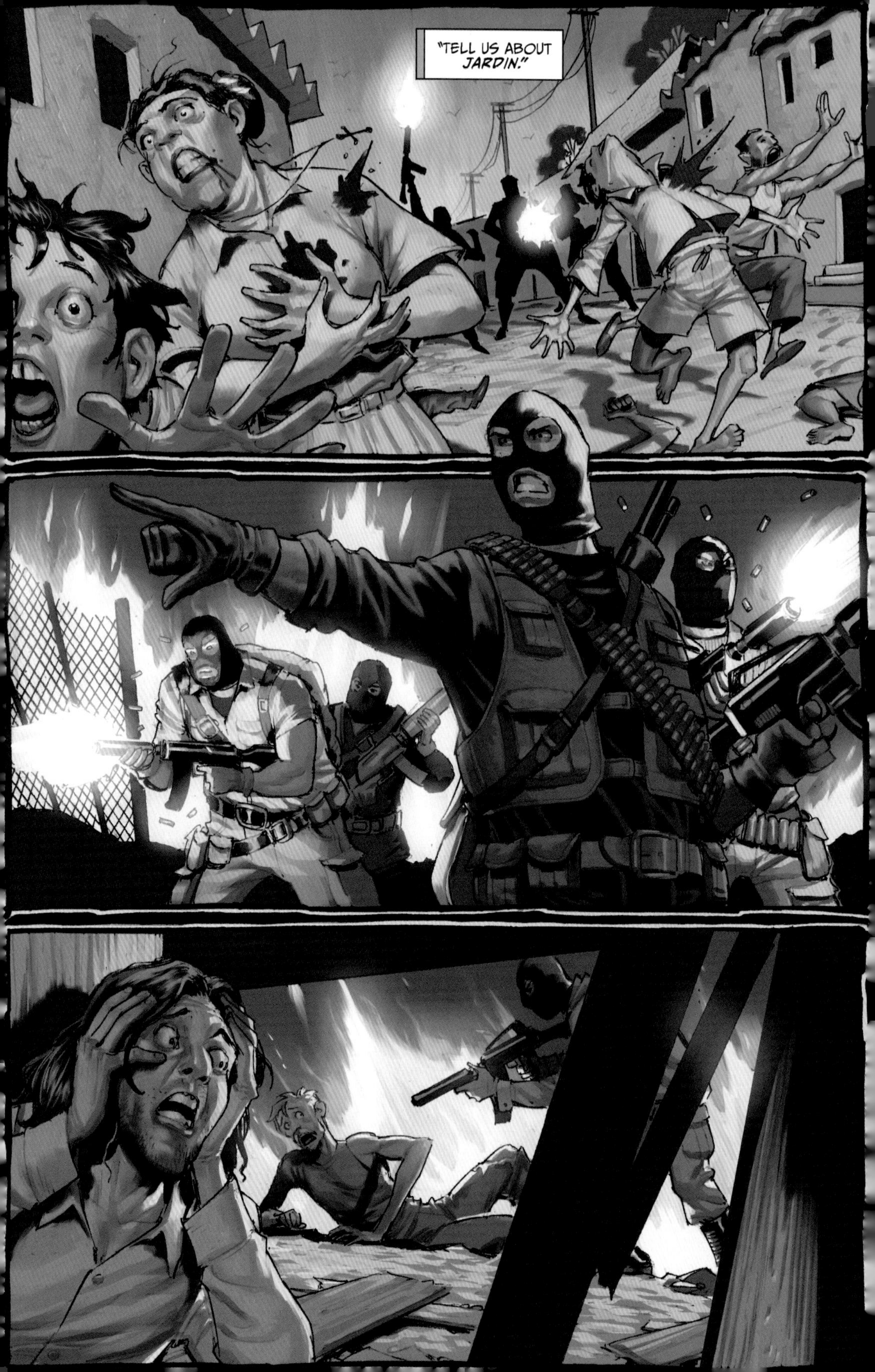
"TELL US ABOUT JARDIN."

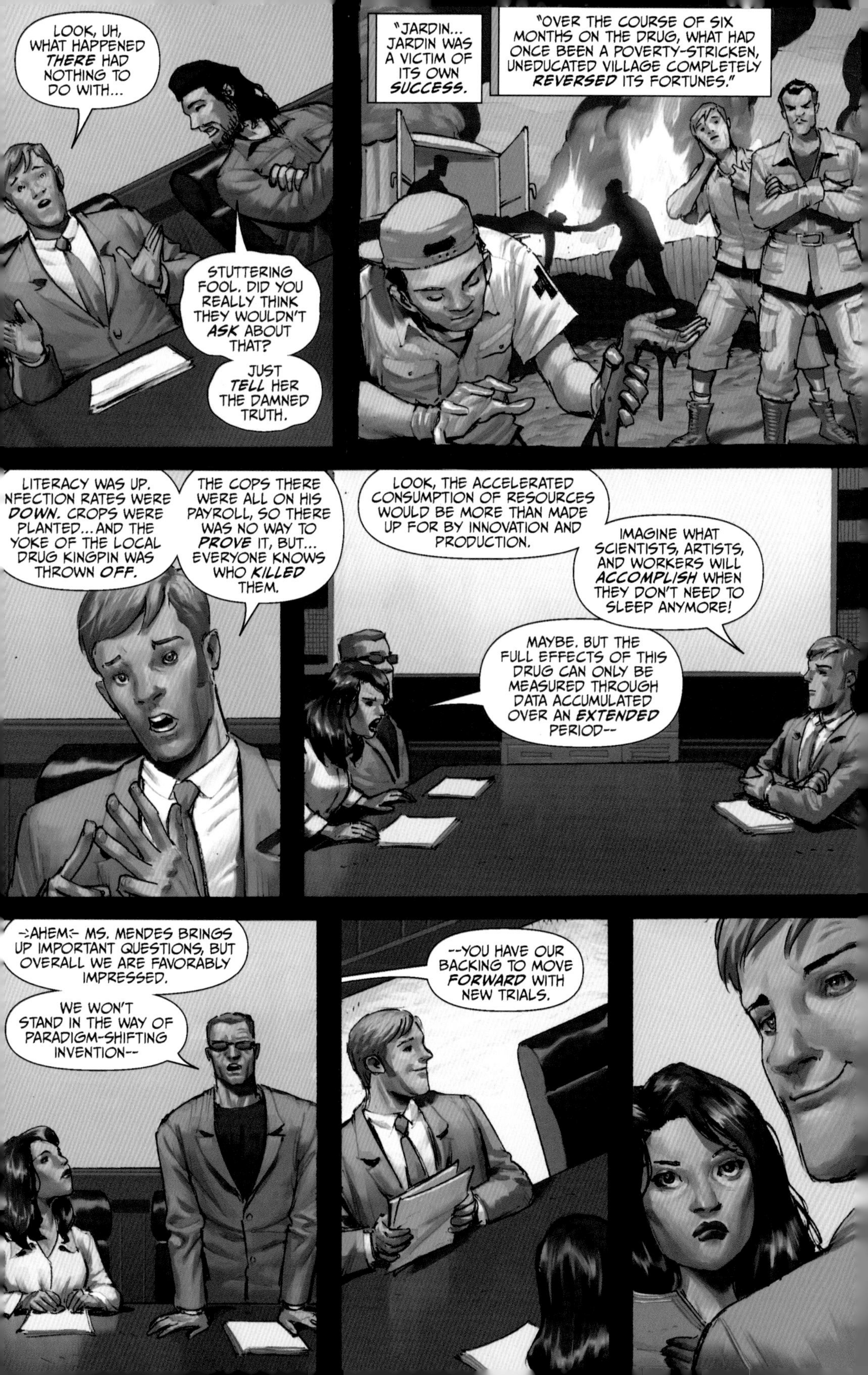
LOOK, UH, WHAT HAPPENED THERE HAD NOTHING TO DO WITH...
STUTTERING FOOL. DID YOU REALLY THINK THEY WOULDN'T ASK ABOUT THAT?
JUST TELL HER THE DAMNED TRUTH.
"JARDIN... JARDIN WAS A VICTIM OF ITS OWN SUCCESS.
"OVER THE COURSE OF SIX MONTHS ON THE DRUG, WHAT HAD ONCE BEEN A POVERTY-STRICKEN, UNEDUCATED VILLAGE COMPLETELY REVERSED ITS FORTUNES."
LITERACY WAS UP. NFECTION RATES WERE DOWN. CROPS WERE PLANTED... AND THE YOKE OF THE LOCAL DRUG KINGPIN WAS THROWN OFF.
THE COPS THERE WERE ALL ON HIS PAYROLL, SO THERE WAS NO WAY TO PROVE IT, BUT... EVERYONE KNOWS WHO KILLED THEM.
LOOK, THE ACCELERATED CONSUMPTION OF RESOURCES WOULD BE MORE THAN MADE UP FOR BY INNOVATION AND PRODUCTION.
IMAGINE WHAT SCIENTISTS, ARTISTS, AND WORKERS WILL ACCOMPLISH WHEN THEY DON'T NEED TO SLEEP ANYMORE!
MAYBE. BUT THE FULL EFFECTS OF THIS DRUG CAN ONLY BE MEASURED THROUGH DATA ACCUMULATED OVER AN EXTENDED PERIOD--
-AHEM- MS. MENDES BRINGS UP IMPORTANT QUESTIONS, BUT OVERALL WE ARE FAVORABLY IMPRESSED.
WE WON'T STAND IN THE WAY OF PARADIGM-SHIFTING INVENTION--
--YOU HAVE OUR BACKING TO MOVE FORWARD WITH NEW TRIALS.

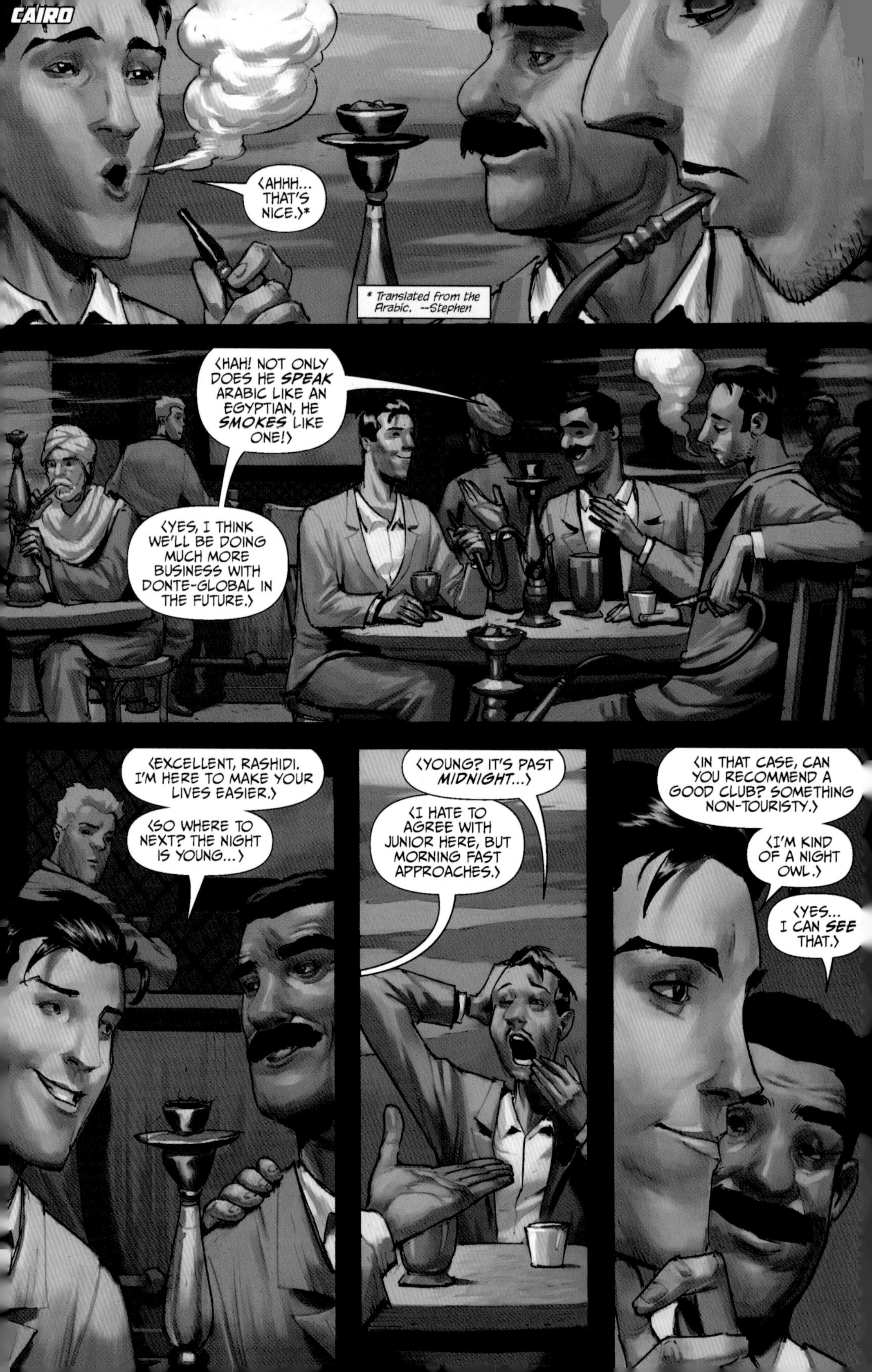
CAIRO
‹AHHH... THAT'S NICE.›*
* Translated from the Arabic. --Stephen
‹HAH! NOT ONLY DOES HE SPEAK ARABIC LIKE AN EGYPTIAN, HE SMOKES LIKE ONE!›
‹YES, I THINK WE'LL BE DOING MUCH MORE BUSINESS WITH DONTE-GLOBAL IN THE FUTURE.›
‹EXCELLENT, RASHIDI. I'M HERE TO MAKE YOUR LIVES EASIER.›
‹SO WHERE TO NEXT? THE NIGHT IS YOUNG...›
‹YOUNG? IT'S PAST MIDNIGHT...›
‹I HATE TO AGREE WITH JUNIOR HERE, BUT MORNING FAST APPROACHES.›
‹IN THAT CASE, CAN YOU RECOMMEND A GOOD CLUB? SOMETHING NON-TOURISTY.›
‹I'M KIND OF A NIGHT OWL.›
‹YES... I CAN SEE THAT.›

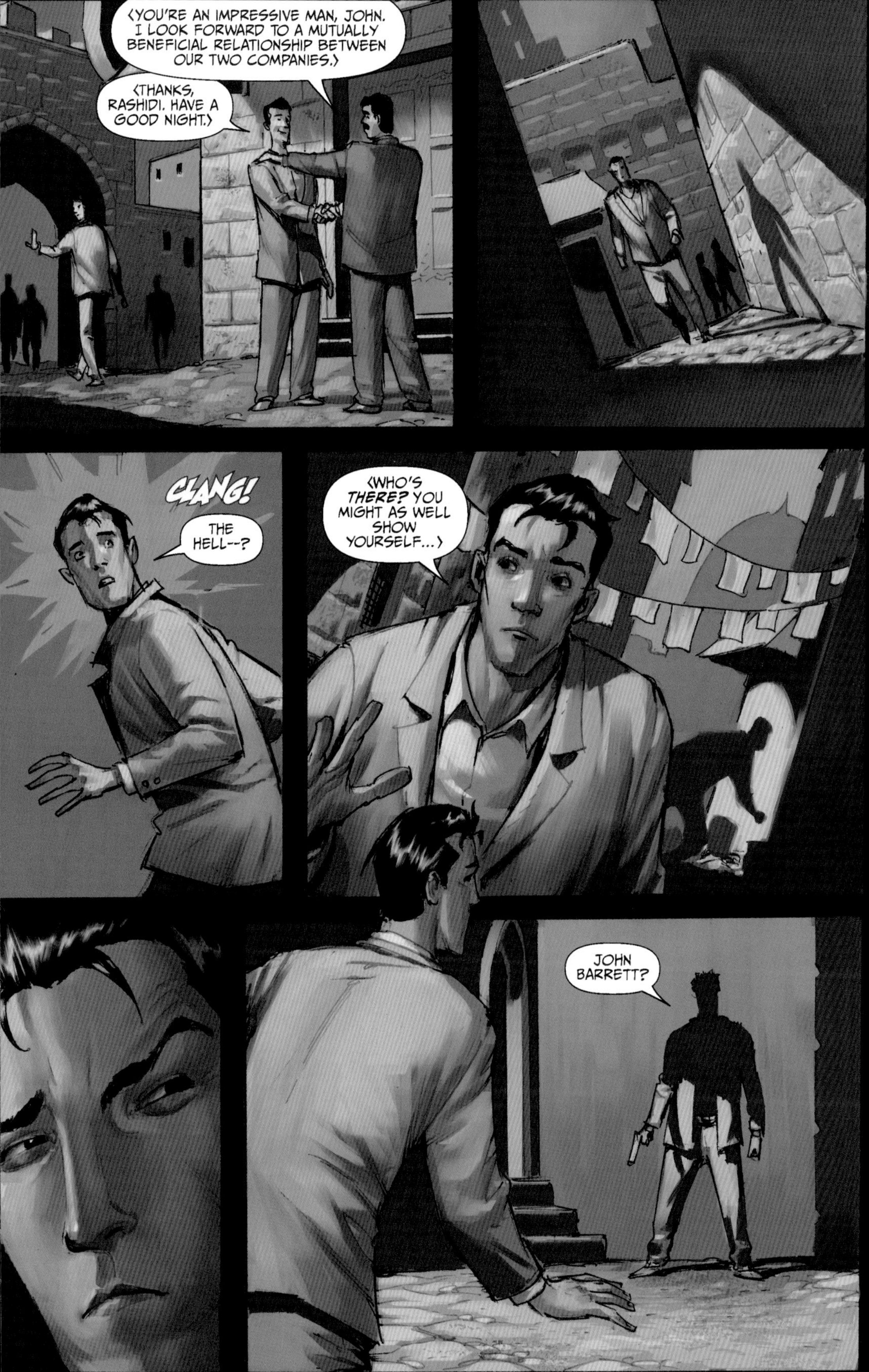

‹YOU'RE AN IMPRESSIVE MAN, JOHN. I LOOK FORWARD TO A MUTUALLY BENEFICIAL RELATIONSHIP BETWEEN OUR TWO COMPANIES.›
‹THANKS, RASHIDI. HAVE A GOOD NIGHT.›
CLANG!
THE HELL--?
‹WHO'S *THERE?* YOU MIGHT AS WELL SHOW YOURSELF...›
JOHN BARRETT?

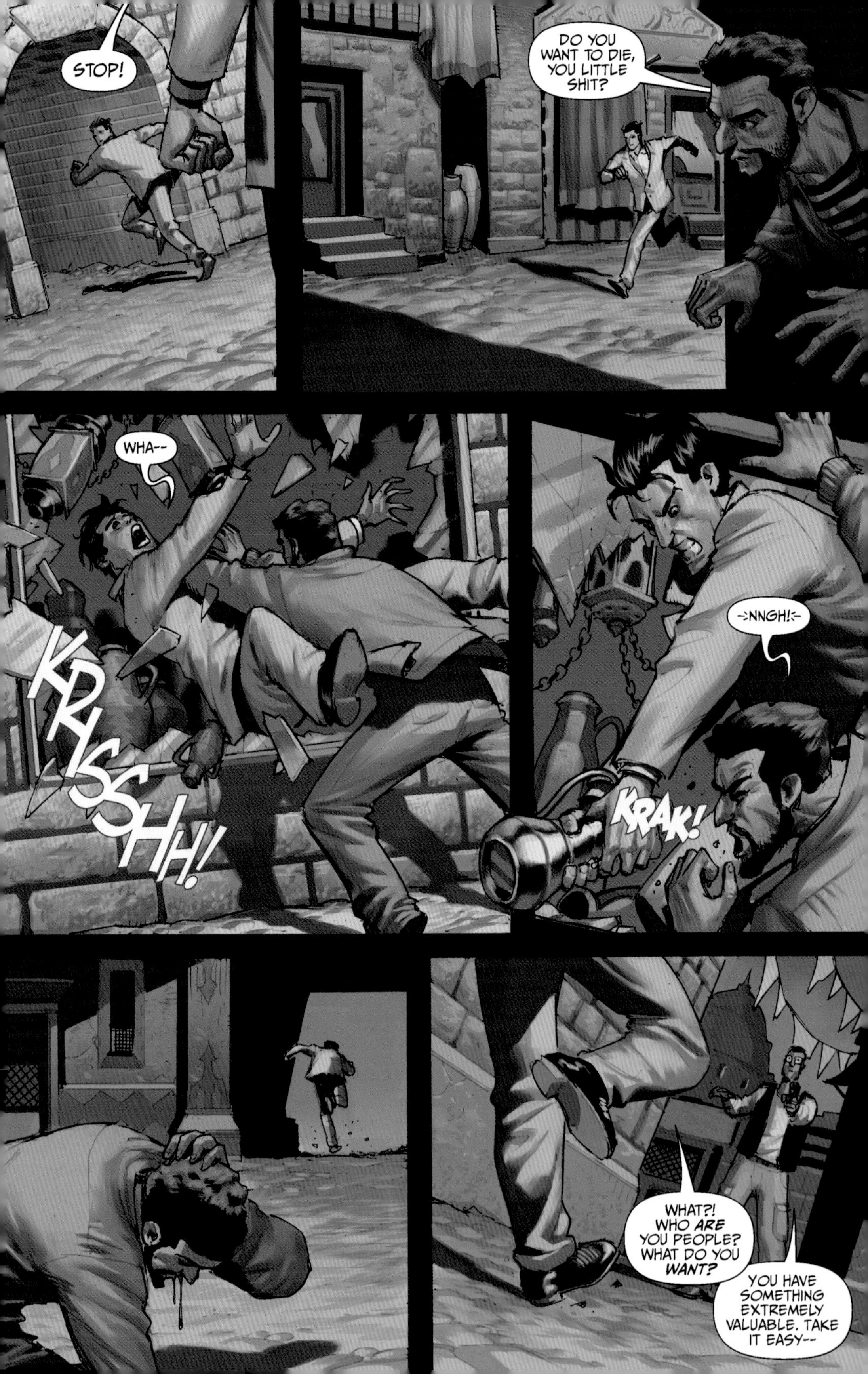
STOP!
DO YOU WANT TO DIE, YOU LITTLE SHIT?
WHA--
KRISSHH!
-NNGH!-
KRAK!
WHAT?! WHO *ARE* YOU PEOPLE? WHAT DO YOU *WANT?*
YOU HAVE SOMETHING EXTREMELY VALUABLE. TAKE IT EASY--

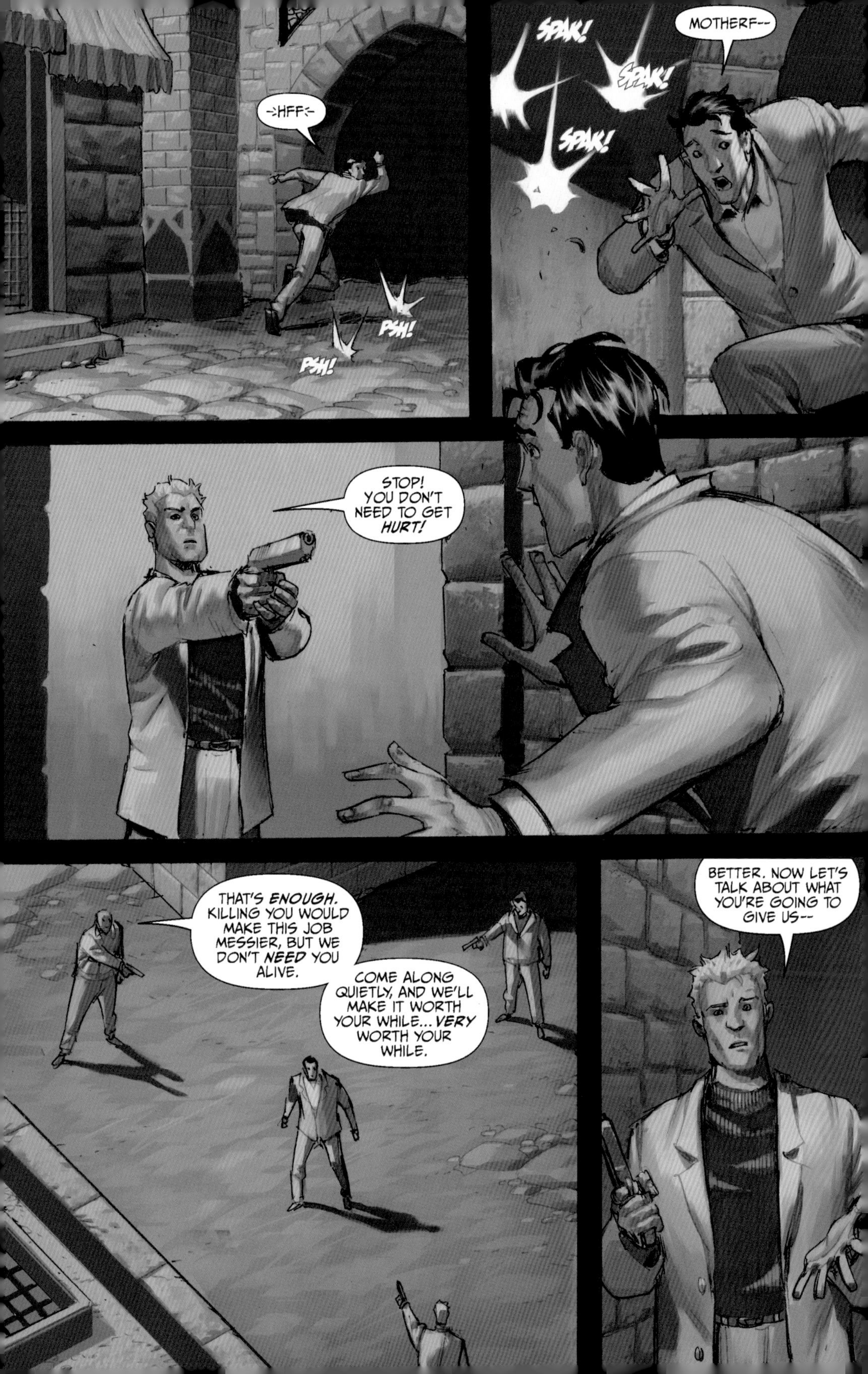
-HFF-
PSH!
PSH!
SPAK!
SPAK!
SPAK!
MOTHERF--
STOP! YOU DON'T NEED TO GET *HURT!*
THAT'S *ENOUGH.* KILLING YOU WOULD MAKE THIS JOB MESSIER, BUT WE DON'T *NEED* YOU ALIVE.
COME ALONG QUIETLY, AND WE'LL MAKE IT WORTH YOUR WHILE... *VERY* WORTH YOUR WHILE.
BETTER. NOW LET'S TALK ABOUT WHAT YOU'RE GOING TO GIVE US--

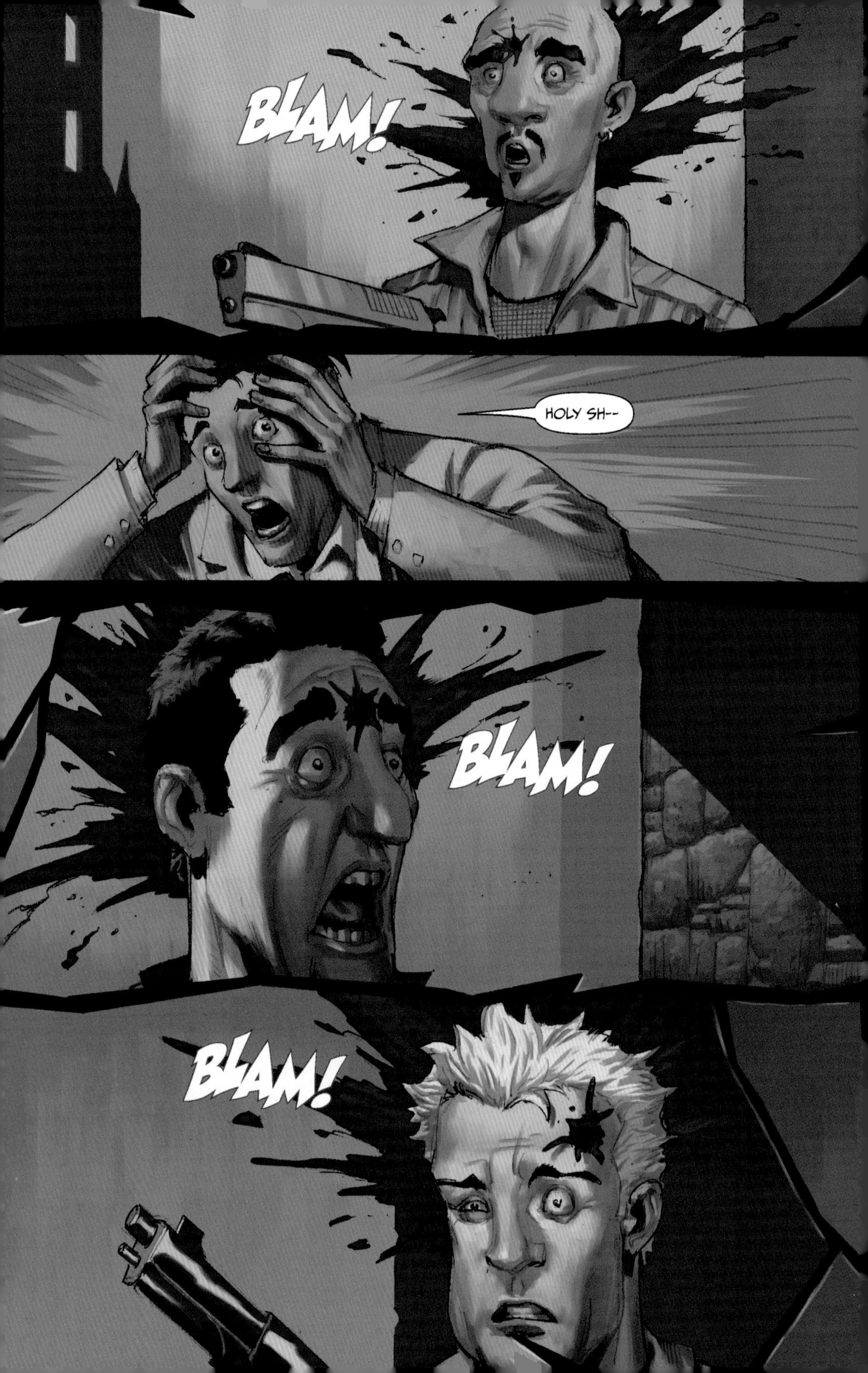
BLAM!
HOLY SH--
BLAM!
BLAM!

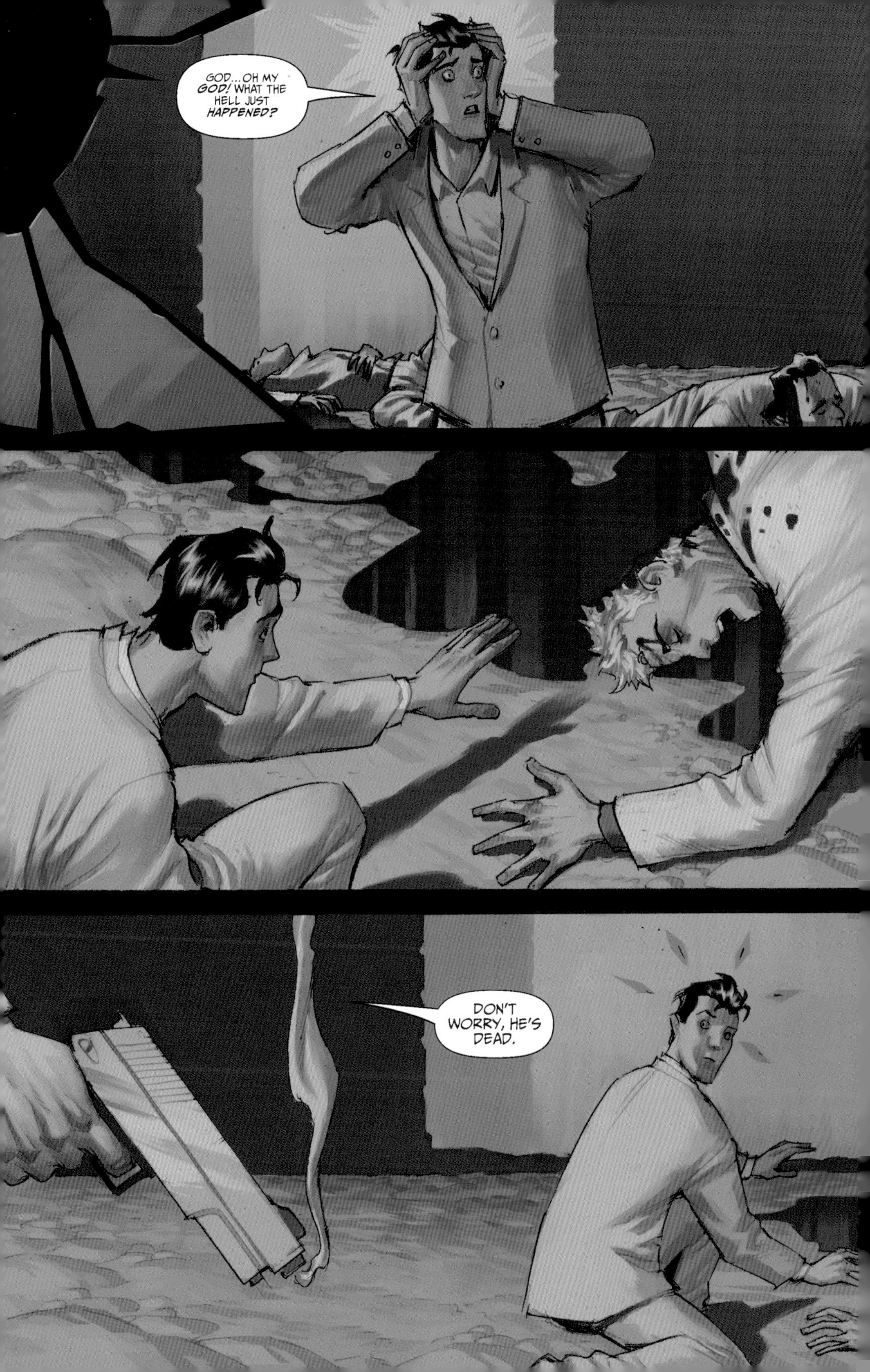
GOD...OH MY GOD! WHAT THE HELL JUST HAPPENED?
DON'T WORRY, HE'S DEAD.

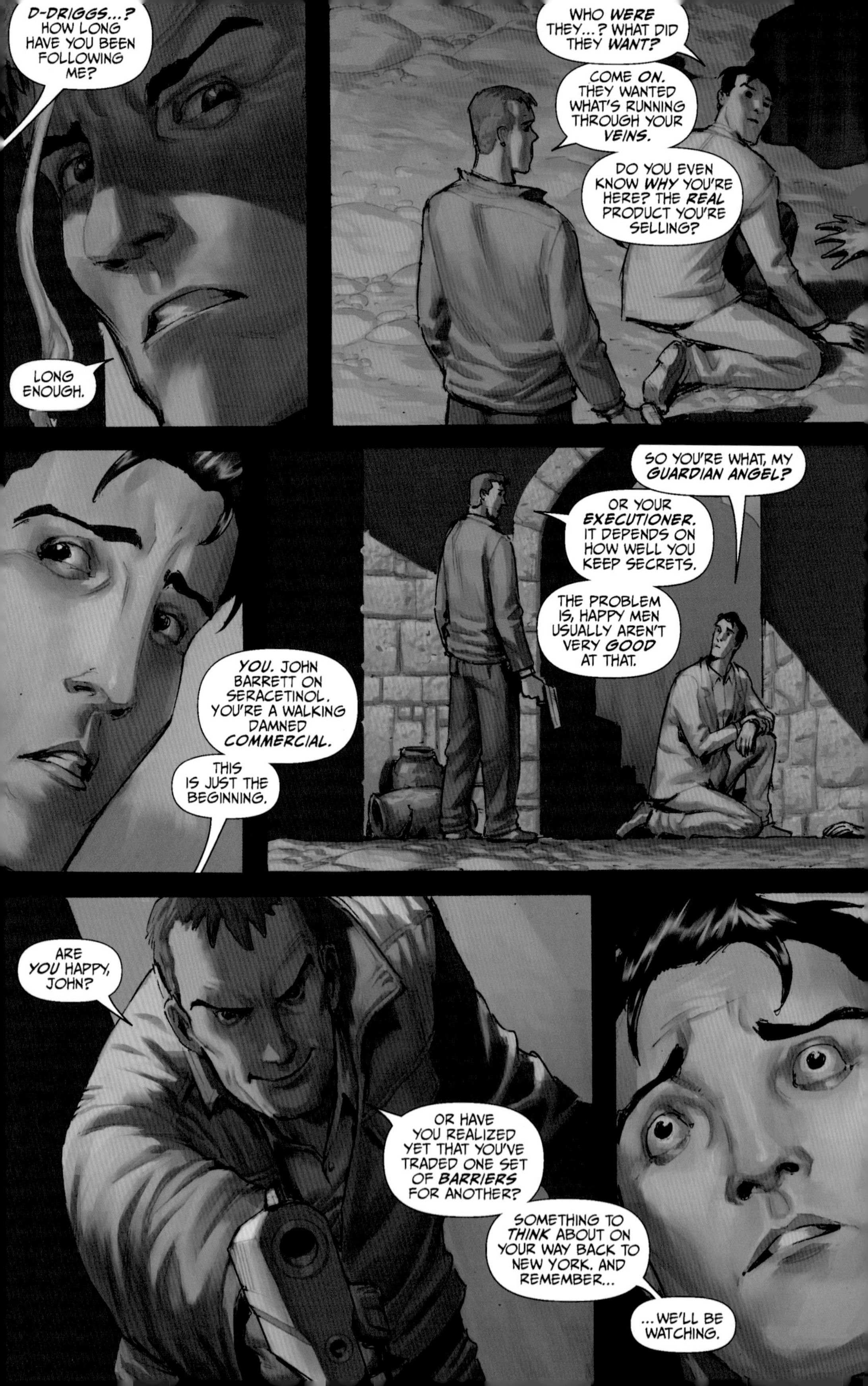

D-DRIGGS...? HOW LONG HAVE YOU BEEN FOLLOWING ME?
LONG ENOUGH.
WHO WERE THEY...? WHAT DID THEY WANT?
COME ON. THEY WANTED WHAT'S RUNNING THROUGH YOUR VEINS.
DO YOU EVEN KNOW WHY YOU'RE HERE? THE REAL PRODUCT YOU'RE SELLING?
YOU. JOHN BARRETT ON SERACETINOL. YOU'RE A WALKING DAMNED COMMERCIAL.
THIS IS JUST THE BEGINNING.
SO YOU'RE WHAT, MY GUARDIAN ANGEL?
OR YOUR EXECUTIONER. IT DEPENDS ON HOW WELL YOU KEEP SECRETS.
THE PROBLEM IS, HAPPY MEN USUALLY AREN'T VERY GOOD AT THAT.
ARE YOU HAPPY, JOHN?
OR HAVE YOU REALIZED YET THAT YOU'VE TRADED ONE SET OF BARRIERS FOR ANOTHER?
SOMETHING TO THINK ABOUT ON YOUR WAY BACK TO NEW YORK. AND REMEMBER...
...WE'LL BE WATCHING.

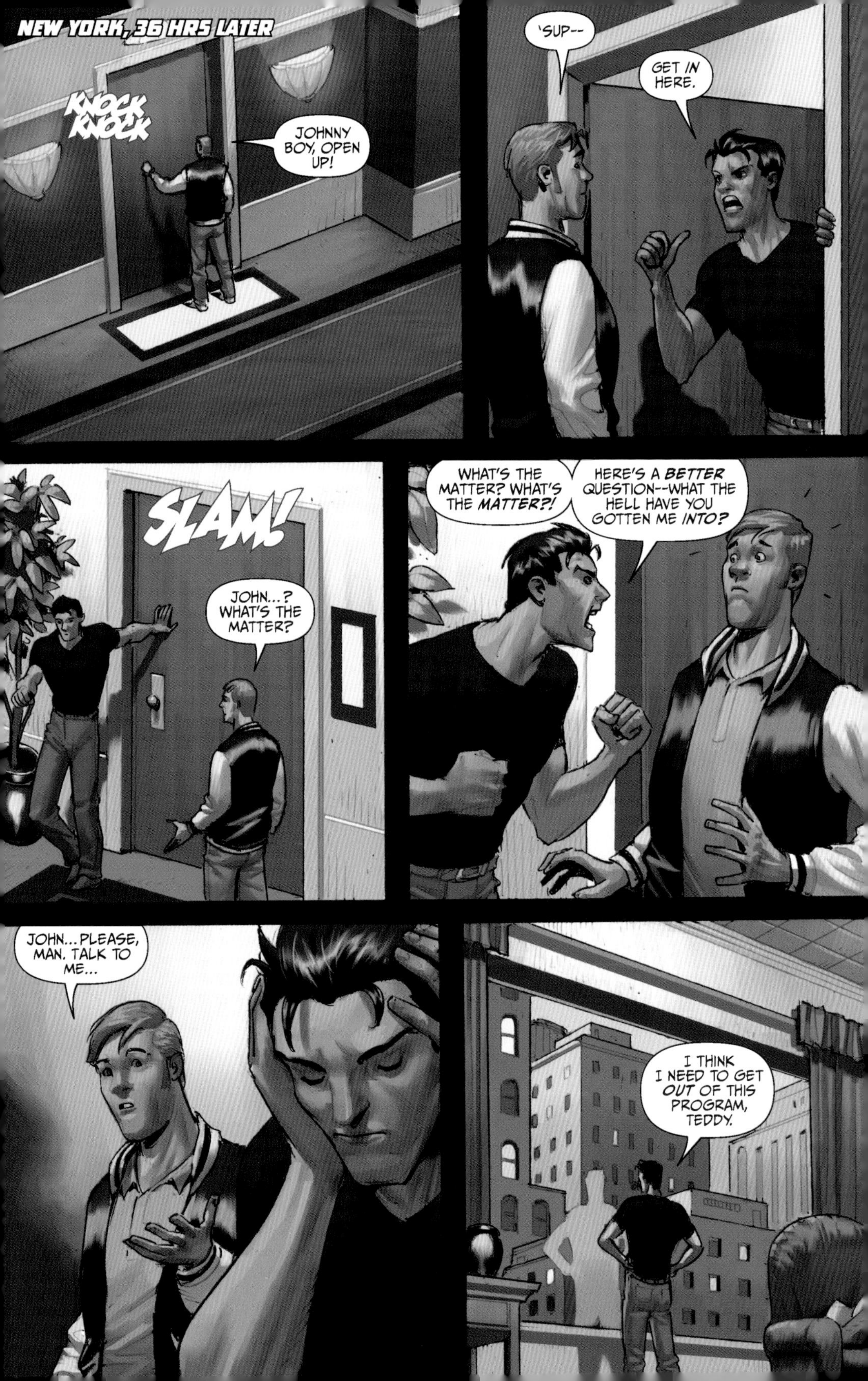
NEW YORK, 36 HRS LATER
KNOCK KNOCK
JOHNNY BOY, OPEN UP!
'SUP--
GET IN HERE.
SLAM!
JOHN...? WHAT'S THE MATTER?
WHAT'S THE MATTER? WHAT'S THE MATTER?!
HERE'S A BETTER QUESTION--WHAT THE HELL HAVE YOU GOTTEN ME INTO?
JOHN...PLEASE, MAN. TALK TO ME...
I THINK I NEED TO GET OUT OF THIS PROGRAM, TEDDY.

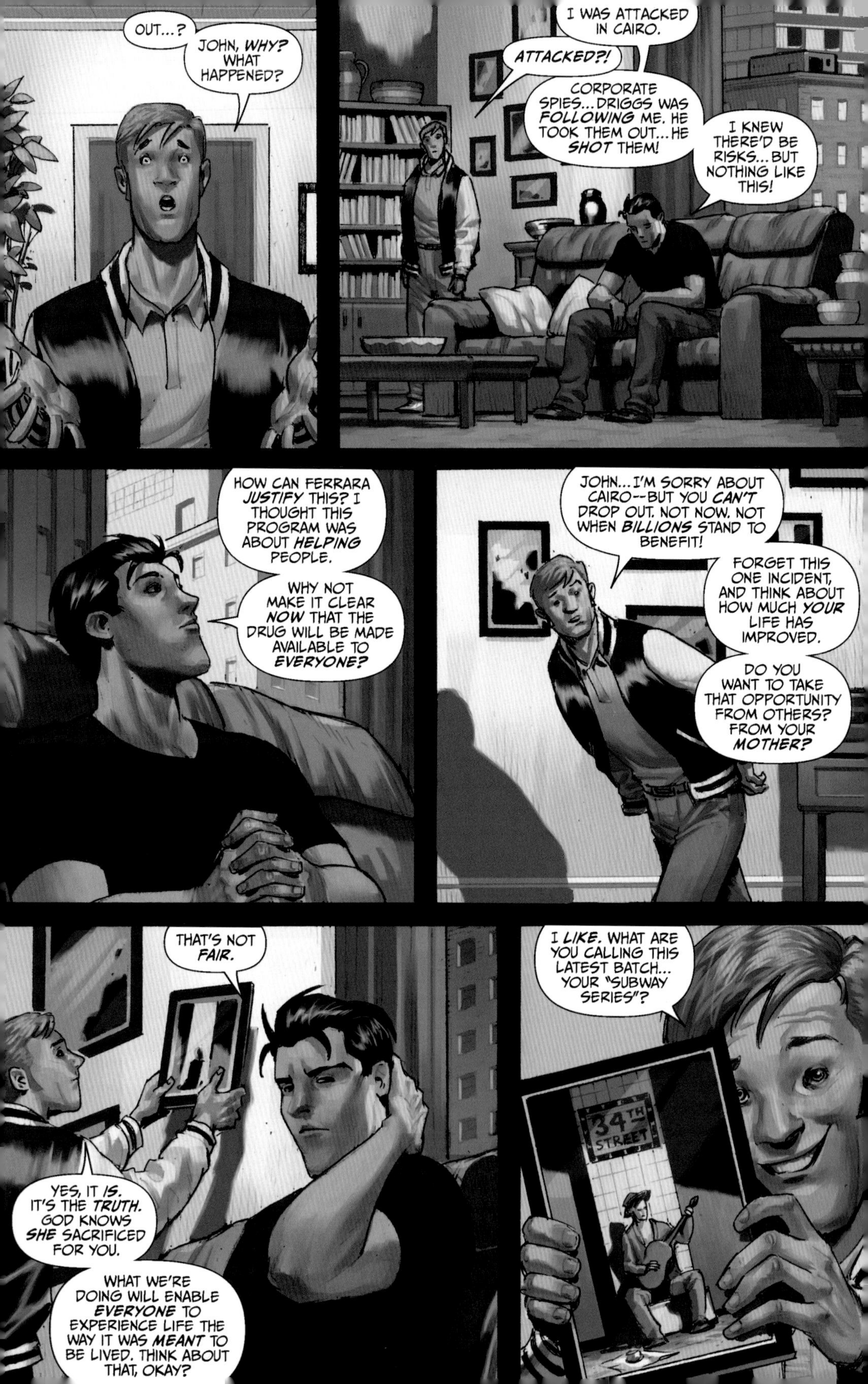
OUT...?
JOHN, WHY? WHAT HAPPENED?
I WAS ATTACKED IN CAIRO.
ATTACKED?!
CORPORATE SPIES...DRIGGS WAS FOLLOWING ME. HE TOOK THEM OUT...HE SHOT THEM!
I KNEW THERE'D BE RISKS...BUT NOTHING LIKE THIS!
HOW CAN FERRARA JUSTIFY THIS? I THOUGHT THIS PROGRAM WAS ABOUT HELPING PEOPLE.
WHY NOT MAKE IT CLEAR NOW THAT THE DRUG WILL BE MADE AVAILABLE TO EVERYONE?
JOHN...I'M SORRY ABOUT CAIRO--BUT YOU CAN'T DROP OUT. NOT NOW. NOT WHEN BILLIONS STAND TO BENEFIT!
FORGET THIS ONE INCIDENT, AND THINK ABOUT HOW MUCH YOUR LIFE HAS IMPROVED.
DO YOU WANT TO TAKE THAT OPPORTUNITY FROM OTHERS? FROM YOUR MOTHER?
THAT'S NOT FAIR.
YES, IT IS. IT'S THE TRUTH. GOD KNOWS SHE SACRIFICED FOR YOU.
WHAT WE'RE DOING WILL ENABLE EVERYONE TO EXPERIENCE LIFE THE WAY IT WAS MEANT TO BE LIVED. THINK ABOUT THAT, OKAY?
I LIKE. WHAT ARE YOU CALLING THIS LATEST BATCH... YOUR "SUBWAY SERIES"?
34TH STREET

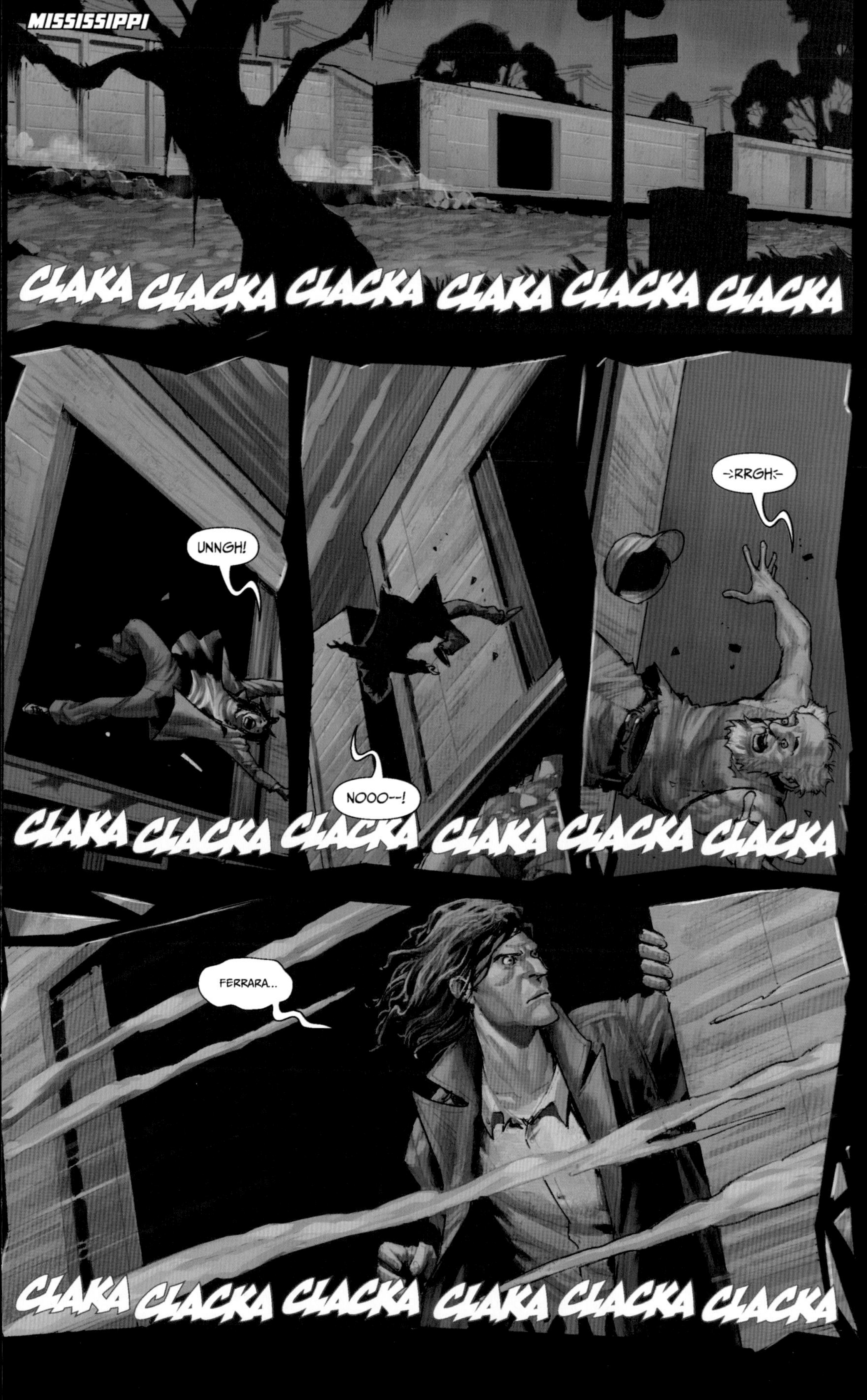
MISSISSIPPI
CLAKA CLACKA CLACKA CLAKA CLACKA CLACKA
UNNGH!
NOOO--!
RRGH
CLAKA CLACKA CLACKA CLAKA CLACKA CLACKA
FERRARA..
CLAKA CLACKA CLACKA CLAKA CLACKA CLACKA

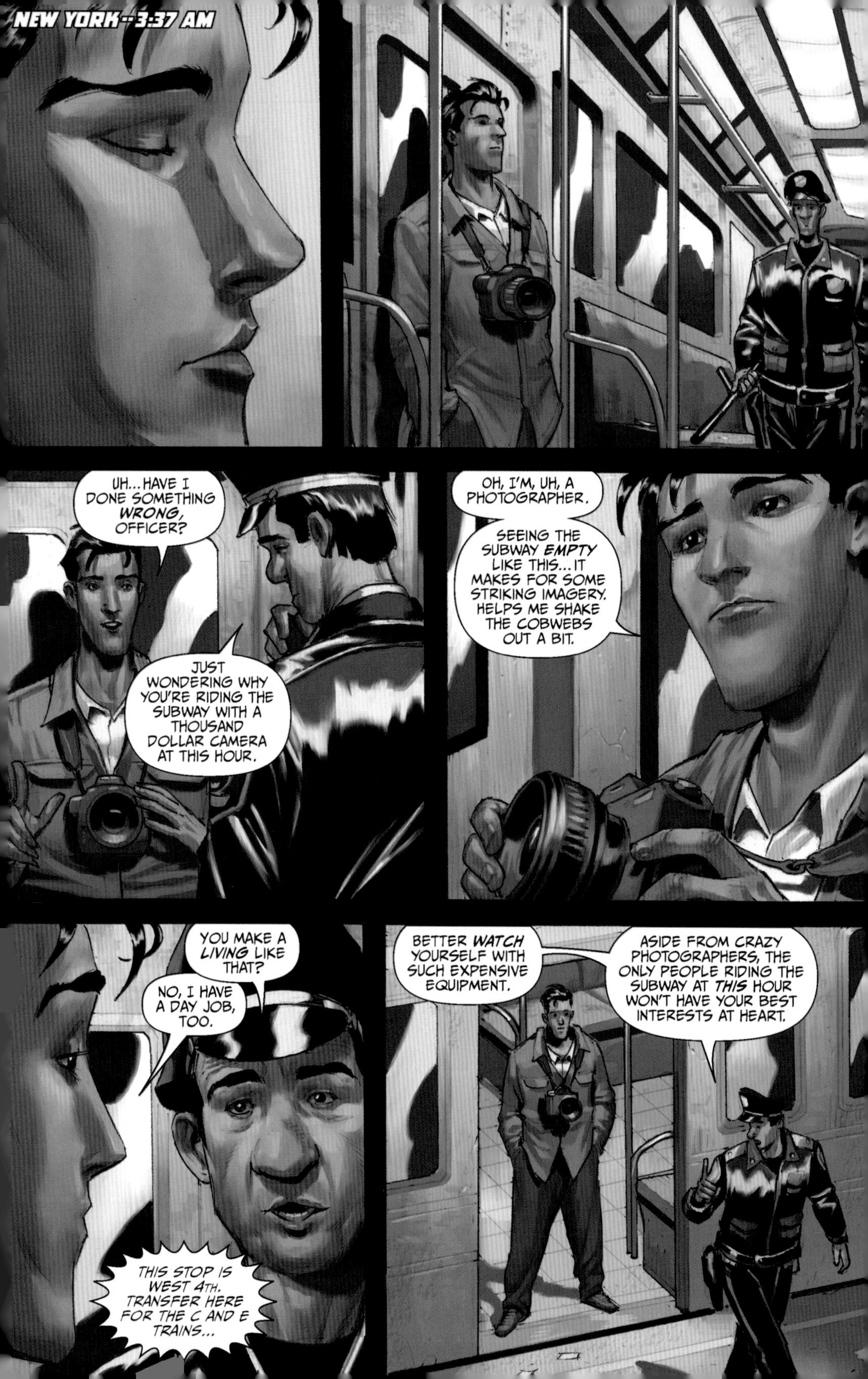
NEW YORK--3:37 AM
UH... HAVE I DONE SOMETHING *WRONG*, OFFICER?
JUST WONDERING WHY YOU'RE RIDING THE SUBWAY WITH A THOUSAND DOLLAR CAMERA AT THIS HOUR.
OH, I'M, UH, A PHOTOGRAPHER.
SEEING THE SUBWAY *EMPTY* LIKE THIS... IT MAKES FOR SOME STRIKING IMAGERY. HELPS ME SHAKE THE COBWEBS OUT A BIT.
YOU MAKE A *LIVING* LIKE THAT?
NO, I HAVE A DAY JOB, TOO.
THIS STOP IS WEST 4TH. TRANSFER HERE FOR THE C AND E TRAINS...
BETTER *WATCH* YOURSELF WITH SUCH EXPENSIVE EQUIPMENT.
ASIDE FROM CRAZY PHOTOGRAPHERS, THE ONLY PEOPLE RIDING THE SUBWAY AT *THIS* HOUR WON'T HAVE YOUR BEST INTERESTS AT HEART.

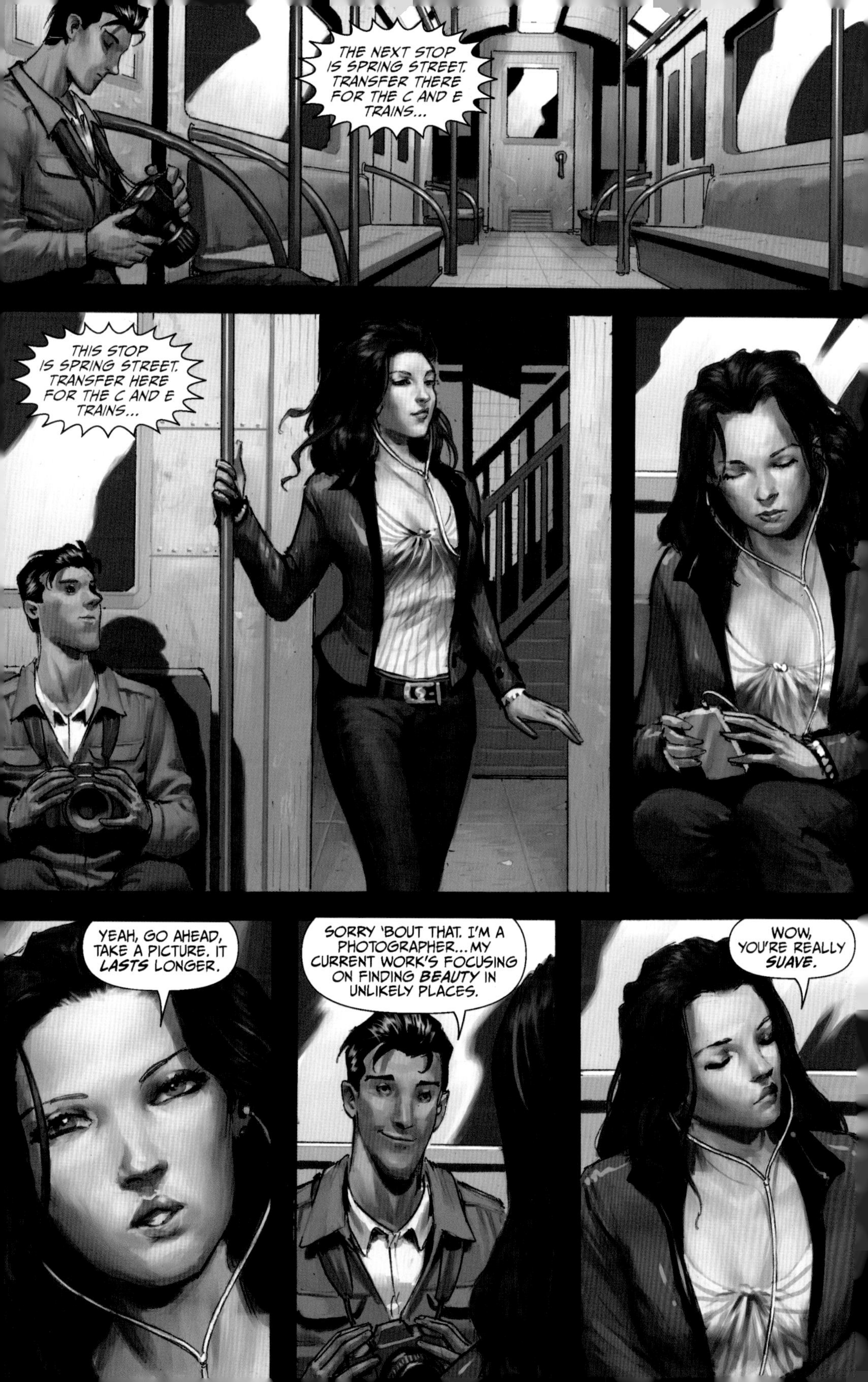
THE NEXT STOP IS SPRING STREET. TRANSFER THERE FOR THE C AND E TRAINS...
THIS STOP IS SPRING STREET. TRANSFER HERE FOR THE C AND E TRAINS...
YEAH, GO AHEAD, TAKE A PICTURE. IT LASTS LONGER.
SORRY 'BOUT THAT. I'M A PHOTOGRAPHER... MY CURRENT WORK'S FOCUSING ON FINDING BEAUTY IN UNLIKELY PLACES.
WOW, YOU'RE REALLY SUAVE.

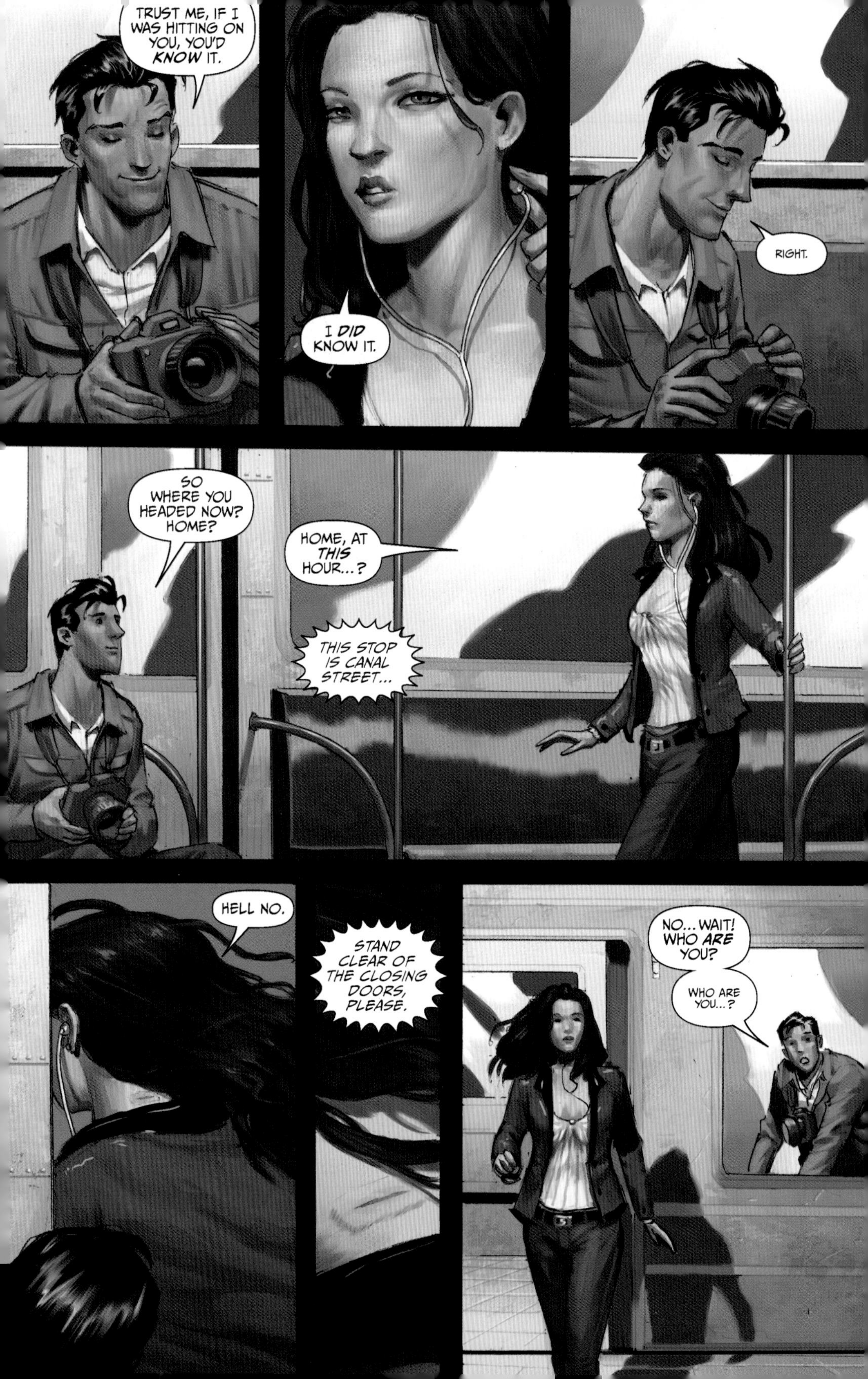
TRUST ME, IF I WAS HITTING ON YOU, YOU'D KNOW IT.
I DID KNOW IT.
RIGHT.
SO WHERE YOU HEADED NOW? HOME?
HOME, AT THIS HOUR...?
THIS STOP IS CANAL STREET...
HELL NO.
STAND CLEAR OF THE CLOSING DOORS, PLEASE.
NO... WAIT! WHO ARE YOU?
WHO ARE YOU...?

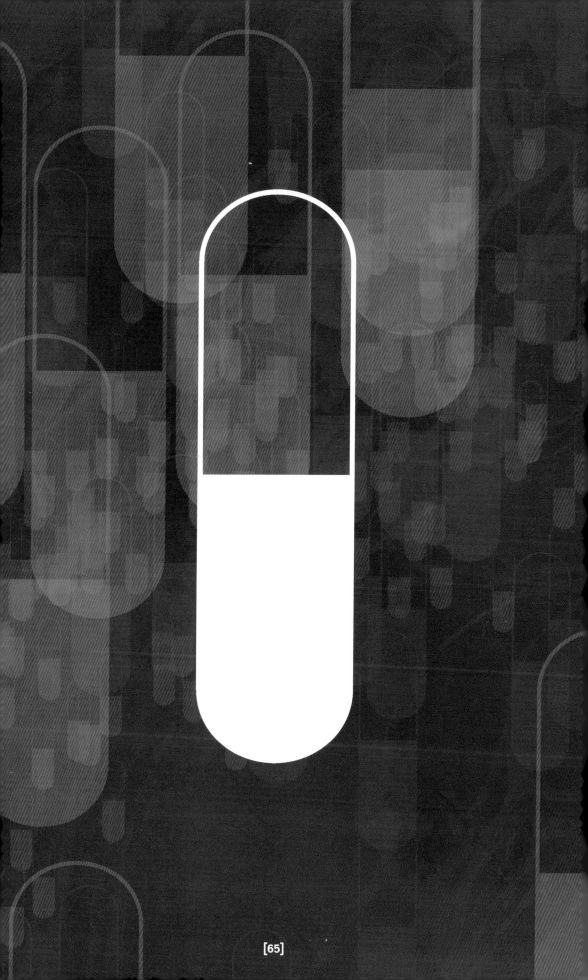

Rest #3

written by: **Mark Powers**
line art by: **Marco Castiello**
colors by: **William Farmer**
letters by: **Troy Peteri**

• • • • •

original edition edited by: **Filip Sablik**
& **Phil Smith**

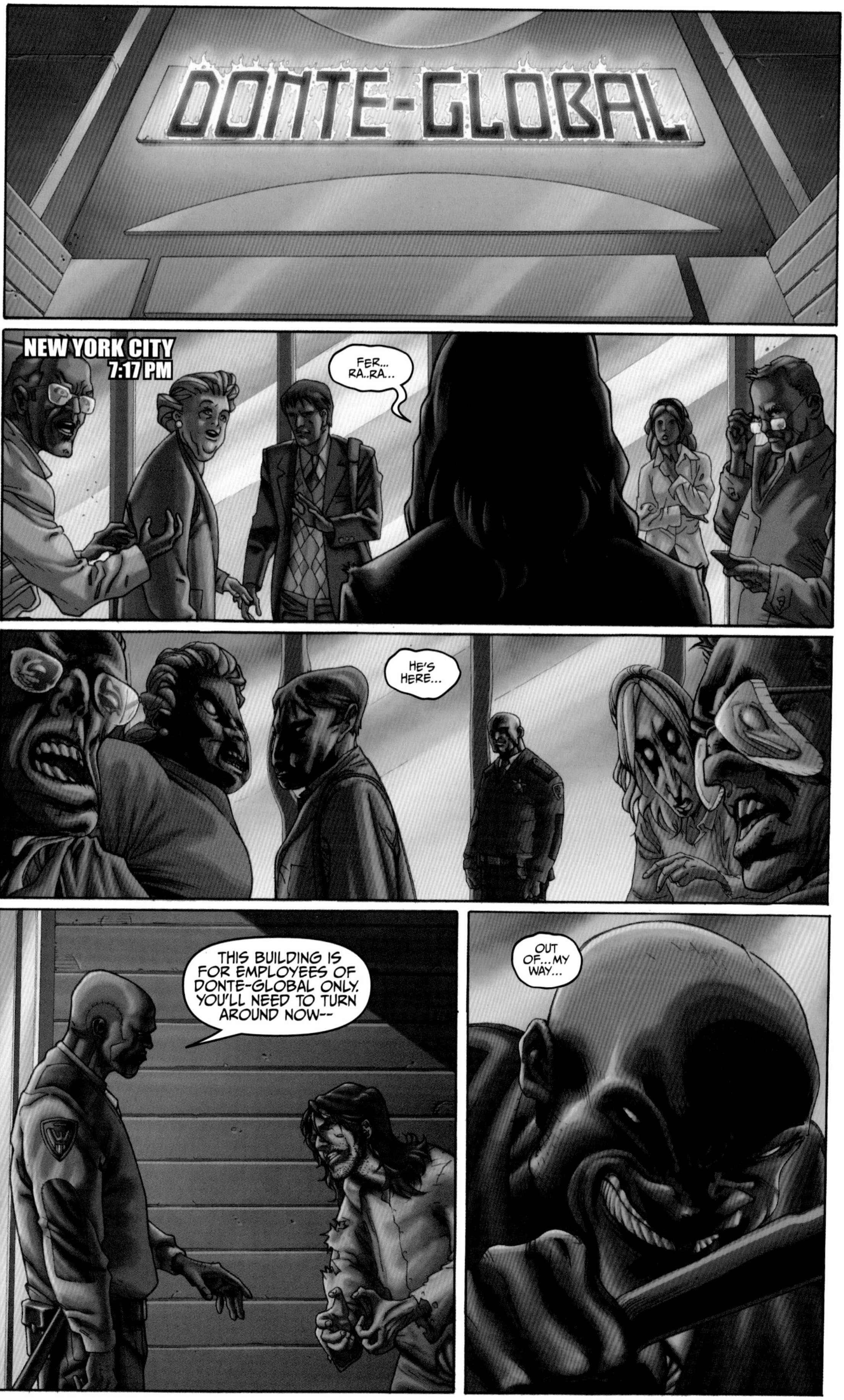
DONTE-GLOBAL
NEW YORK CITY 7:17 PM
FER... RA..RA...
HE'S HERE...
THIS BUILDING IS FOR EMPLOYEES OF DONTE-GLOBAL ONLY. YOU'LL NEED TO TURN AROUND NOW--
OUT OF...MY WAY...

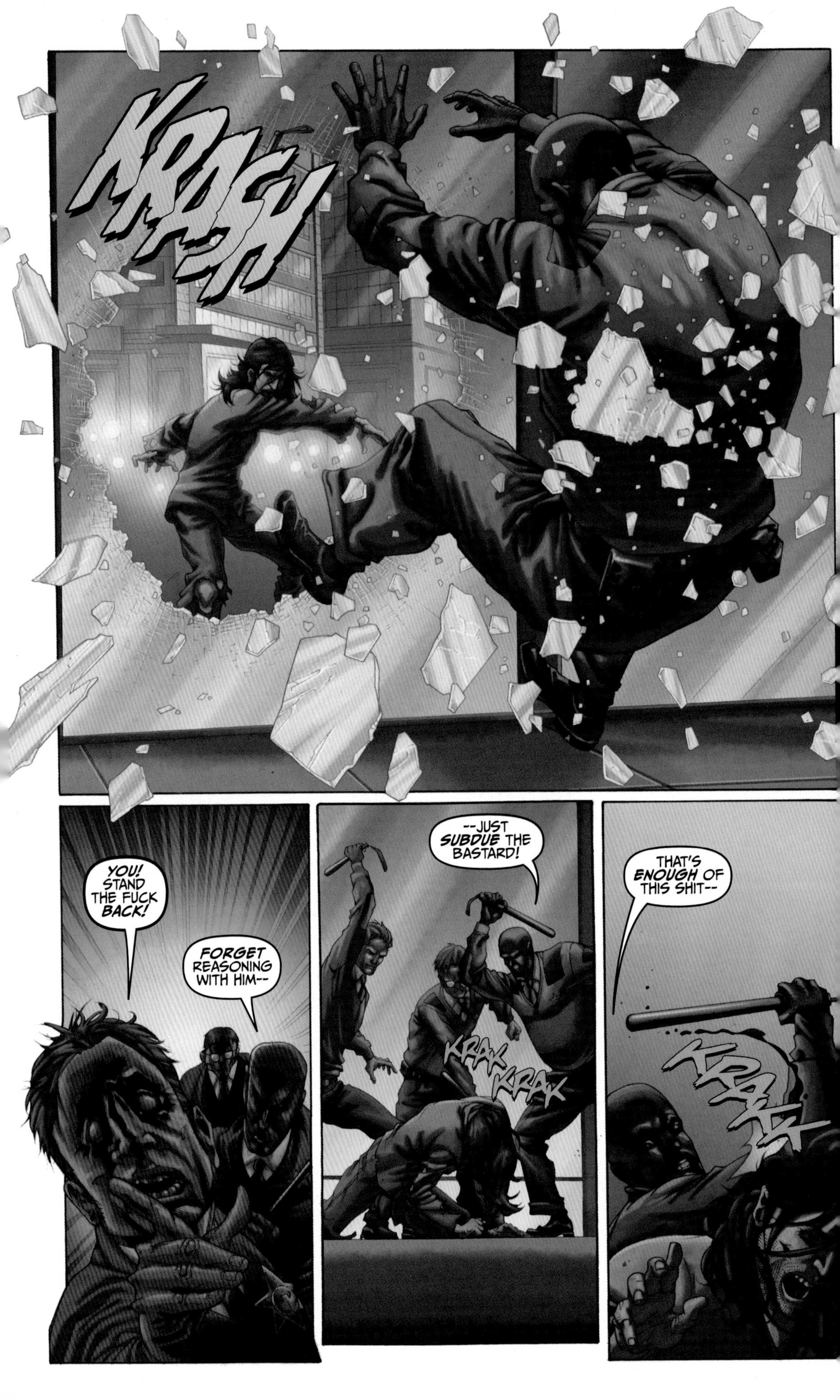
KRASH
YOU! STAND THE FUCK BACK!
FORGET REASONING WITH HIM--
--JUST SUBDUE THE BASTARD!
KRAK KRAK
THAT'S ENOUGH OF THIS SHIT--
KRAKK

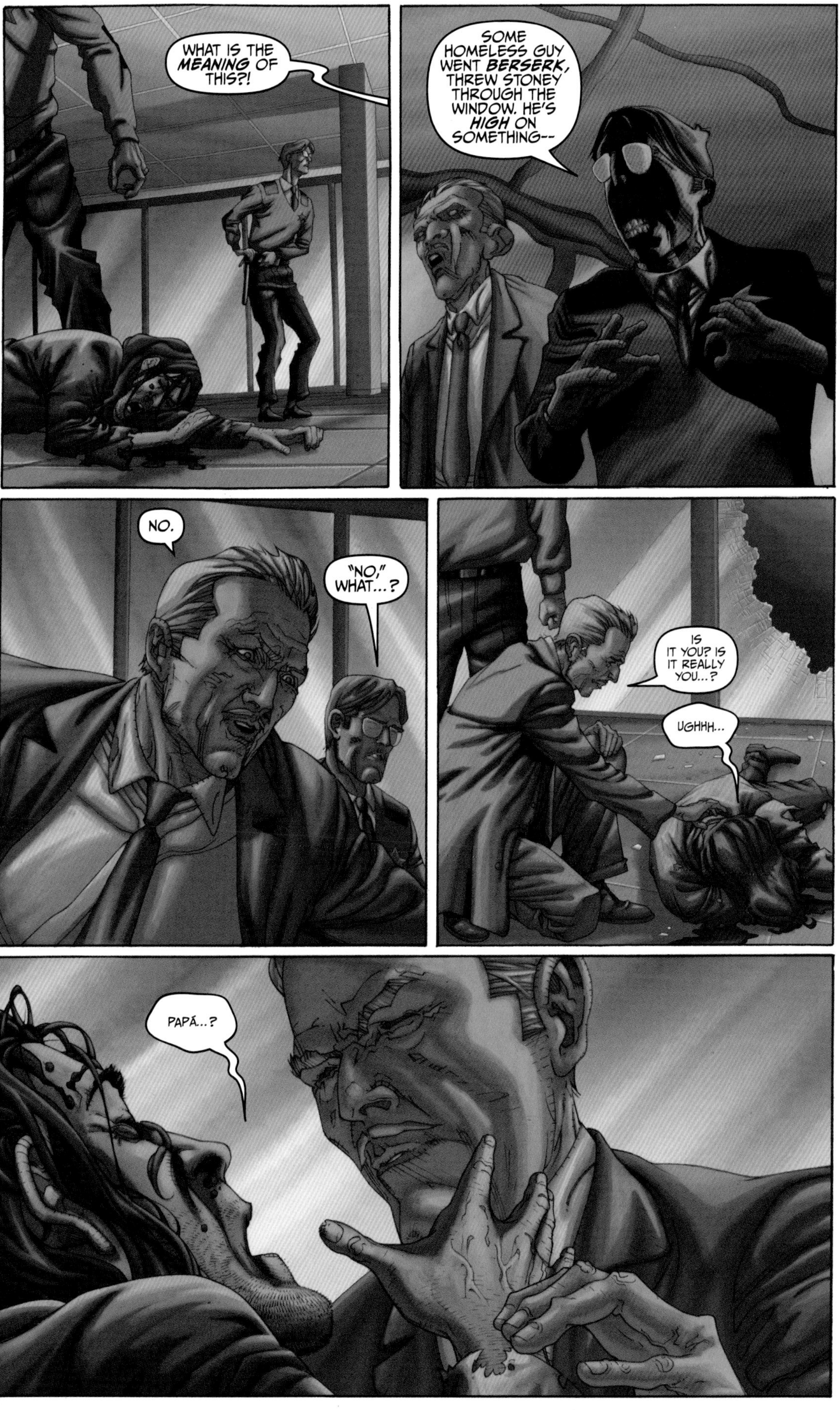
WHAT IS THE MEANING OF THIS?!
SOME HOMELESS GUY WENT BERSERK, THREW STONEY THROUGH THE WINDOW. HE'S HIGH ON SOMETHING--
NO.
"NO," WHAT...?
IS IT YOU? IS IT REALLY YOU...?
UGHHH...
PAPÁ...?

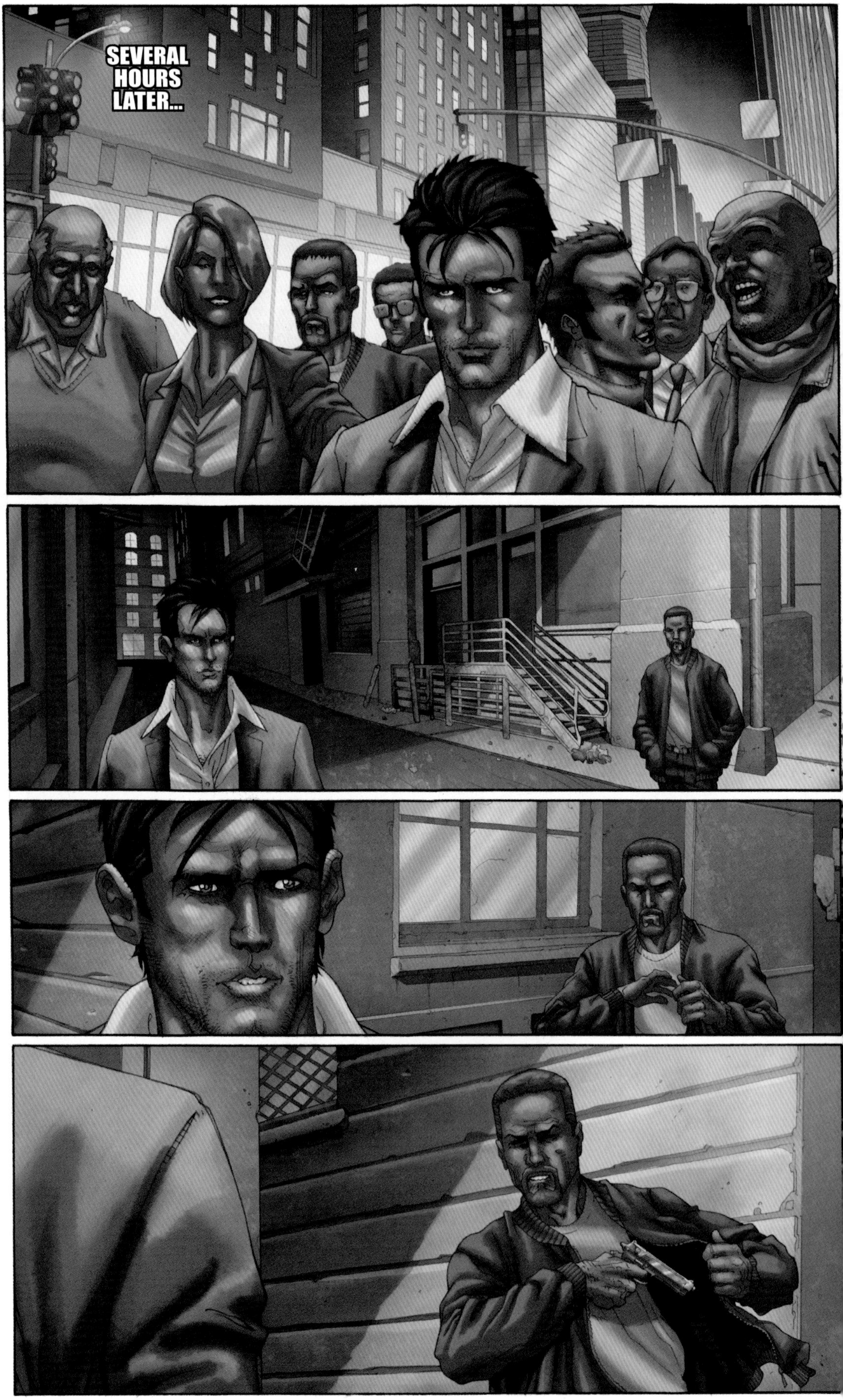
SEVERAL HOURS LATER...

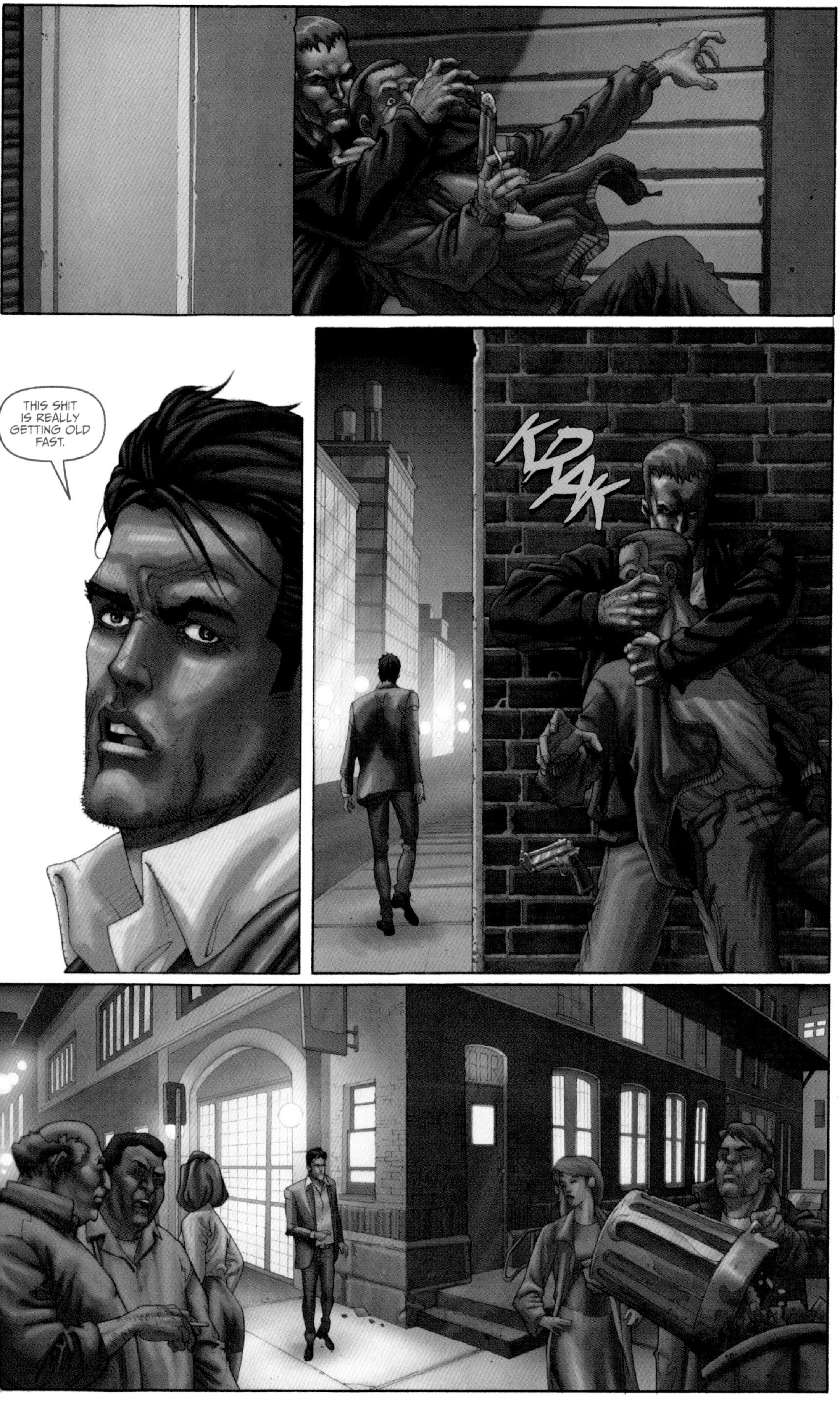
THIS SHIT IS REALLY GETTING OLD FAST.
KRAK

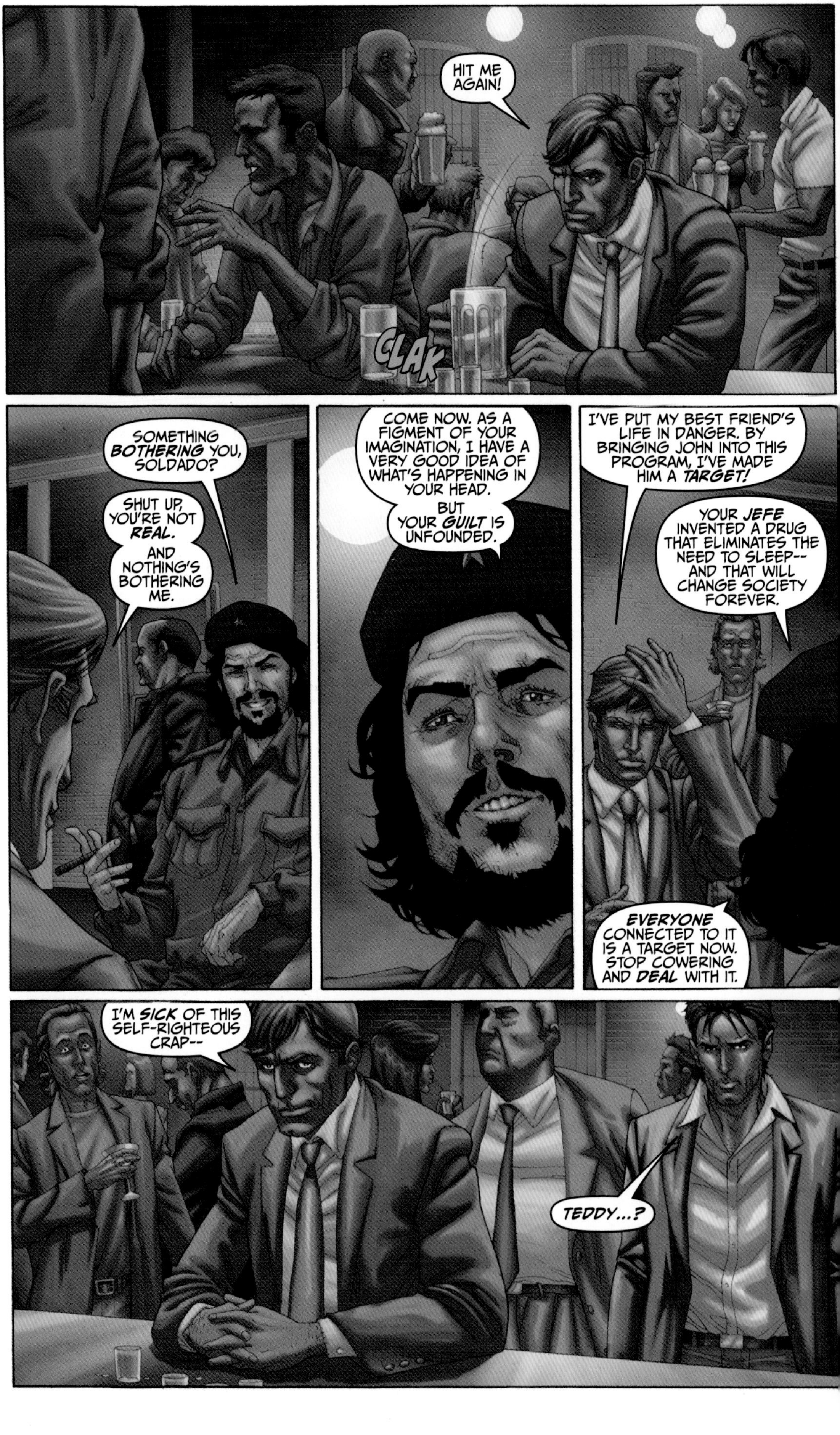
HIT ME AGAIN!
CLAK
SOMETHING BOTHERING YOU, SOLDADO?
SHUT UP, YOU'RE NOT REAL.
AND NOTHING'S BOTHERING ME.
COME NOW. AS A FIGMENT OF YOUR IMAGINATION, I HAVE A VERY GOOD IDEA OF WHAT'S HAPPENING IN YOUR HEAD.
BUT YOUR GUILT IS UNFOUNDED.
I'VE PUT MY BEST FRIEND'S LIFE IN DANGER. BY BRINGING JOHN INTO THIS PROGRAM, I'VE MADE HIM A TARGET!
YOUR JEFE INVENTED A DRUG THAT ELIMINATES THE NEED TO SLEEP-- AND THAT WILL CHANGE SOCIETY FOREVER.
EVERYONE CONNECTED TO IT IS A TARGET NOW. STOP COWERING AND DEAL WITH IT.
I'M SICK OF THIS SELF-RIGHTEOUS CRAP--
TEDDY...?

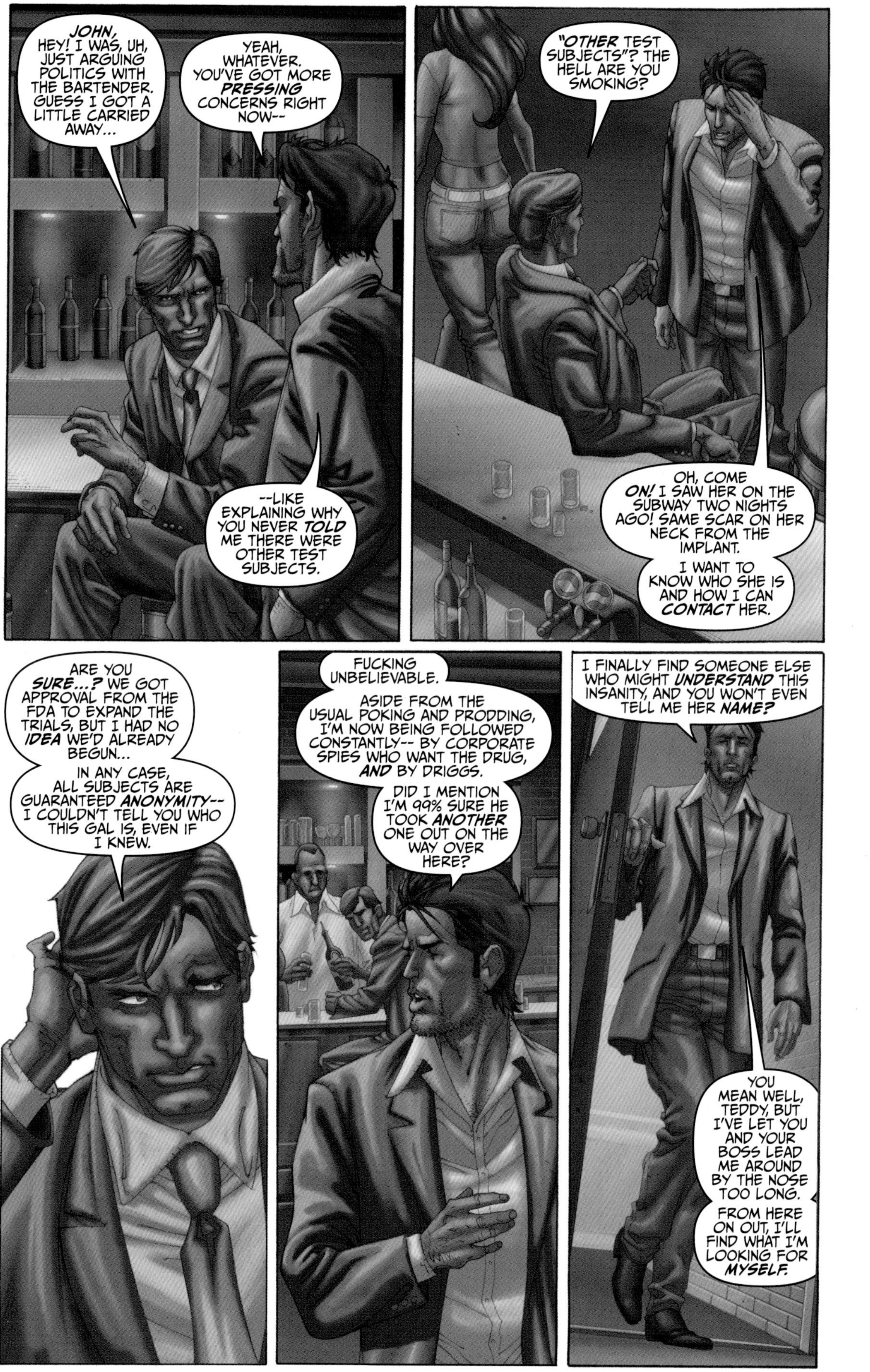
JOHN, HEY! I WAS, UH, JUST ARGUING POLITICS WITH THE BARTENDER. GUESS I GOT A LITTLE CARRIED AWAY...
YEAH, WHATEVER. YOU'VE GOT MORE PRESSING CONCERNS RIGHT NOW--
--LIKE EXPLAINING WHY YOU NEVER TOLD ME THERE WERE OTHER TEST SUBJECTS.
"OTHER TEST SUBJECTS"? THE HELL ARE YOU SMOKING?
OH, COME ON! I SAW HER ON THE SUBWAY TWO NIGHTS AGO! SAME SCAR ON HER NECK FROM THE IMPLANT.
I WANT TO KNOW WHO SHE IS AND HOW I CAN CONTACT HER.
ARE YOU SURE...? WE GOT APPROVAL FROM THE FDA TO EXPAND THE TRIALS, BUT I HAD NO IDEA WE'D ALREADY BEGUN...
IN ANY CASE, ALL SUBJECTS ARE GUARANTEED ANONYMITY-- I COULDN'T TELL YOU WHO THIS GAL IS, EVEN IF I KNEW.
FUCKING UNBELIEVABLE.
ASIDE FROM THE USUAL POKING AND PRODDING, I'M NOW BEING FOLLOWED CONSTANTLY-- BY CORPORATE SPIES WHO WANT THE DRUG, AND BY DRIGGS.
DID I MENTION I'M 99% SURE HE TOOK ANOTHER ONE OUT ON THE WAY OVER HERE?
I FINALLY FIND SOMEONE ELSE WHO MIGHT UNDERSTAND THIS INSANITY, AND YOU WON'T EVEN TELL ME HER NAME?
YOU MEAN WELL, TEDDY, BUT I'VE LET YOU AND YOUR BOSS LEAD ME AROUND BY THE NOSE TOO LONG.
FROM HERE ON OUT, I'LL FIND WHAT I'M LOOKING FOR MYSELF.

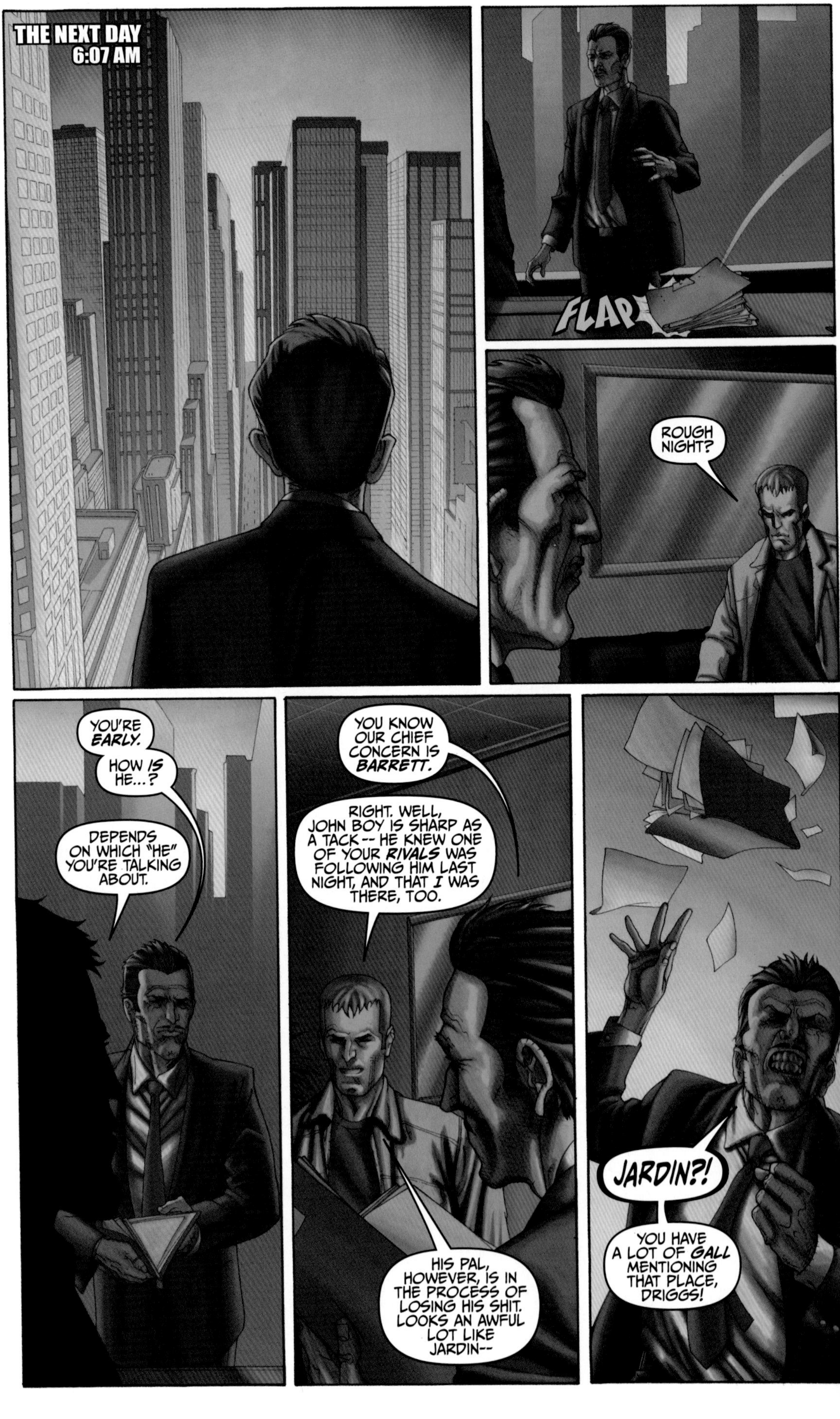
THE NEXT DAY
6:07 AM
FLAP
ROUGH NIGHT?
YOU'RE EARLY.
HOW IS HE...?
DEPENDS ON WHICH "HE" YOU'RE TALKING ABOUT.
YOU KNOW OUR CHIEF CONCERN IS BARRETT.
RIGHT. WELL, JOHN BOY IS SHARP AS A TACK-- HE KNEW ONE OF YOUR RIVALS WAS FOLLOWING HIM LAST NIGHT, AND THAT I WAS THERE, TOO.
HIS PAL, HOWEVER, IS IN THE PROCESS OF LOSING HIS SHIT. LOOKS AN AWFUL LOT LIKE JARDIN--
JARDIN?!
YOU HAVE A LOT OF GALL MENTIONING THAT PLACE, DRIGGS!

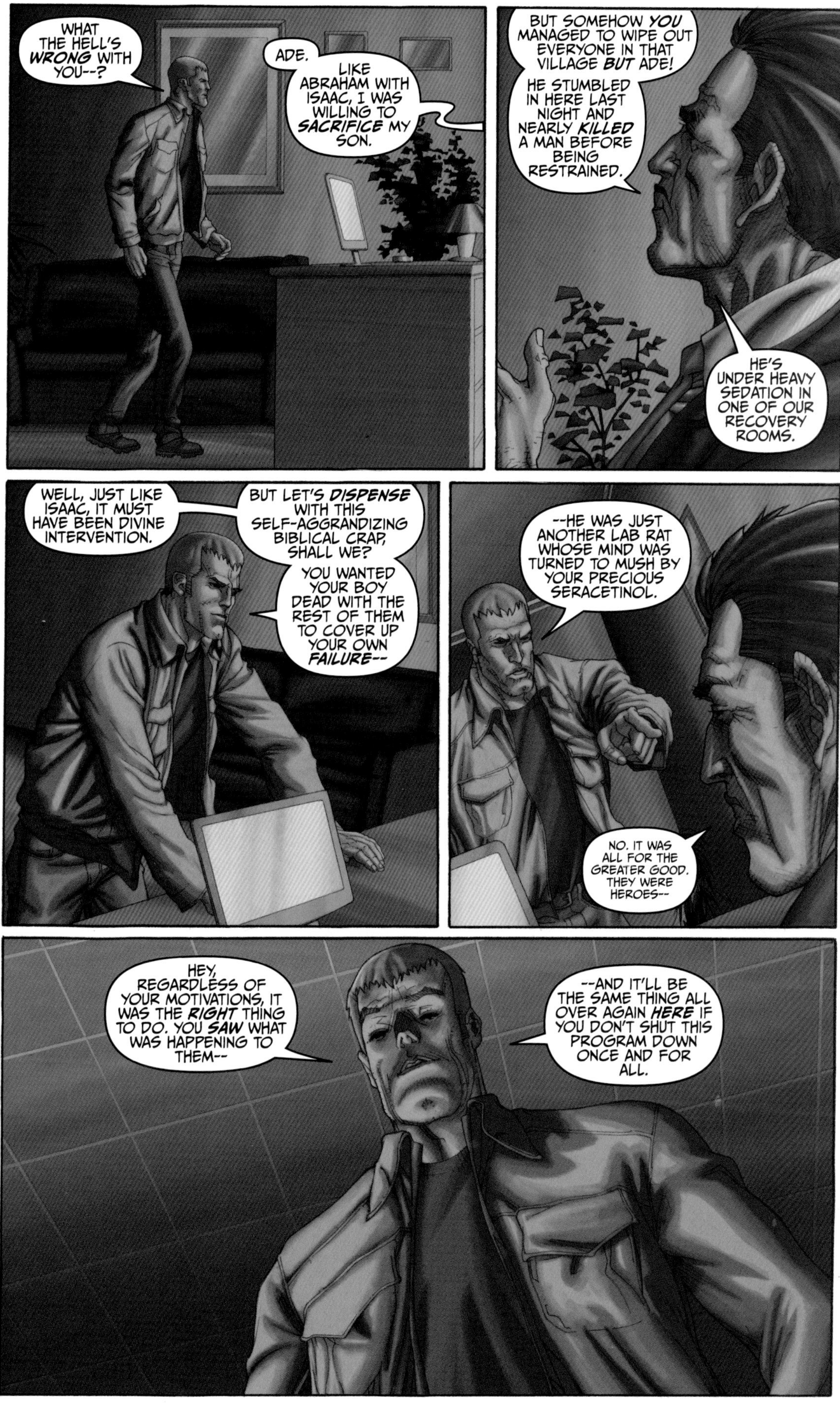
WHAT THE HELL'S *WRONG* WITH YOU--?
ADE.
LIKE ABRAHAM WITH ISAAC, I WAS WILLING TO *SACRIFICE* MY SON.
BUT SOMEHOW *YOU* MANAGED TO WIPE OUT EVERYONE IN THAT VILLAGE *BUT* ADE!
HE STUMBLED IN HERE LAST NIGHT AND NEARLY *KILLED* A MAN BEFORE BEING RESTRAINED.
HE'S UNDER HEAVY SEDATION IN ONE OF OUR RECOVERY ROOMS.
WELL, JUST LIKE ISAAC, IT MUST HAVE BEEN DIVINE INTERVENTION.
BUT LET'S *DISPENSE* WITH THIS SELF-AGGRANDIZING BIBLICAL CRAP, SHALL WE?
YOU WANTED YOUR BOY DEAD WITH THE REST OF THEM TO COVER UP YOUR OWN *FAILURE*--
--HE WAS JUST ANOTHER LAB RAT WHOSE MIND WAS TURNED TO MUSH BY YOUR PRECIOUS SERACETINOL.
NO. IT WAS ALL FOR THE GREATER GOOD. THEY WERE HEROES--
HEY, REGARDLESS OF YOUR MOTIVATIONS, IT WAS THE *RIGHT* THING TO DO. YOU *SAW* WHAT WAS HAPPENING TO THEM--
--AND IT'LL BE THE SAME THING ALL OVER AGAIN *HERE* IF YOU DON'T SHUT THIS PROGRAM DOWN ONCE AND FOR ALL.

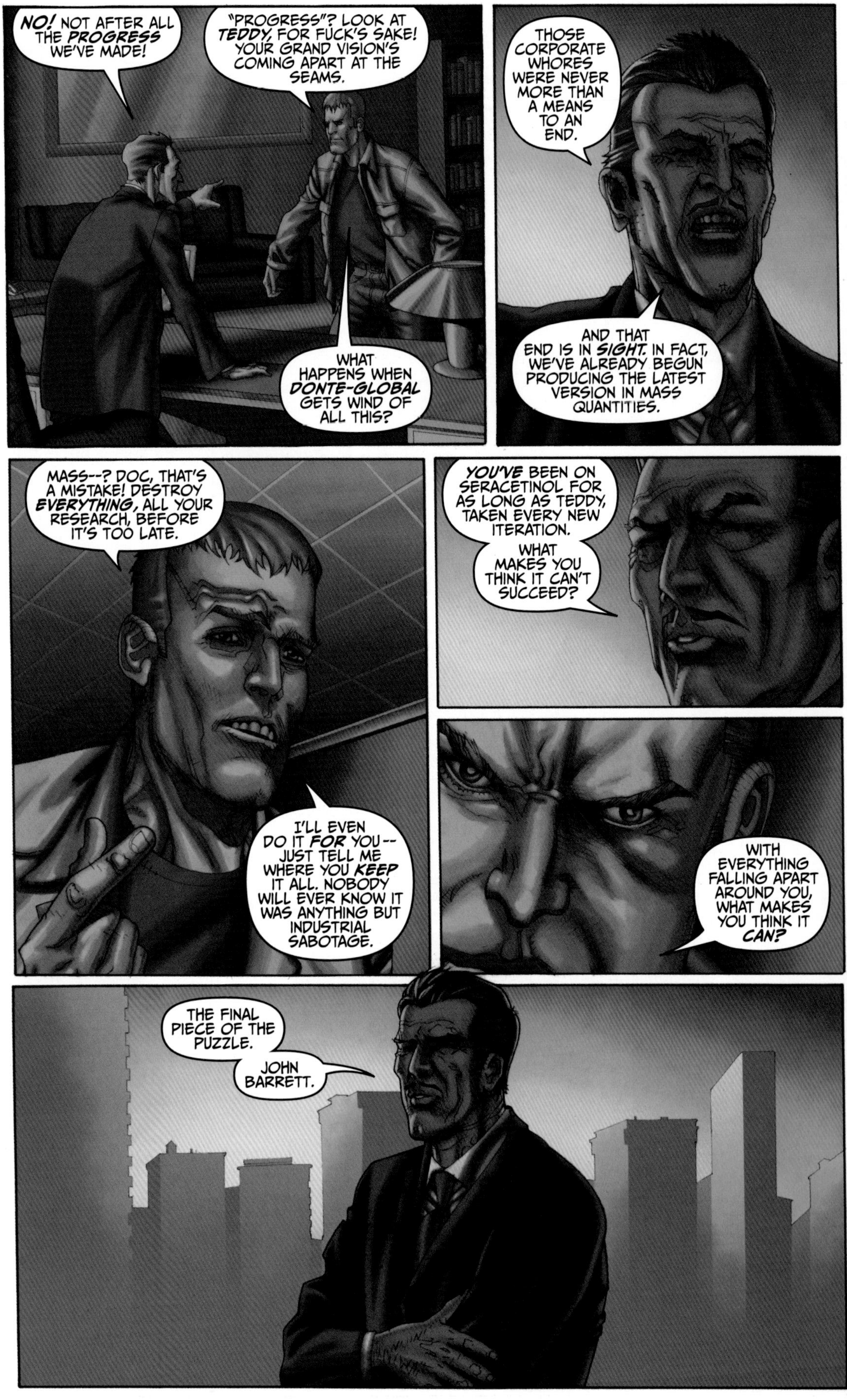
NO! NOT AFTER ALL THE PROGRESS WE'VE MADE!
"PROGRESS"? LOOK AT TEDDY, FOR FUCK'S SAKE! YOUR GRAND VISION'S COMING APART AT THE SEAMS.
WHAT HAPPENS WHEN DONTE-GLOBAL GETS WIND OF ALL THIS?
THOSE CORPORATE WHORES WERE NEVER MORE THAN A MEANS TO AN END.
AND THAT END IS IN SIGHT. IN FACT, WE'VE ALREADY BEGUN PRODUCING THE LATEST VERSION IN MASS QUANTITIES.
MASS--? DOC, THAT'S A MISTAKE! DESTROY EVERYTHING, ALL YOUR RESEARCH, BEFORE IT'S TOO LATE.
I'LL EVEN DO IT FOR YOU--JUST TELL ME WHERE YOU KEEP IT ALL. NOBODY WILL EVER KNOW IT WAS ANYTHING BUT INDUSTRIAL SABOTAGE.
YOU'VE BEEN ON SERACETINOL FOR AS LONG AS TEDDY, TAKEN EVERY NEW ITERATION.
WHAT MAKES YOU THINK IT CAN'T SUCCEED?
WITH EVERYTHING FALLING APART AROUND YOU, WHAT MAKES YOU THINK IT CAN?
THE FINAL PIECE OF THE PUZZLE.
JOHN BARRETT.

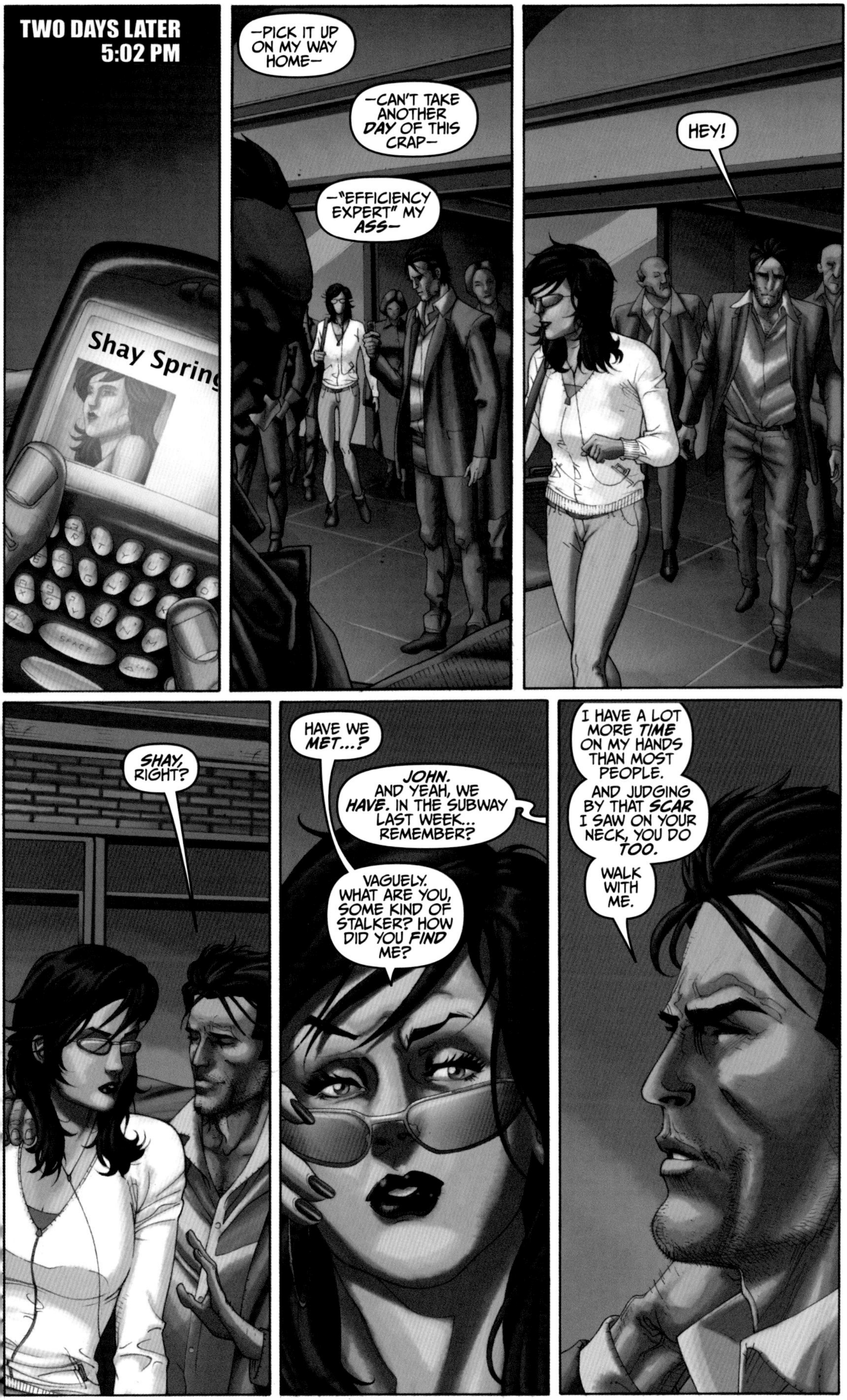
TWO DAYS LATER 5:02 PM
Shay Spring
—PICK IT UP ON MY WAY HOME—
—CAN'T TAKE ANOTHER DAY OF THIS CRAP—
—"EFFICIENCY EXPERT" MY ASS—
HEY!
SHAY, RIGHT?
HAVE WE MET...?
JOHN. AND YEAH, WE HAVE. IN THE SUBWAY LAST WEEK... REMEMBER?
VAGUELY. WHAT ARE YOU, SOME KIND OF STALKER? HOW DID YOU FIND ME?
I HAVE A LOT MORE TIME ON MY HANDS THAN MOST PEOPLE.
AND JUDGING BY THAT SCAR I SAW ON YOUR NECK, YOU DO TOO.
WALK WITH ME.

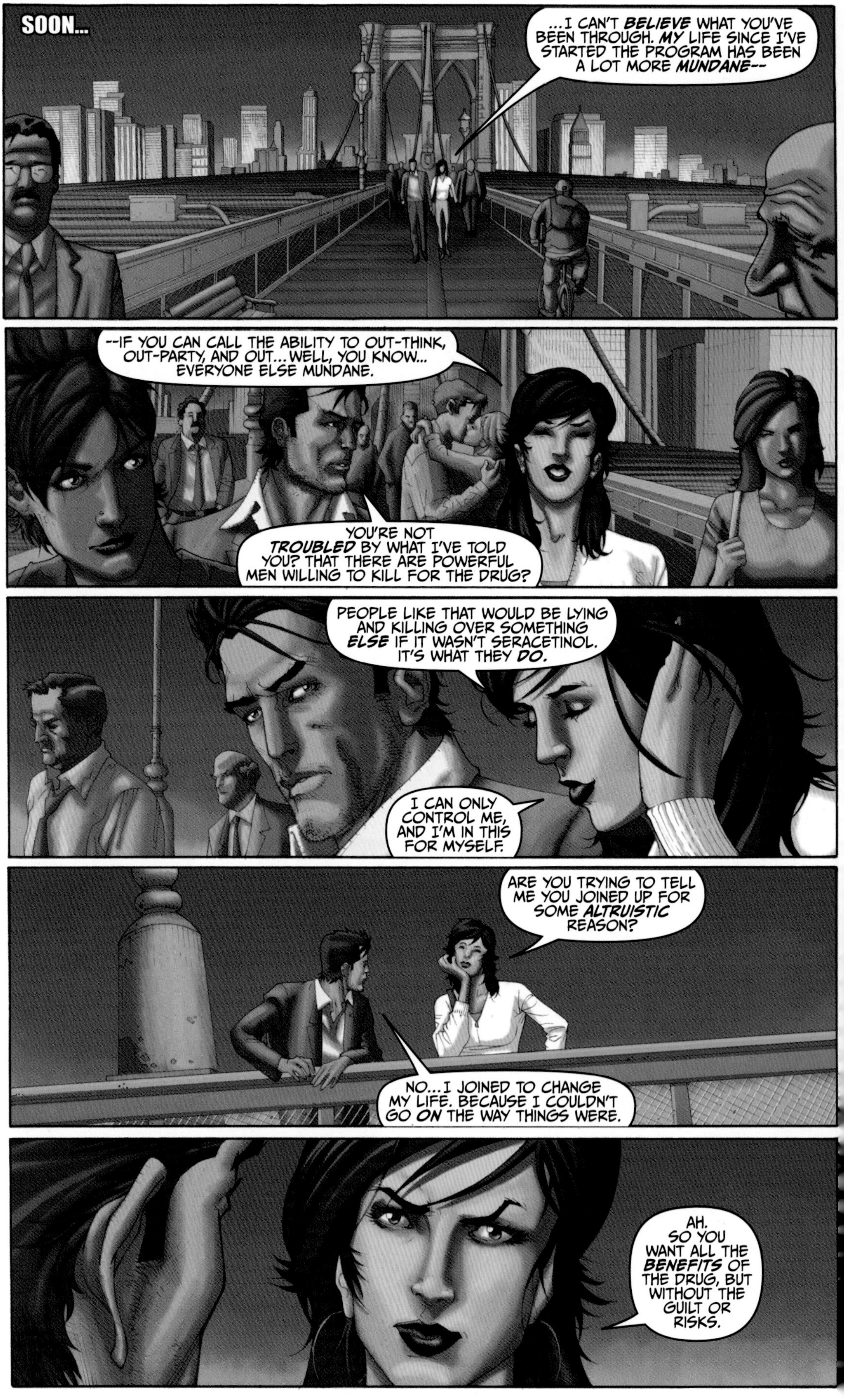
SOON...
...I CAN'T BELIEVE WHAT YOU'VE BEEN THROUGH. MY LIFE SINCE I'VE STARTED THE PROGRAM HAS BEEN A LOT MORE MUNDANE--
--IF YOU CAN CALL THE ABILITY TO OUT-THINK, OUT-PARTY, AND OUT...WELL, YOU KNOW... EVERYONE ELSE MUNDANE.
YOU'RE NOT TROUBLED BY WHAT I'VE TOLD YOU? THAT THERE ARE POWERFUL MEN WILLING TO KILL FOR THE DRUG?
PEOPLE LIKE THAT WOULD BE LYING AND KILLING OVER SOMETHING ELSE IF IT WASN'T SERACETINOL. IT'S WHAT THEY DO.
I CAN ONLY CONTROL ME, AND I'M IN THIS FOR MYSELF.
ARE YOU TRYING TO TELL ME YOU JOINED UP FOR SOME ALTRUISTIC REASON?
NO...I JOINED TO CHANGE MY LIFE. BECAUSE I COULDN'T GO ON THE WAY THINGS WERE.
AH. SO YOU WANT ALL THE BENEFITS OF THE DRUG, BUT WITHOUT THE GUILT OR RISKS.

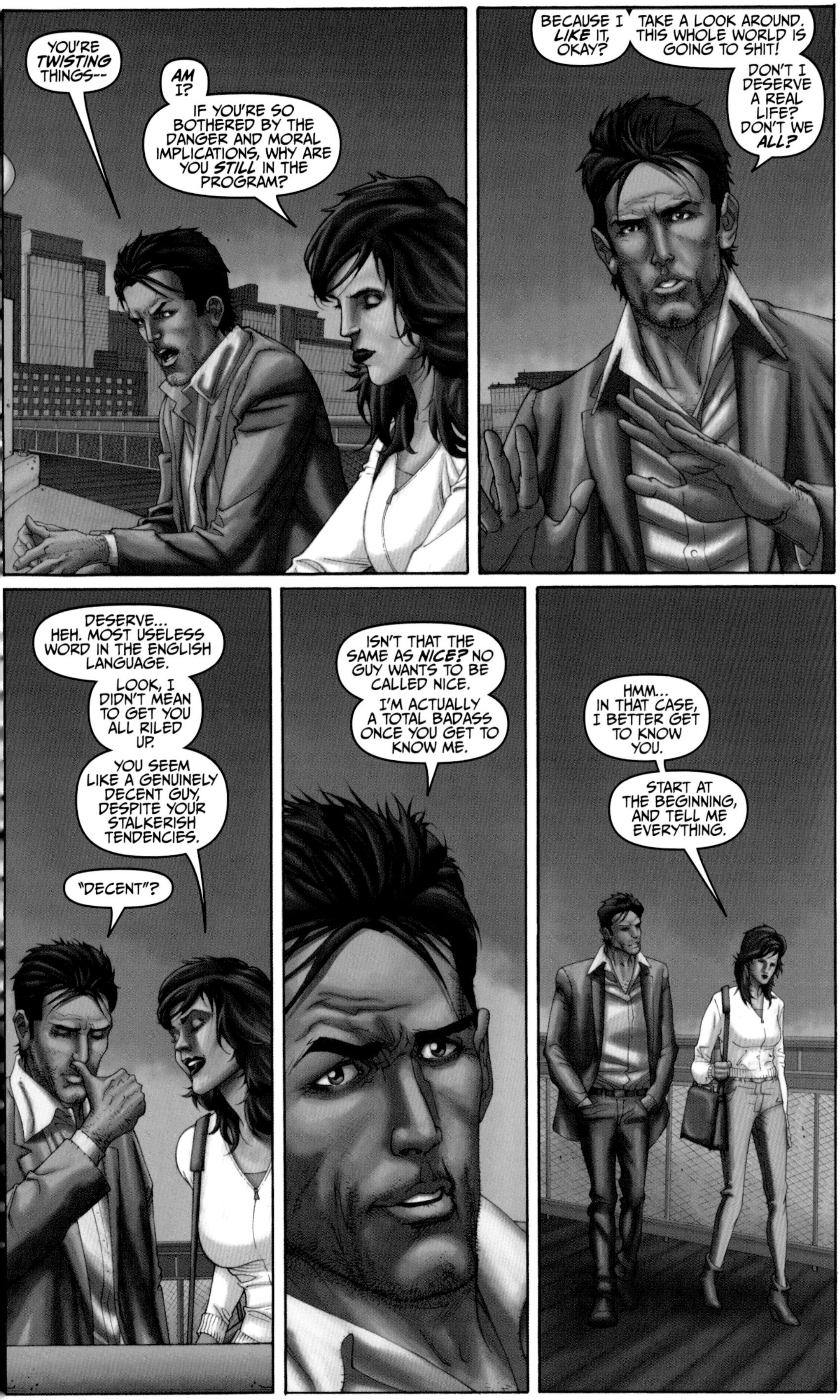
YOU'RE TWISTING THINGS--
AM I?
IF YOU'RE SO BOTHERED BY THE DANGER AND MORAL IMPLICATIONS, WHY ARE YOU STILL IN THE PROGRAM?
BECAUSE I LIKE IT, OKAY?
TAKE A LOOK AROUND. THIS WHOLE WORLD IS GOING TO SHIT!
DON'T I DESERVE A REAL LIFE? DON'T WE ALL?
DESERVE... HEH. MOST USELESS WORD IN THE ENGLISH LANGUAGE.
LOOK, I DIDN'T MEAN TO GET YOU ALL RILED UP.
YOU SEEM LIKE A GENUINELY DECENT GUY, DESPITE YOUR STALKERISH TENDENCIES.
"DECENT"?
ISN'T THAT THE SAME AS NICE? NO GUY WANTS TO BE CALLED NICE.
I'M ACTUALLY A TOTAL BADASS ONCE YOU GET TO KNOW ME.
HMM... IN THAT CASE, I BETTER GET TO KNOW YOU.
START AT THE BEGINNING, AND TELL ME EVERYTHING.

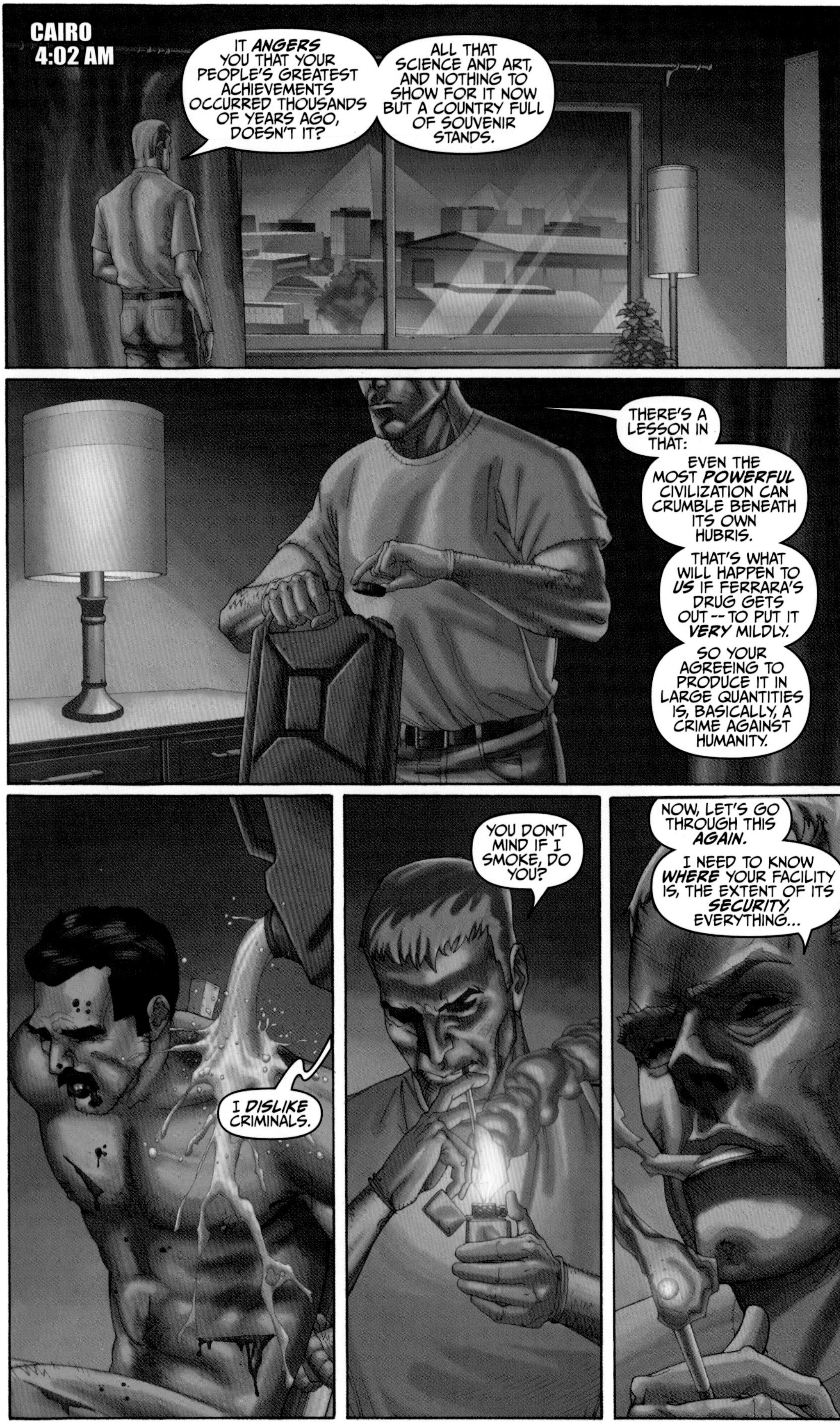
CAIRO 4:02 AM
IT ANGERS YOU THAT YOUR PEOPLE'S GREATEST ACHIEVEMENTS OCCURRED THOUSANDS OF YEARS AGO, DOESN'T IT?
ALL THAT SCIENCE AND ART, AND NOTHING TO SHOW FOR IT NOW BUT A COUNTRY FULL OF SOUVENIR STANDS.
THERE'S A LESSON IN THAT:
EVEN THE MOST POWERFUL CIVILIZATION CAN CRUMBLE BENEATH ITS OWN HUBRIS.
THAT'S WHAT WILL HAPPEN TO US IF FERRARA'S DRUG GETS OUT -- TO PUT IT VERY MILDLY.
SO YOUR AGREEING TO PRODUCE IT IN LARGE QUANTITIES IS, BASICALLY, A CRIME AGAINST HUMANITY.
I DISLIKE CRIMINALS.
YOU DON'T MIND IF I SMOKE, DO YOU?
NOW, LET'S GO THROUGH THIS AGAIN.
I NEED TO KNOW WHERE YOUR FACILITY IS, THE EXTENT OF ITS SECURITY, EVERYTHING...

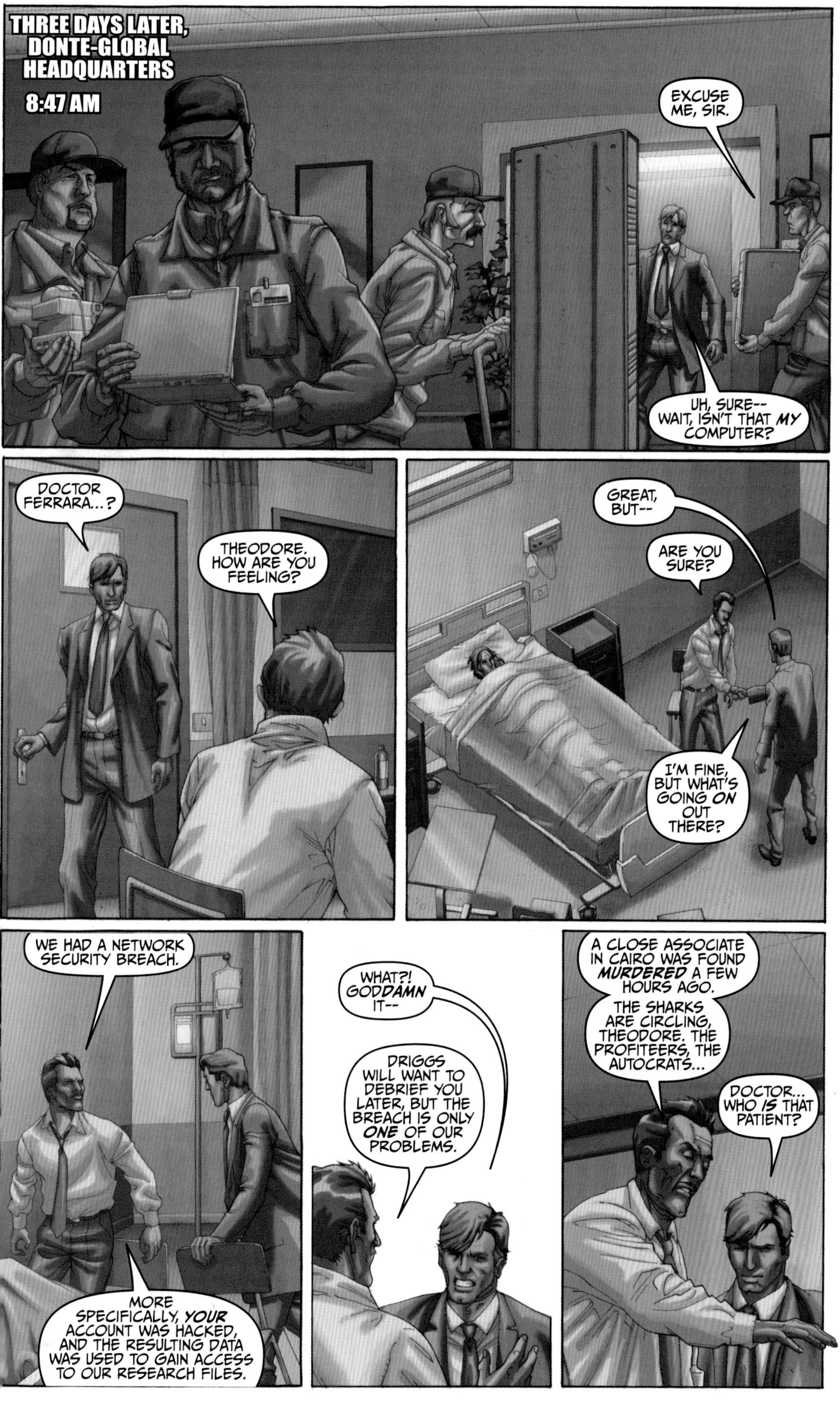
THREE DAYS LATER, DONTE-GLOBAL HEADQUARTERS
8:47 AM
EXCUSE ME, SIR.
UH, SURE-- WAIT, ISN'T THAT MY COMPUTER?
DOCTOR FERRARA...?
THEODORE. HOW ARE YOU FEELING?
GREAT, BUT--
ARE YOU SURE?
I'M FINE, BUT WHAT'S GOING ON OUT THERE?
WE HAD A NETWORK SECURITY BREACH.
MORE SPECIFICALLY, YOUR ACCOUNT WAS HACKED, AND THE RESULTING DATA WAS USED TO GAIN ACCESS TO OUR RESEARCH FILES.
WHAT?! GODDAMN IT--
DRIGGS WILL WANT TO DEBRIEF YOU LATER, BUT THE BREACH IS ONLY ONE OF OUR PROBLEMS.
A CLOSE ASSOCIATE IN CAIRO WAS FOUND MURDERED A FEW HOURS AGO.
THE SHARKS ARE CIRCLING, THEODORE. THE PROFITEERS, THE AUTOCRATS...
DOCTOR... WHO IS THAT PATIENT?

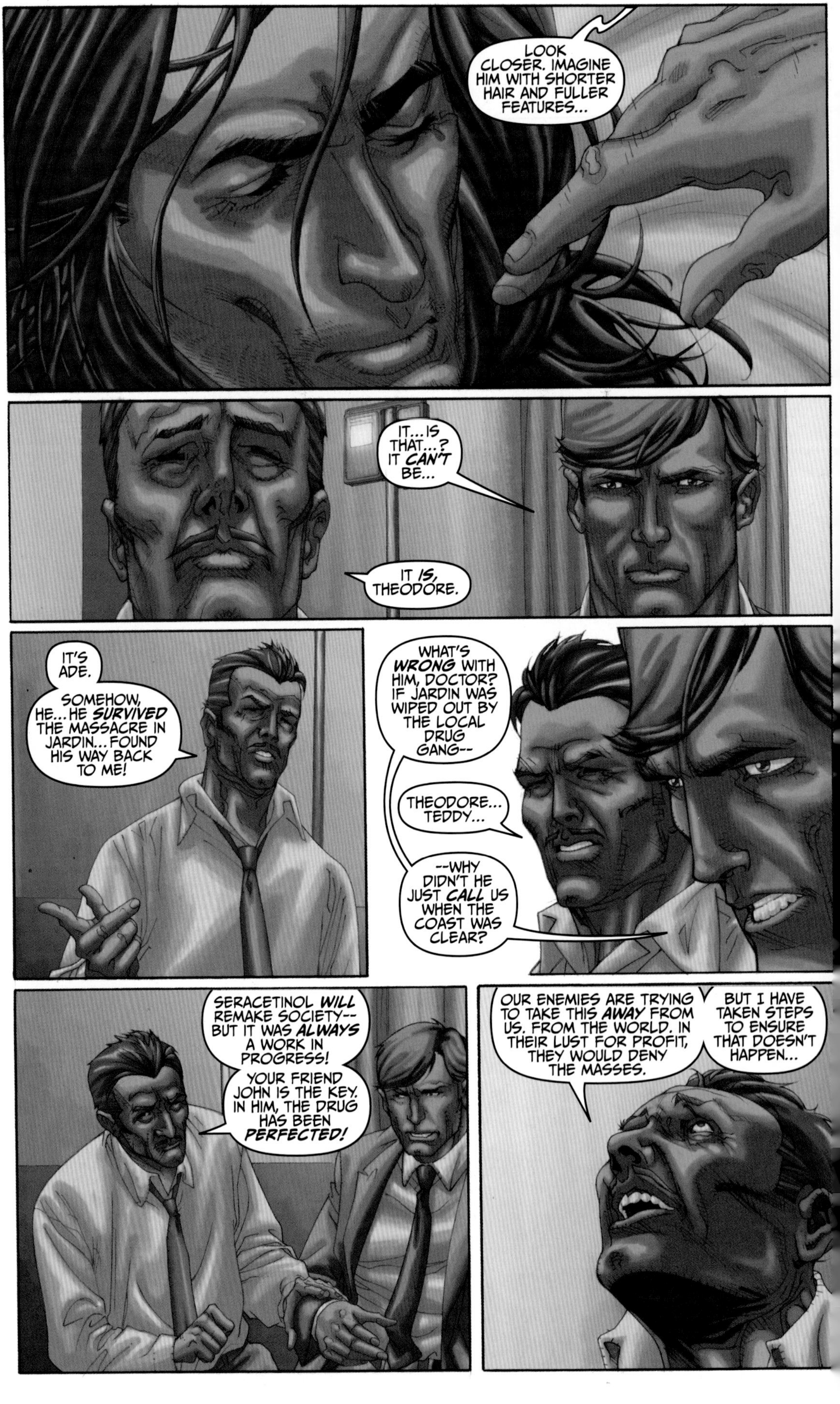
LOOK CLOSER. IMAGINE HIM WITH SHORTER HAIR AND FULLER FEATURES...
IT...IS THAT...? IT *CAN'T* BE...
IT *IS*, THEODORE.
IT'S ADE.
SOMEHOW, HE...HE *SURVIVED* THE MASSACRE IN JARDIN...FOUND HIS WAY BACK TO ME!
WHAT'S *WRONG* WITH HIM, DOCTOR? IF JARDIN WAS WIPED OUT BY THE LOCAL DRUG GANG--
THEODORE... TEDDY...
--WHY DIDN'T HE JUST *CALL* US WHEN THE COAST WAS CLEAR?
SERACETINOL *WILL* REMAKE SOCIETY--BUT IT WAS *ALWAYS* A WORK IN PROGRESS!
YOUR FRIEND JOHN IS THE KEY. IN HIM, THE DRUG HAS BEEN *PERFECTED!*
OUR ENEMIES ARE TRYING TO TAKE THIS *AWAY* FROM US. FROM THE WORLD. IN THEIR LUST FOR PROFIT, THEY WOULD DENY THE MASSES.
BUT I HAVE TAKEN STEPS TO ENSURE THAT DOESN'T HAPPEN...

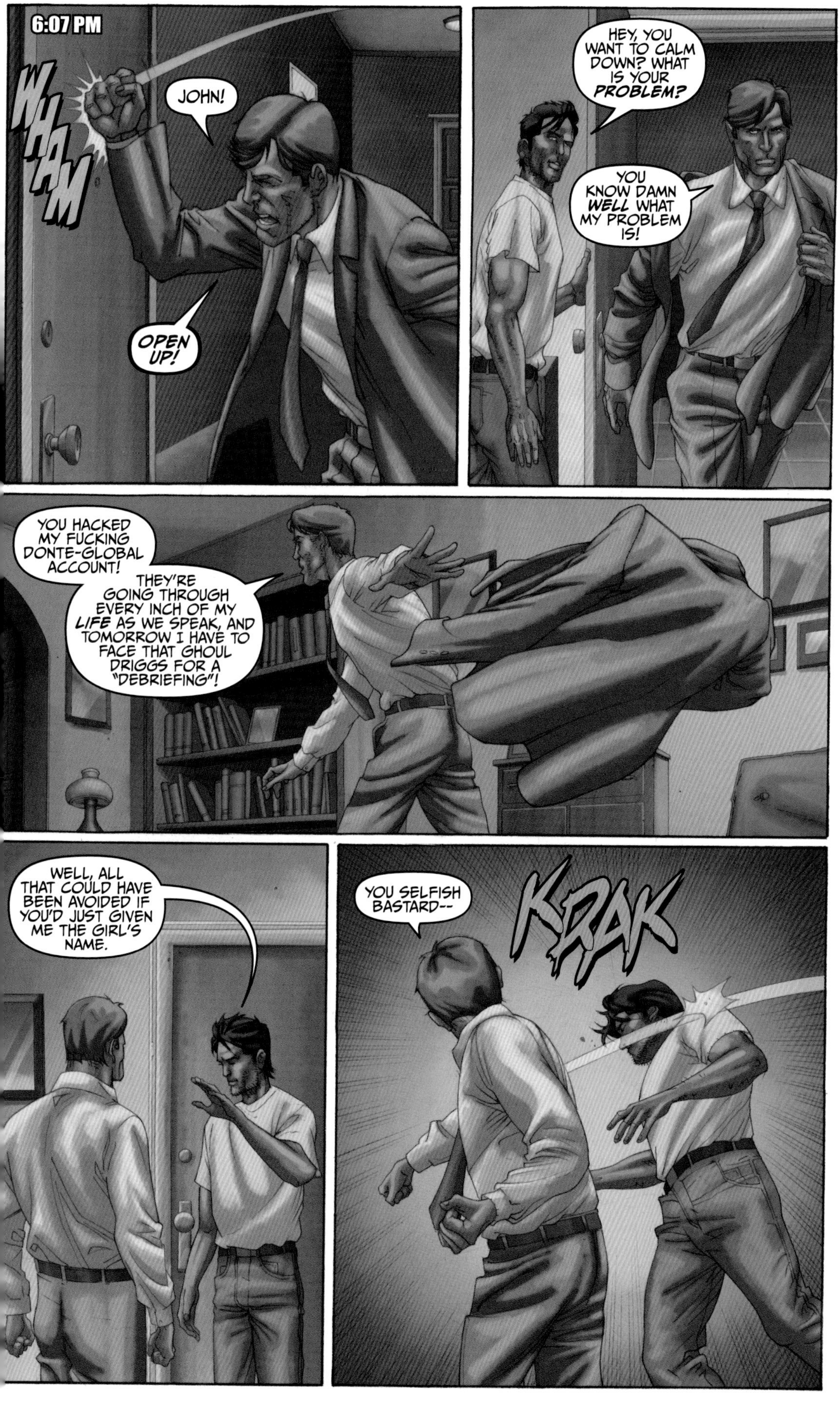
6:07 PM
WHAM
JOHN!
OPEN UP!
HEY, YOU WANT TO CALM DOWN? WHAT IS YOUR PROBLEM?
YOU KNOW DAMN WELL WHAT MY PROBLEM IS!
YOU HACKED MY FUCKING DONTE-GLOBAL ACCOUNT!
THEY'RE GOING THROUGH EVERY INCH OF MY LIFE AS WE SPEAK, AND TOMORROW I HAVE TO FACE THAT GHOUL DRIGGS FOR A "DEBRIEFING"!
WELL, ALL THAT COULD HAVE BEEN AVOIDED IF YOU'D JUST GIVEN ME THE GIRL'S NAME.
YOU SELFISH BASTARD--
KRAK

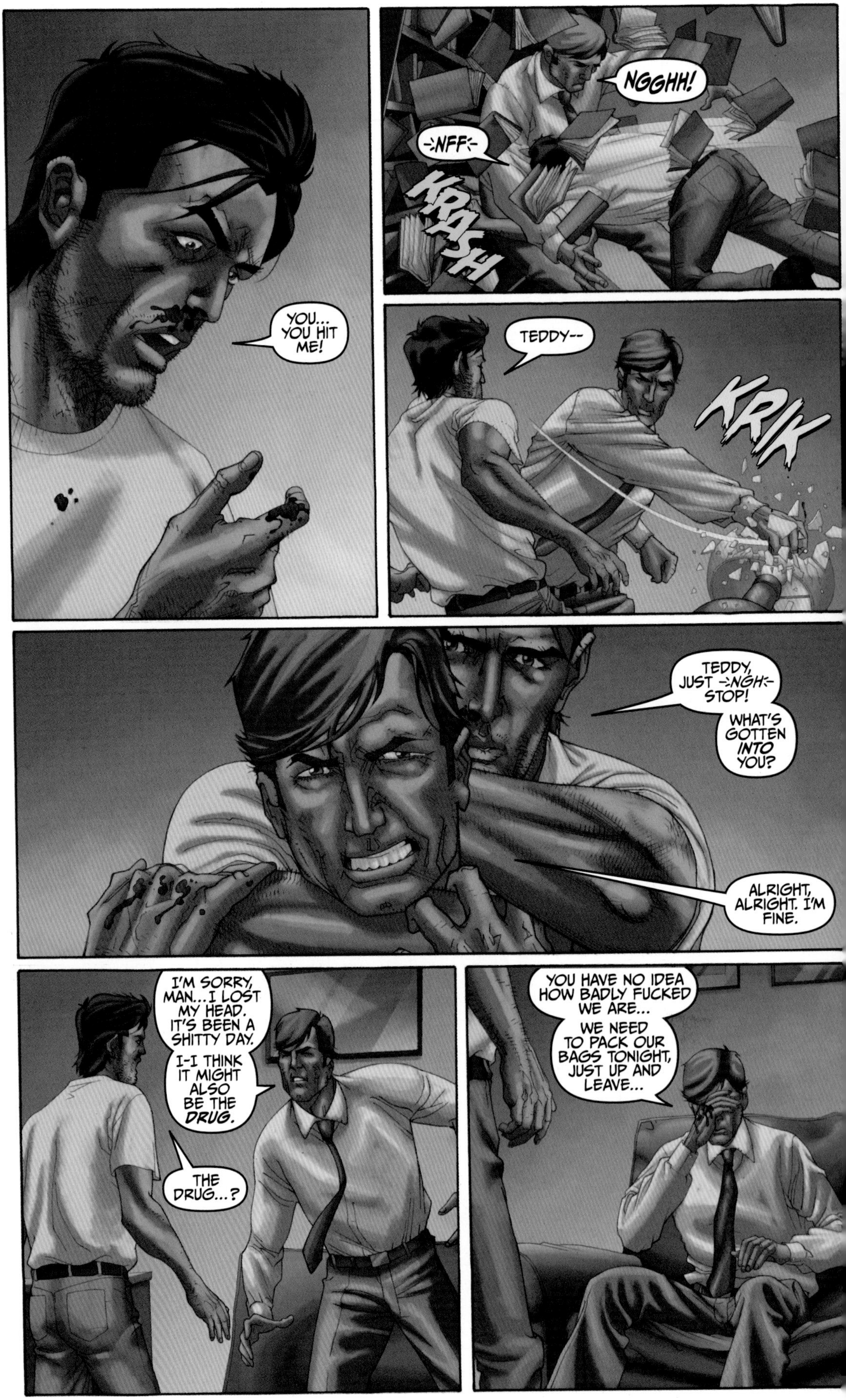
YOU... YOU HIT ME!
NGGHH!
-NFF-
KRASH
TEDDY--
KRIK
TEDDY, JUST -NGH- STOP!
WHAT'S GOTTEN INTO YOU?
ALRIGHT, ALRIGHT. I'M FINE.
I'M SORRY, MAN... I LOST MY HEAD. IT'S BEEN A SHITTY DAY.
I-I THINK IT MIGHT ALSO BE THE DRUG.
THE DRUG...?
YOU HAVE NO IDEA HOW BADLY FUCKED WE ARE...
WE NEED TO PACK OUR BAGS TONIGHT, JUST UP AND LEAVE...

WHOA, WHOA, *WHOA* -- "UP AND LEAVE"?

TALK TO ME. WHATEVER IT IS, WE'LL HANDLE IT *TOGETHER*.

I... I'VE BEEN HAVING HALLUCINATIONS. OFF AND ON FOR A COUPLE MONTHS NOW.

I TRIED TO CONVINCE MYSELF IT WAS A PASSING EFFECT, OR TOO MUCH DRINKING, ESPECIALLY SINCE YOU'VE BEEN DOING SO GREAT, BUT...

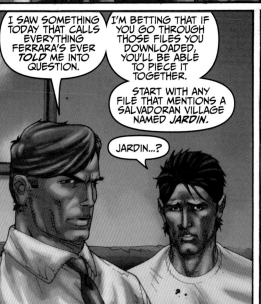

I SAW SOMETHING TODAY THAT CALLS EVERYTHING FERRARA'S EVER *TOLD* ME INTO QUESTION.

I'M BETTING THAT IF YOU GO THROUGH THOSE FILES YOU DOWNLOADED, YOU'LL BE ABLE TO PIECE IT TOGETHER.

START WITH ANY FILE THAT MENTIONS A SALVADORAN VILLAGE NAMED *JARDIN*.

JARDIN...?

PROMISE ME YOU'LL LEAVE TONIGHT, ONE WAY OR THE OTHER.

I WON'T BE A *LIABILITY* TO YOU ANY LONGER.

I DON'T LIKE HOW YOU'RE *TALKING*. I'M COMING WITH YOU--

NO. I GOTTA TRY AND GET MY *HEAD* STRAIGHT, AND I CAN'T DO THAT WITH YOU ACTING AS MY CRUTCH.

COME BY MY PLACE IN TWO HOURS.

ALL I EVER WANTED OUT OF THIS WAS TO SEE YOU HAPPY.

I JUST HOPE YOU CAN *FORGIVE* ME SOMEDAY FOR WHAT I'VE DONE TO YOU.

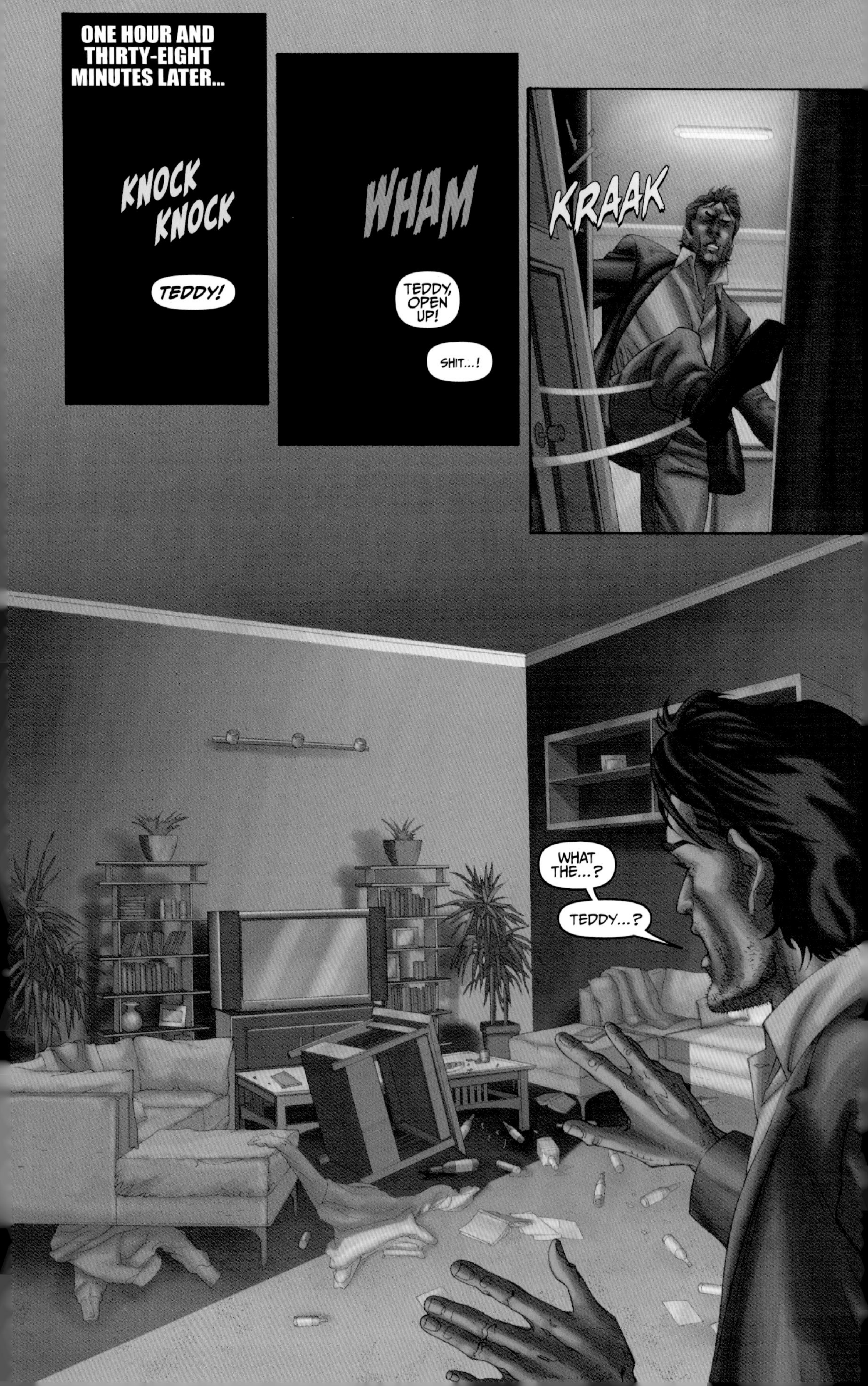
ONE HOUR AND THIRTY-EIGHT MINUTES LATER...
KNOCK KNOCK
TEDDY!
WHAM
TEDDY, OPEN UP!
SHIT...!
KRAAK
WHAT THE...?
TEDDY...?

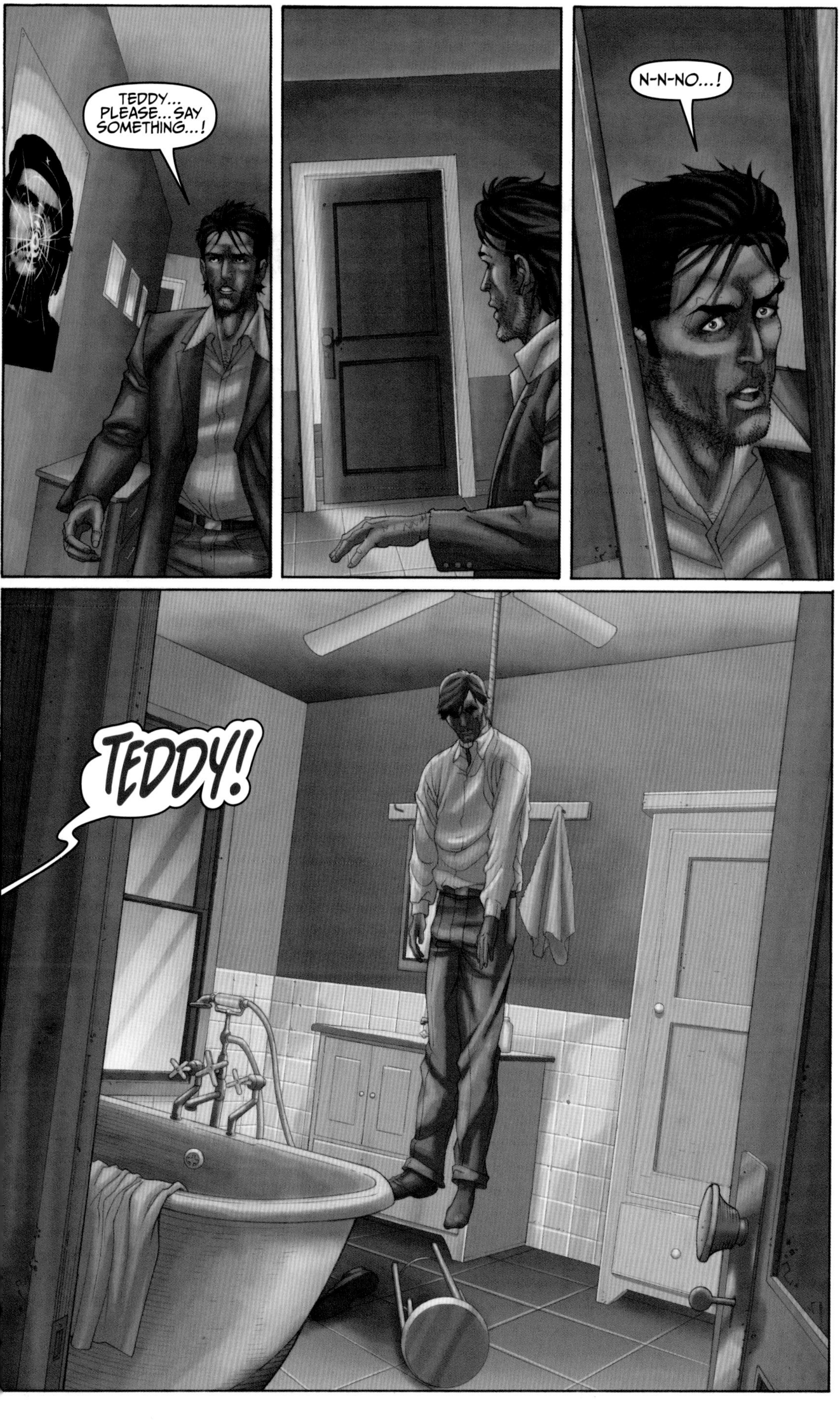
TEDDY... PLEASE... SAY SOMETHING...!
N-N-NO...!
TEDDY!

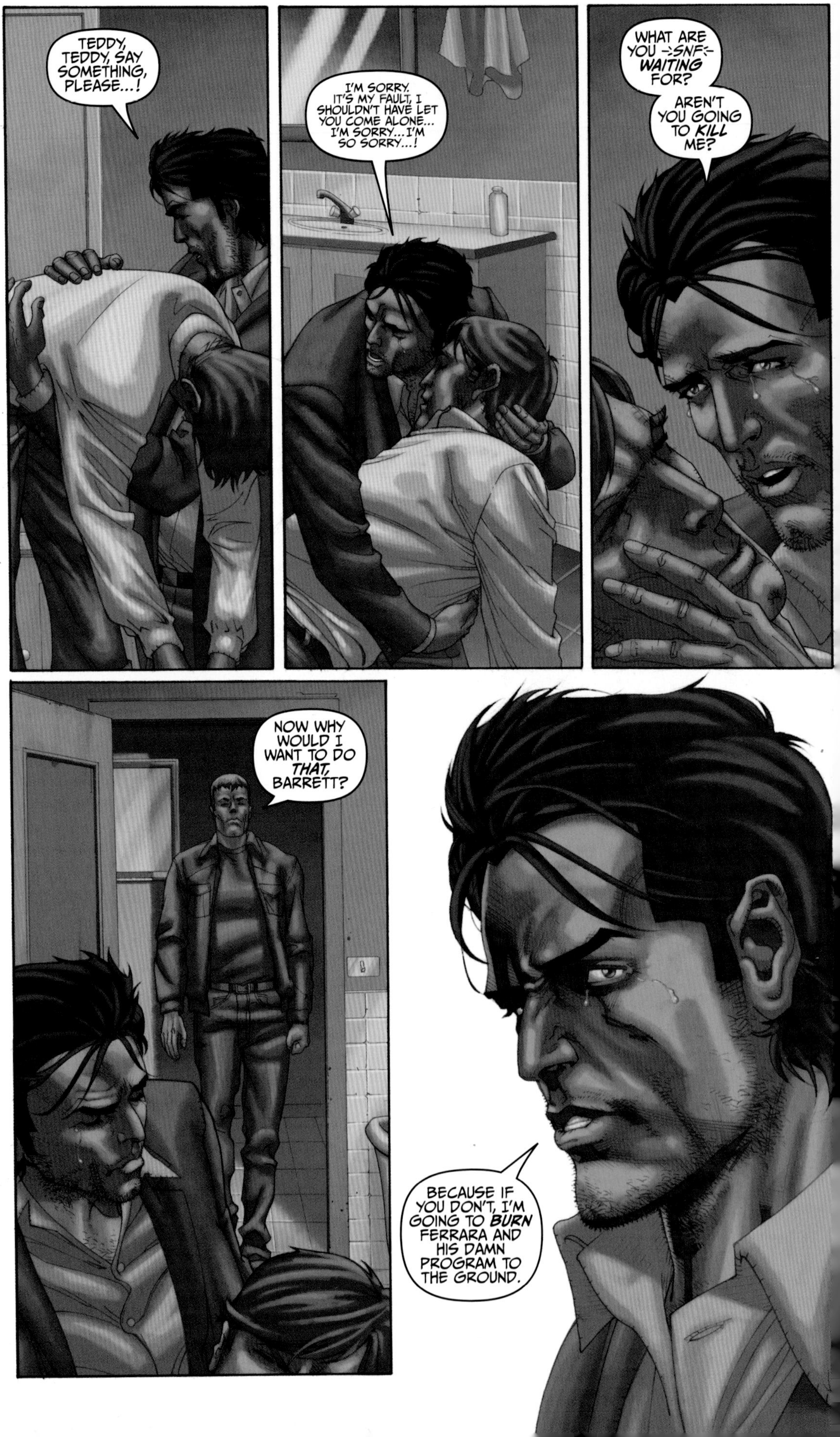
TEDDY, TEDDY, SAY SOMETHING, PLEASE...!
I'M SORRY. IT'S MY FAULT, I SHOULDN'T HAVE LET YOU COME ALONE... I'M SORRY...I'M SO SORRY...!
WHAT ARE YOU ~SNF~ WAITING FOR?
AREN'T YOU GOING TO KILL ME?
NOW WHY WOULD I WANT TO DO THAT, BARRETT?
BECAUSE IF YOU DON'T, I'M GOING TO BURN FERRARA AND HIS DAMN PROGRAM TO THE GROUND.

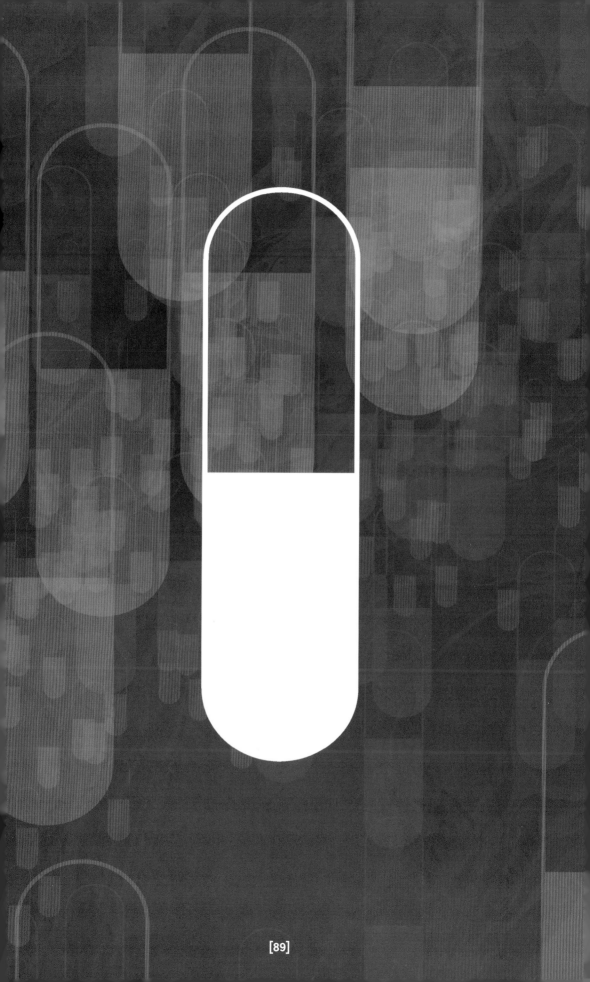

Rest #4

written by: **Mark Powers**
line art by: **Marco Castiello**
colors by: **Carlos Lopez**
letters by: **Troy Peteri**
• • • • •
original edition edited by: **Filip Sablik**
& **Phil Smith**

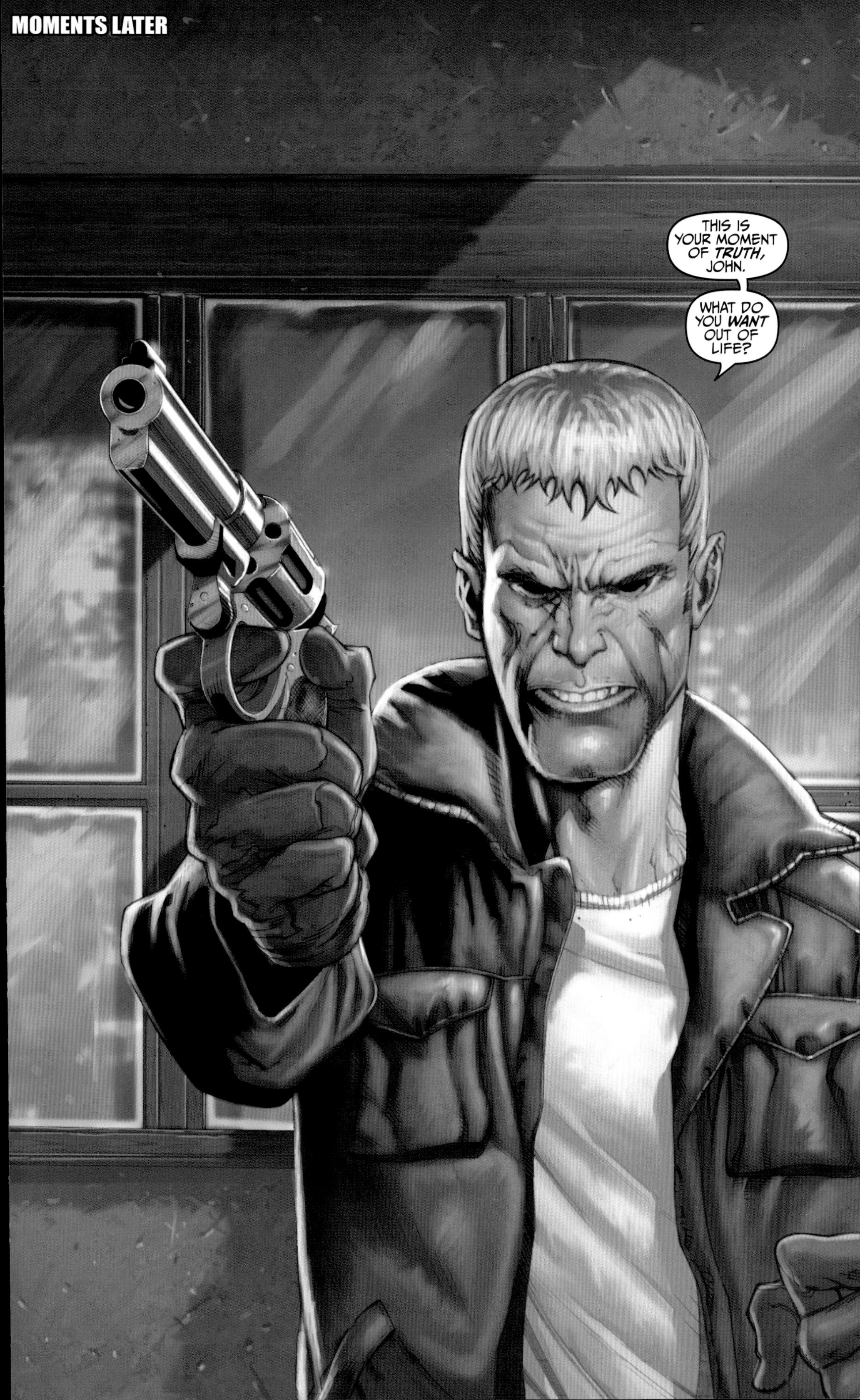
MOMENTS LATER
THIS IS YOUR MOMENT OF TRUTH, JOHN.
WHAT DO YOU WANT OUT OF LIFE?

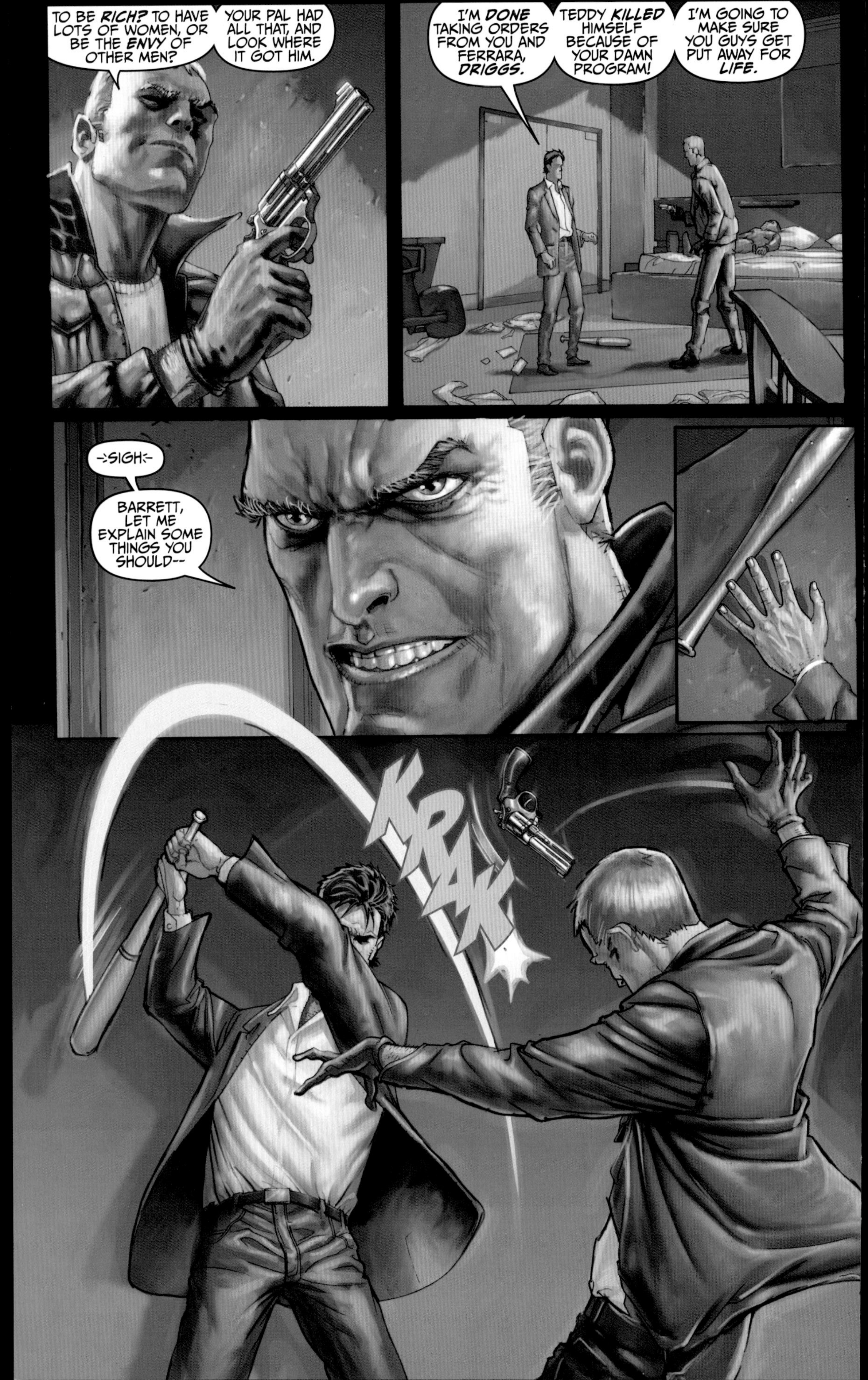
TO BE RICH? TO HAVE LOTS OF WOMEN, OR BE THE ENVY OF OTHER MEN?
YOUR PAL HAD ALL THAT, AND LOOK WHERE IT GOT HIM.
I'M DONE TAKING ORDERS FROM YOU AND FERRARA, DRIGGS.
TEDDY KILLED HIMSELF BECAUSE OF YOUR DAMN PROGRAM!
I'M GOING TO MAKE SURE YOU GUYS GET PUT AWAY FOR LIFE.
-SIGH-
BARRETT, LET ME EXPLAIN SOME THINGS YOU SHOULD--
KRAK

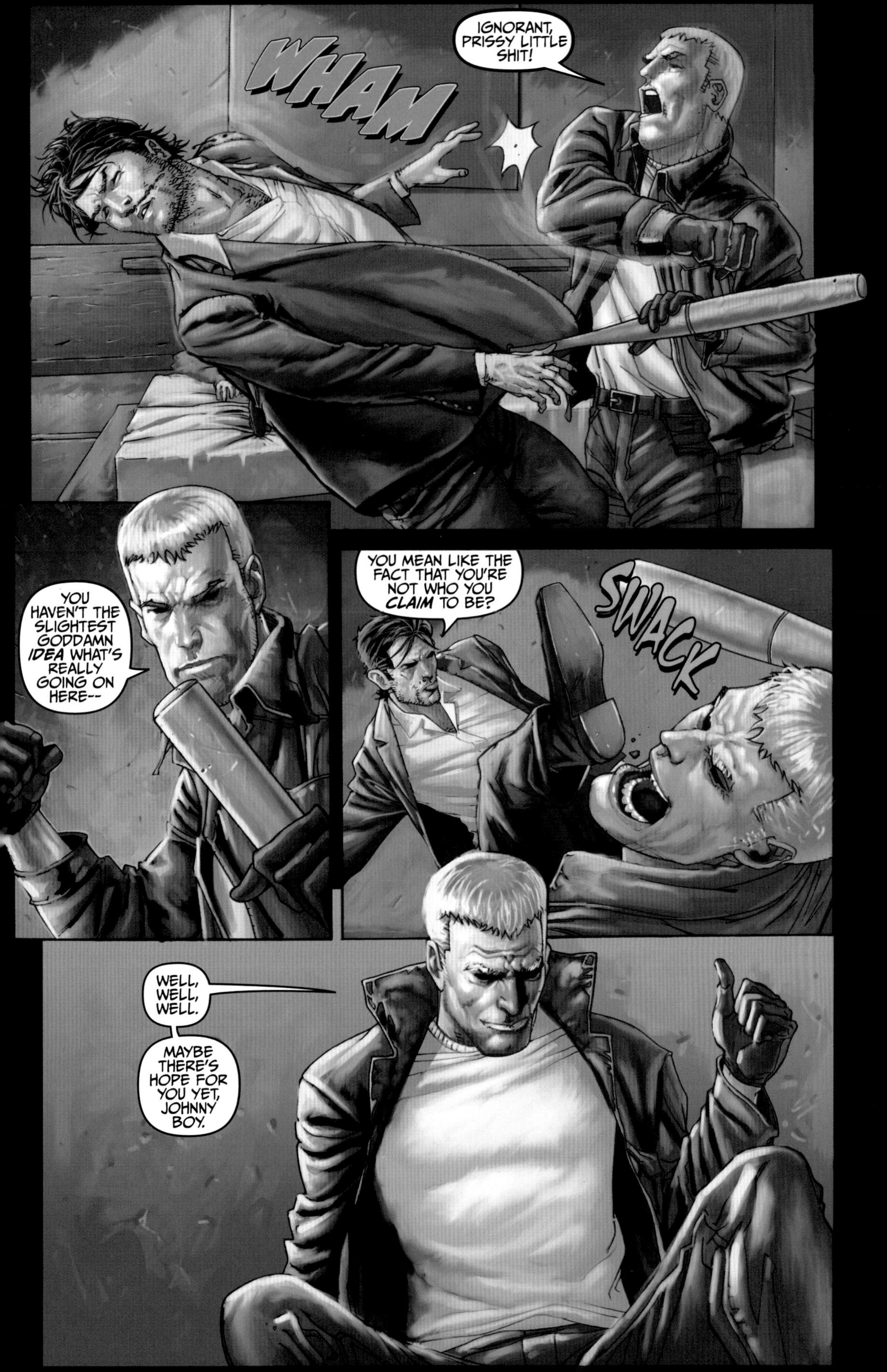
WHAM
IGNORANT, PRISSY LITTLE SHIT!
YOU HAVEN'T THE SLIGHTEST GODDAMN *IDEA* WHAT'S REALLY GOING ON HERE--
YOU MEAN LIKE THE FACT THAT YOU'RE NOT WHO YOU *CLAIM* TO BE?
SWACK
WELL, WELL, WELL.
MAYBE THERE'S HOPE FOR YOU YET, JOHNNY BOY.

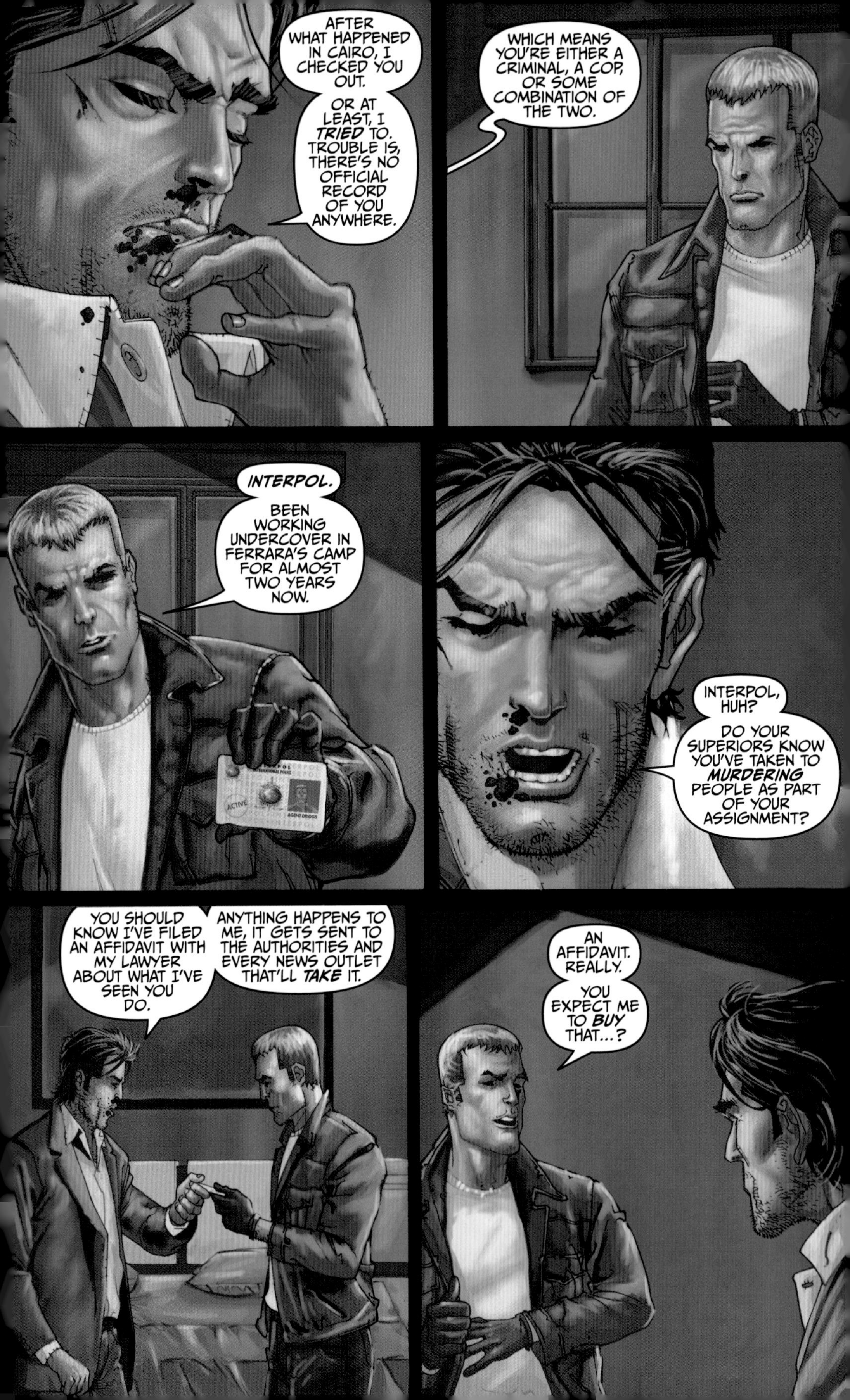
AFTER WHAT HAPPENED IN CAIRO, I CHECKED YOU OUT.
OR AT LEAST, I *TRIED* TO. TROUBLE IS, THERE'S NO OFFICIAL RECORD OF YOU ANYWHERE.
WHICH MEANS YOU'RE EITHER A CRIMINAL, A COP, OR SOME COMBINATION OF THE TWO.
INTERPOL.
BEEN WORKING UNDERCOVER IN FERRARA'S CAMP FOR ALMOST TWO YEARS NOW.
INTERPOL, HUH?
DO YOUR SUPERIORS KNOW YOU'VE TAKEN TO *MURDERING* PEOPLE AS PART OF YOUR ASSIGNMENT?
YOU SHOULD KNOW I'VE FILED AN AFFIDAVIT WITH MY LAWYER ABOUT WHAT I'VE SEEN YOU DO.
ANYTHING HAPPENS TO ME, IT GETS SENT TO THE AUTHORITIES AND EVERY NEWS OUTLET THAT'LL *TAKE* IT.
AN AFFIDAVIT. REALLY.
YOU EXPECT ME TO *BUY* THAT...?

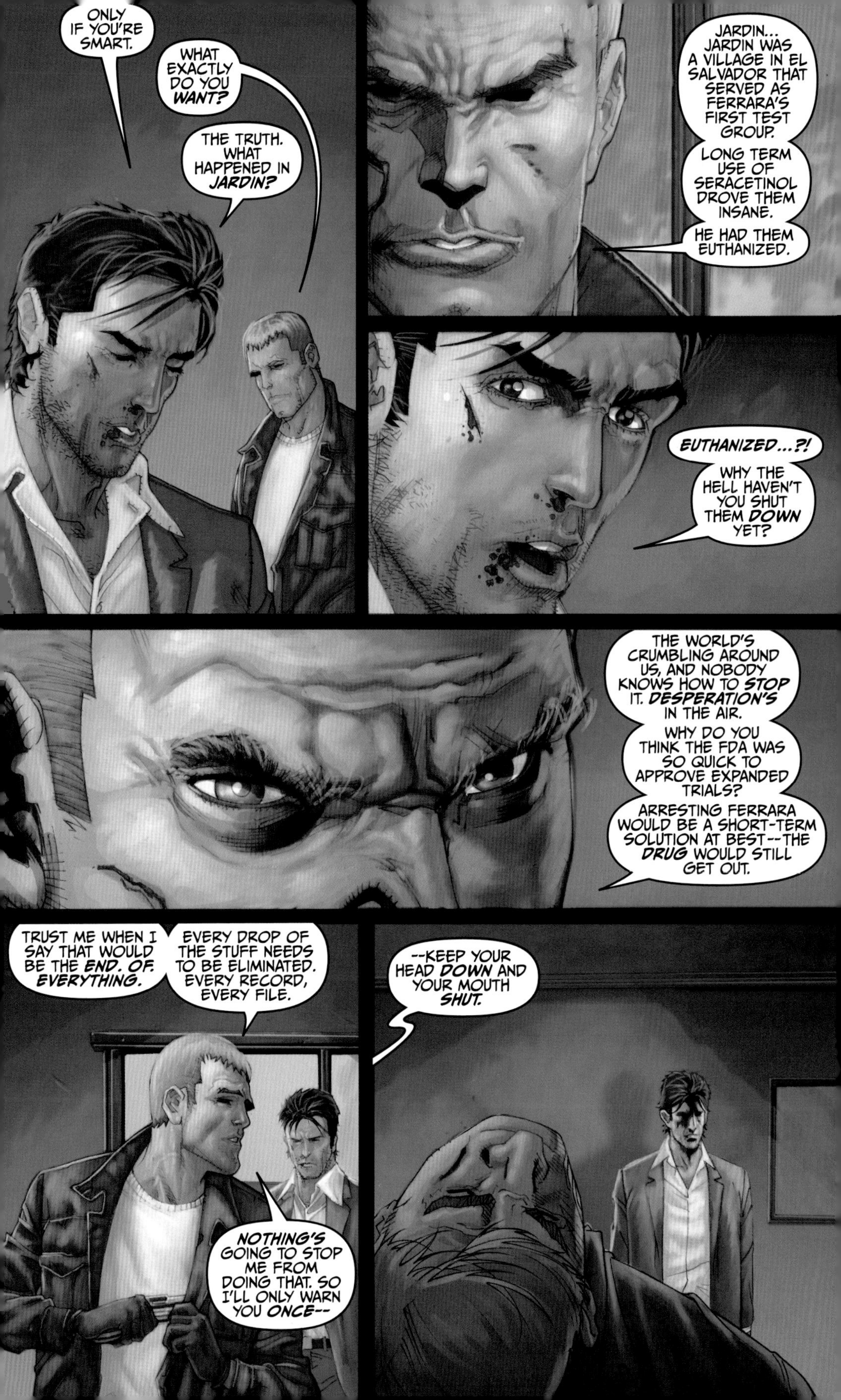
ONLY IF YOU'RE SMART.
WHAT EXACTLY DO YOU *WANT?*
THE TRUTH. WHAT HAPPENED IN *JARDIN?*
JARDIN... JARDIN WAS A VILLAGE IN EL SALVADOR THAT SERVED AS FERRARA'S FIRST TEST GROUP.
LONG TERM USE OF SERACETINOL DROVE THEM INSANE.
HE HAD THEM EUTHANIZED.
EUTHANIZED...?!
WHY THE HELL HAVEN'T YOU SHUT THEM *DOWN* YET?
THE WORLD'S CRUMBLING AROUND US, AND NOBODY KNOWS HOW TO *STOP* IT. *DESPERATION'S* IN THE AIR.
WHY DO YOU THINK THE FDA WAS SO QUICK TO APPROVE EXPANDED TRIALS?
ARRESTING FERRARA WOULD BE A SHORT-TERM SOLUTION AT BEST--THE *DRUG* WOULD STILL GET OUT.
TRUST ME WHEN I SAY THAT WOULD BE THE *END. OF. EVERYTHING.*
EVERY DROP OF THE STUFF NEEDS TO BE ELIMINATED. EVERY RECORD, EVERY FILE.
NOTHING'S GOING TO STOP ME FROM DOING THAT. SO I'LL ONLY WARN YOU *ONCE*--
--KEEP YOUR HEAD *DOWN* AND YOUR MOUTH *SHUT.*

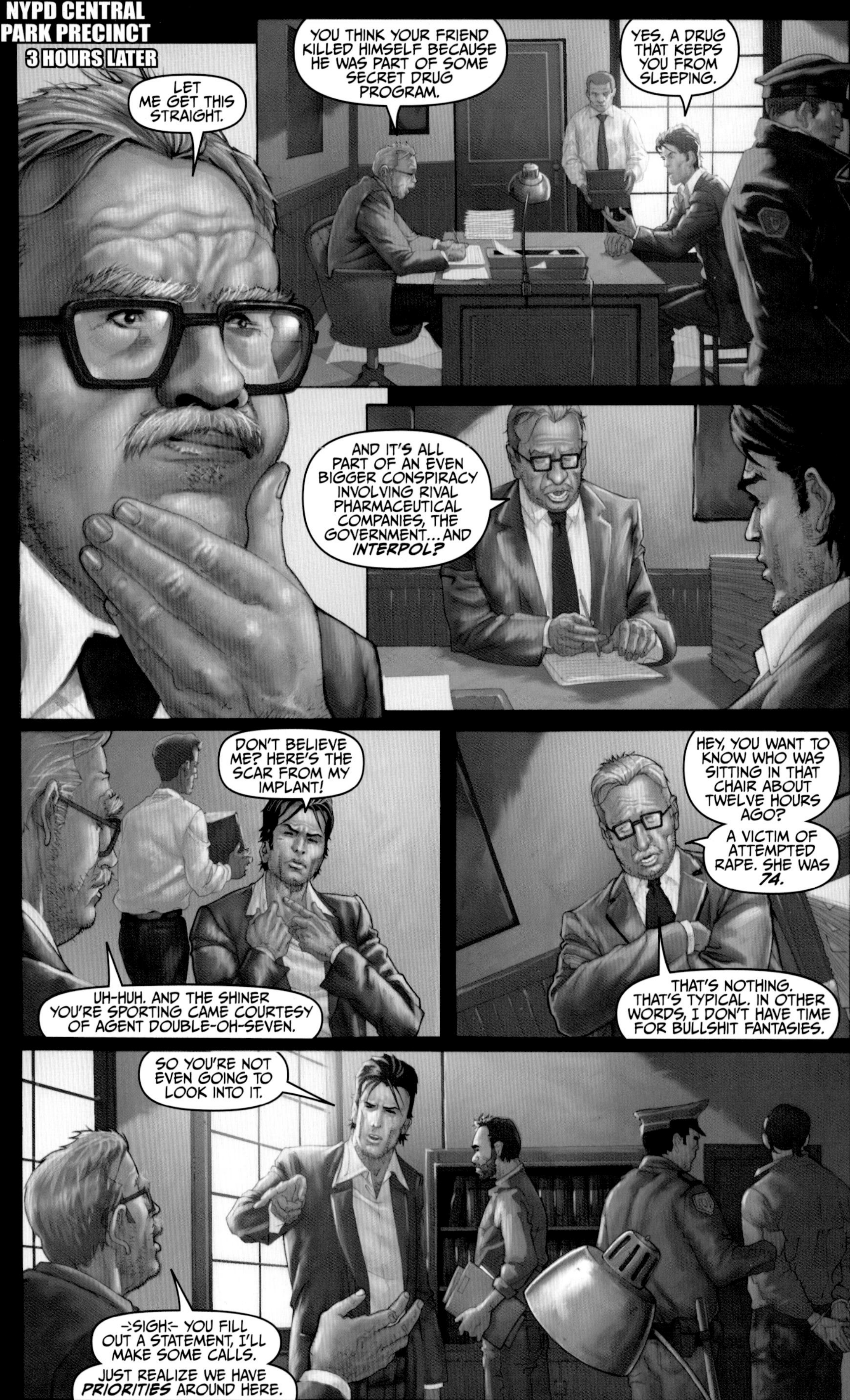
NYPD CENTRAL PARK PRECINCT
3 HOURS LATER
LET ME GET THIS STRAIGHT.
YOU THINK YOUR FRIEND KILLED HIMSELF BECAUSE HE WAS PART OF SOME SECRET DRUG PROGRAM.
YES. A DRUG THAT KEEPS YOU FROM SLEEPING.
AND IT'S ALL PART OF AN EVEN BIGGER CONSPIRACY INVOLVING RIVAL PHARMACEUTICAL COMPANIES, THE GOVERNMENT...AND INTERPOL?
DON'T BELIEVE ME? HERE'S THE SCAR FROM MY IMPLANT!
UH-HUH. AND THE SHINER YOU'RE SPORTING CAME COURTESY OF AGENT DOUBLE-OH-SEVEN.
HEY, YOU WANT TO KNOW WHO WAS SITTING IN THAT CHAIR ABOUT TWELVE HOURS AGO?
A VICTIM OF ATTEMPTED RAPE. SHE WAS 74.
THAT'S NOTHING. THAT'S TYPICAL. IN OTHER WORDS, I DON'T HAVE TIME FOR BULLSHIT FANTASIES.
SO YOU'RE NOT EVEN GOING TO LOOK INTO IT.
-SIGH- YOU FILL OUT A STATEMENT, I'LL MAKE SOME CALLS.
JUST REALIZE WE HAVE PRIORITIES AROUND HERE.

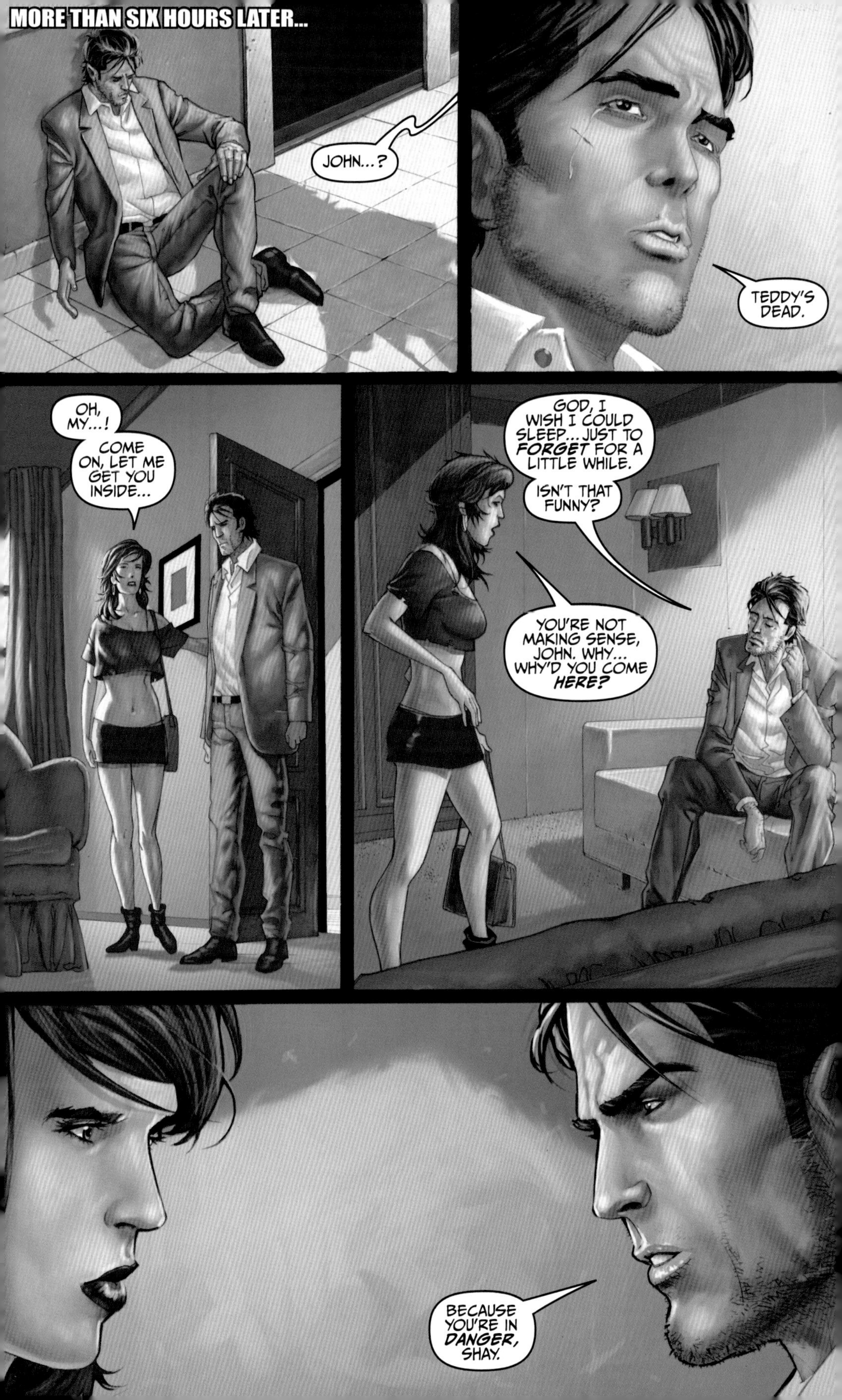
MORE THAN SIX HOURS LATER...
JOHN...?
TEDDY'S DEAD.
OH, MY...!
COME ON, LET ME GET YOU INSIDE...
GOD, I WISH I COULD SLEEP... JUST TO FORGET FOR A LITTLE WHILE.
ISN'T THAT FUNNY?
YOU'RE NOT MAKING SENSE, JOHN. WHY... WHY'D YOU COME HERE?
BECAUSE YOU'RE IN DANGER, SHAY.

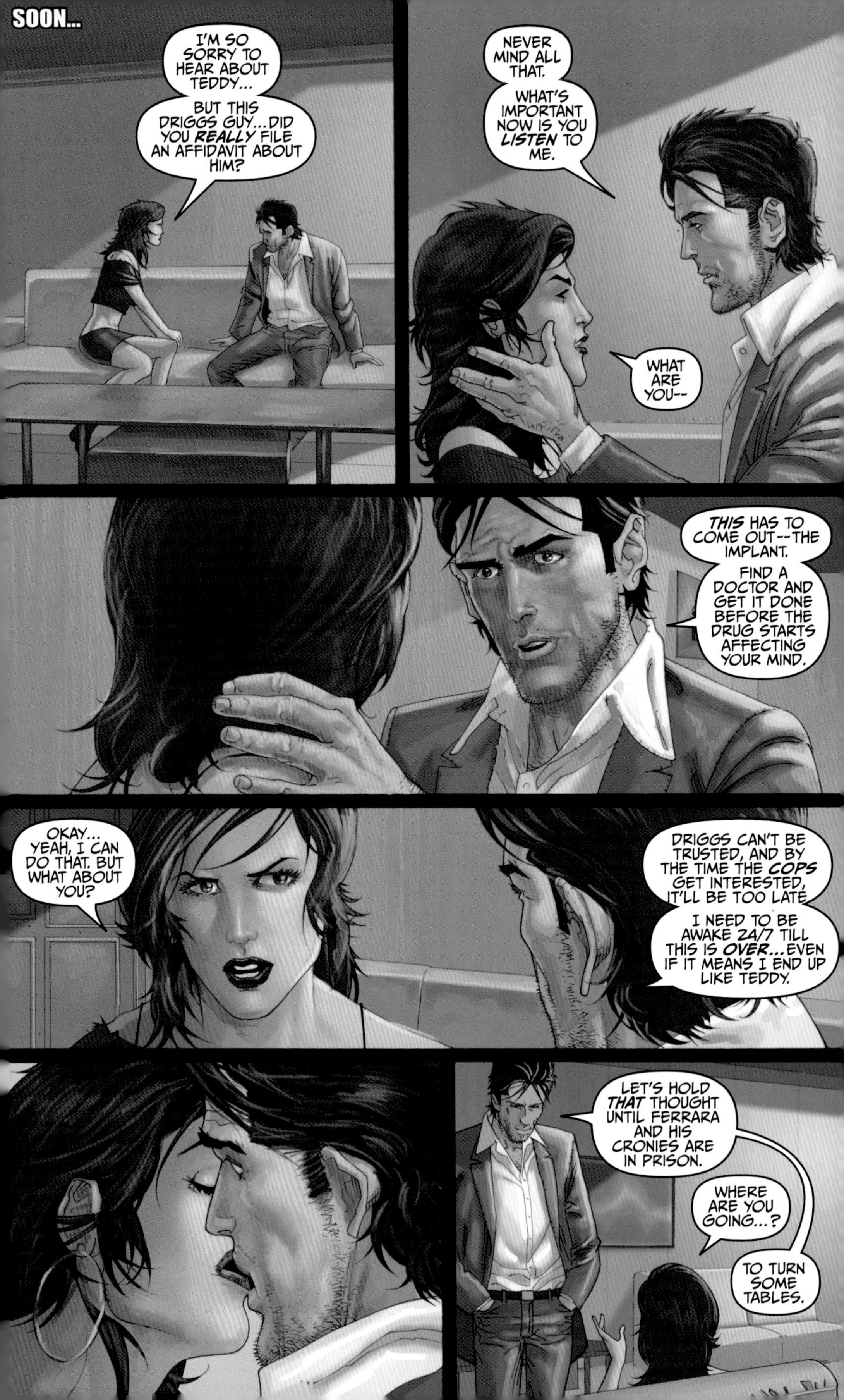
SOON...
I'M SO SORRY TO HEAR ABOUT TEDDY...
BUT THIS DRIGGS GUY...DID YOU REALLY FILE AN AFFIDAVIT ABOUT HIM?
NEVER MIND ALL THAT.
WHAT'S IMPORTANT NOW IS YOU LISTEN TO ME.
WHAT ARE YOU--
THIS HAS TO COME OUT--THE IMPLANT.
FIND A DOCTOR AND GET IT DONE BEFORE THE DRUG STARTS AFFECTING YOUR MIND.
OKAY... YEAH, I CAN DO THAT. BUT WHAT ABOUT YOU?
DRIGGS CAN'T BE TRUSTED, AND BY THE TIME THE COPS GET INTERESTED, IT'LL BE TOO LATE.
I NEED TO BE AWAKE 24/7 TILL THIS IS OVER...EVEN IF IT MEANS I END UP LIKE TEDDY.
LET'S HOLD THAT THOUGHT UNTIL FERRARA AND HIS CRONIES ARE IN PRISON.
WHERE ARE YOU GOING...?
TO TURN SOME TABLES.

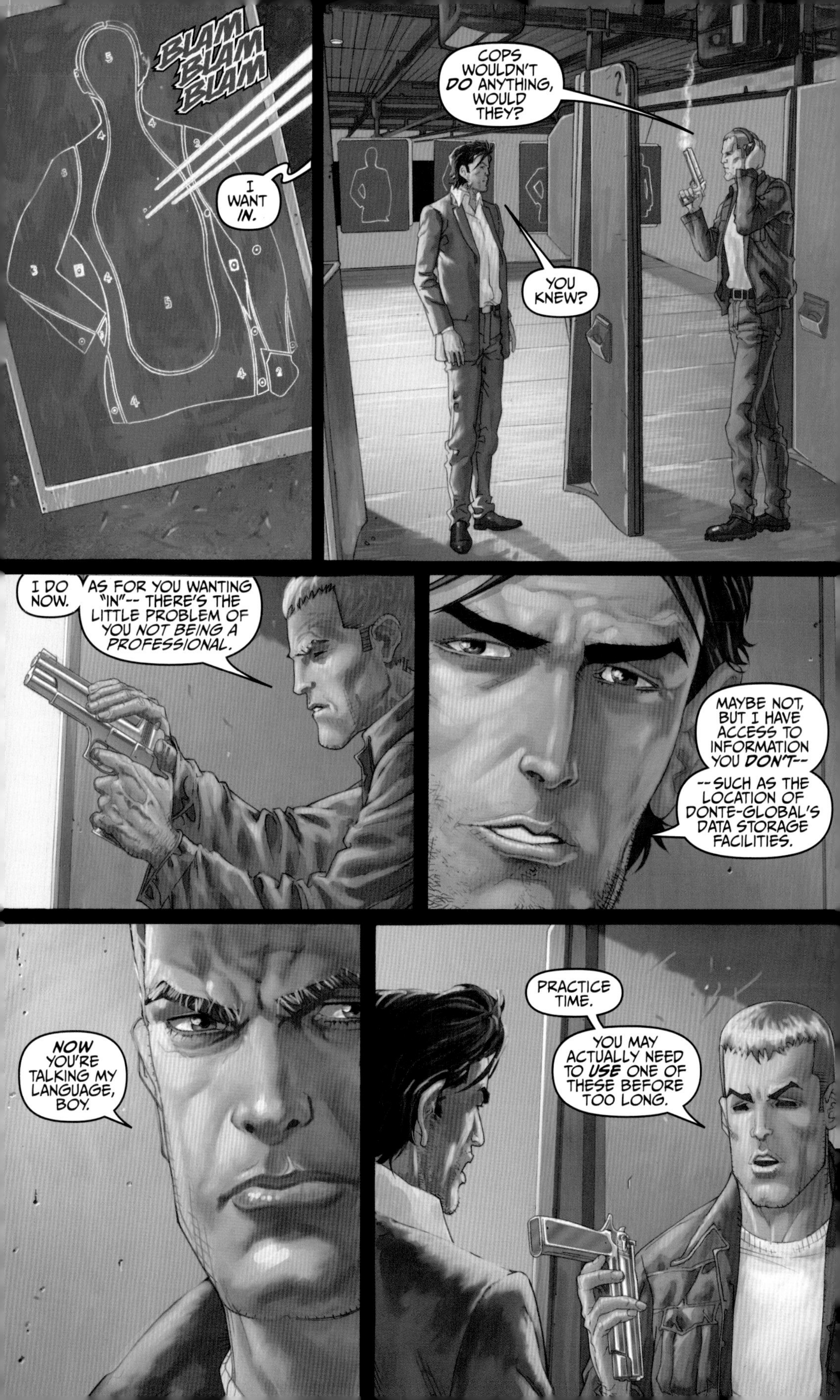
BLAM BLAM BLAM
I WANT IN.
COPS WOULDN'T DO ANYTHING, WOULD THEY?
YOU KNEW?
I DO NOW.
AS FOR YOU WANTING "IN"-- THERE'S THE LITTLE PROBLEM OF YOU NOT BEING A PROFESSIONAL.
MAYBE NOT, BUT I HAVE ACCESS TO INFORMATION YOU DON'T--
--SUCH AS THE LOCATION OF DONTE-GLOBAL'S DATA STORAGE FACILITIES.
NOW YOU'RE TALKING MY LANGUAGE, BOY.
PRACTICE TIME.
YOU MAY ACTUALLY NEED TO USE ONE OF THESE BEFORE TOO LONG.

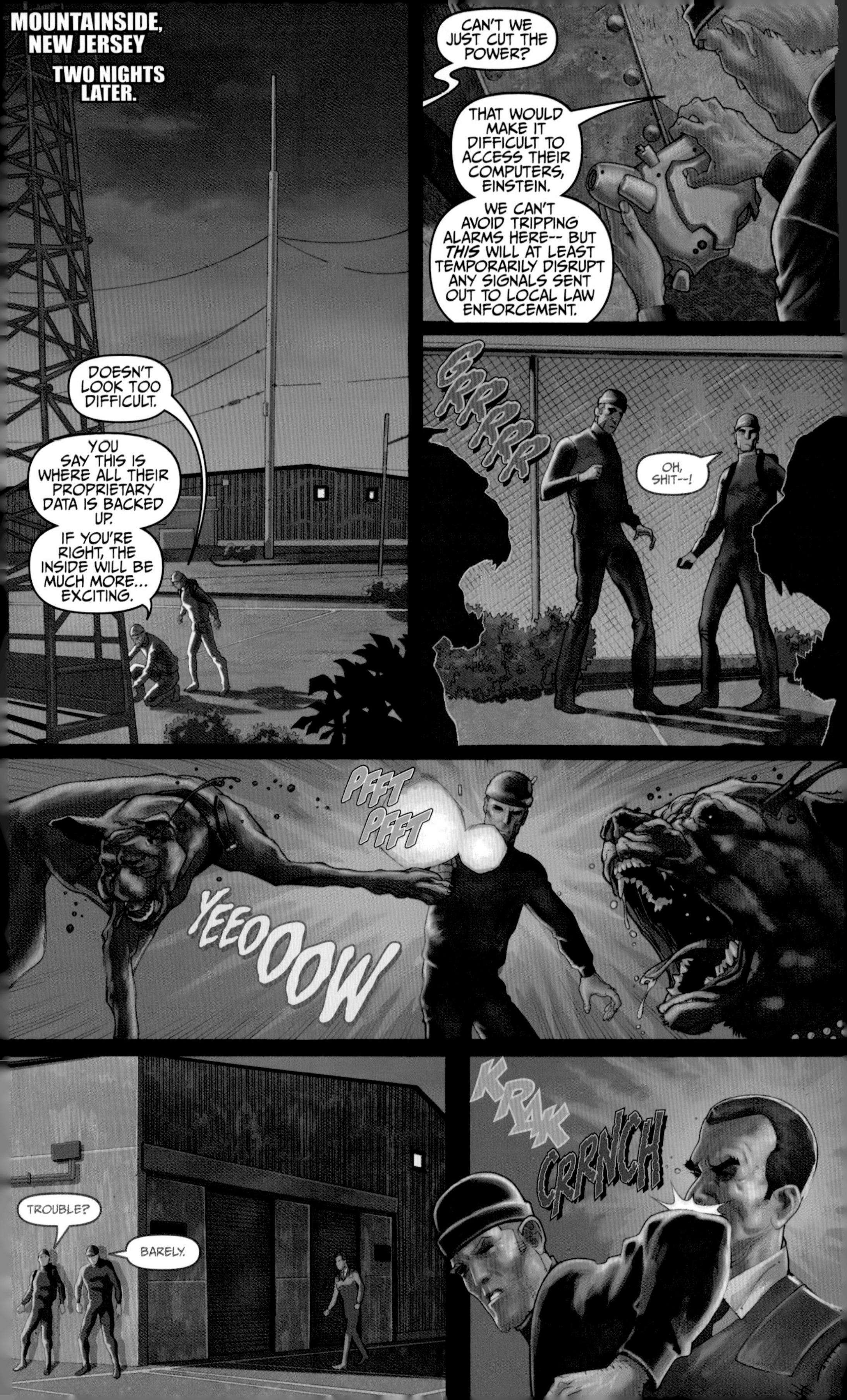
MOUNTAINSIDE, NEW JERSEY
TWO NIGHTS LATER.
DOESN'T LOOK TOO DIFFICULT.
YOU SAY THIS IS WHERE ALL THEIR PROPRIETARY DATA IS BACKED UP.
IF YOU'RE RIGHT, THE INSIDE WILL BE MUCH MORE... EXCITING.
CAN'T WE JUST CUT THE POWER?
THAT WOULD MAKE IT DIFFICULT TO ACCESS THEIR COMPUTERS, EINSTEIN.
WE CAN'T AVOID TRIPPING ALARMS HERE-- BUT *THIS* WILL AT LEAST TEMPORARILY DISRUPT ANY SIGNALS SENT OUT TO LOCAL LAW ENFORCEMENT.
GRRRRR
OH, SHIT--!
PFFT
PFFT
YEEOOOW
TROUBLE?
BARELY.
KRAK
CRRNCH

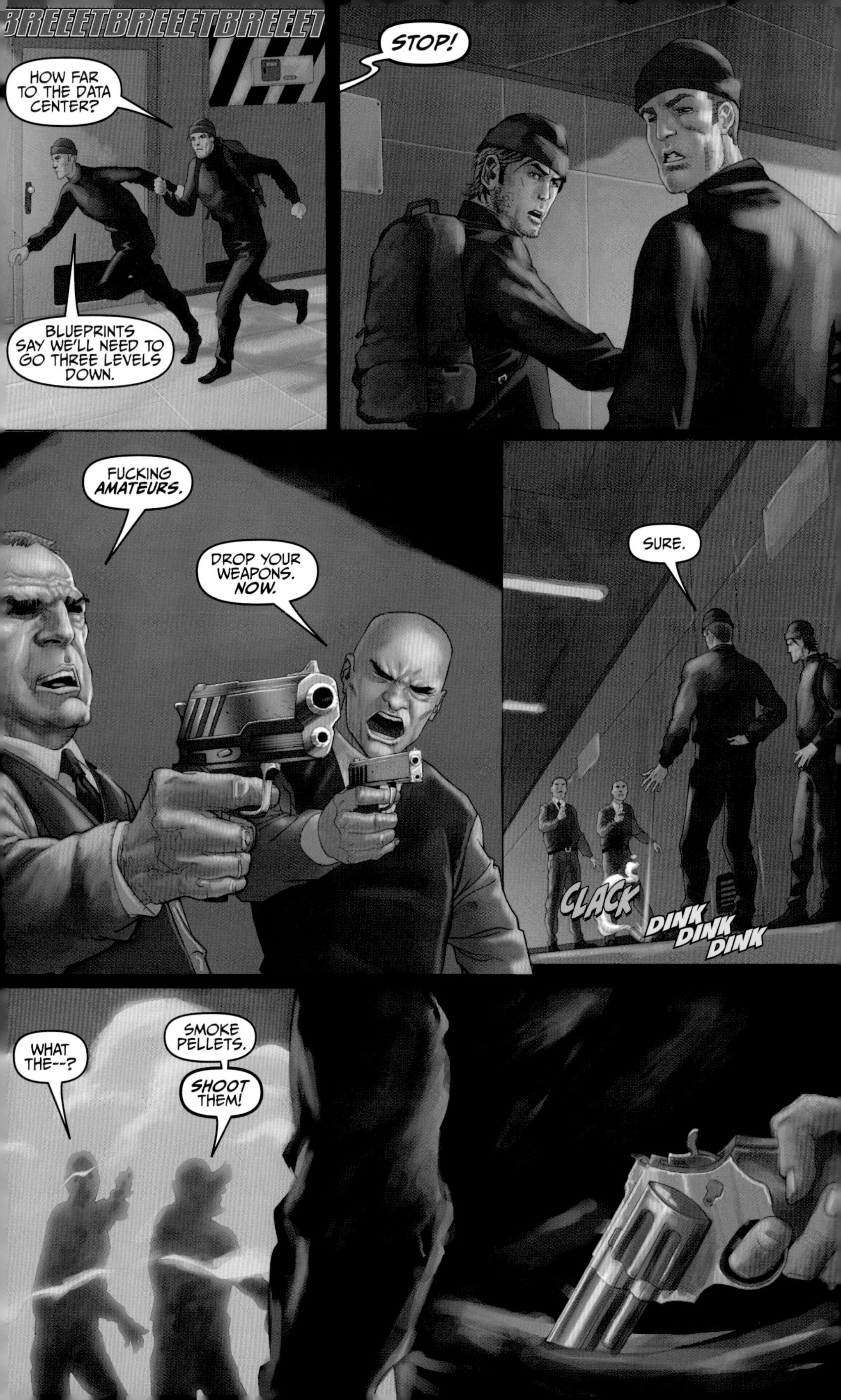
BREEETBREEETBREEET
HOW FAR TO THE DATA CENTER?
BLUEPRINTS SAY WE'LL NEED TO GO THREE LEVELS DOWN.
STOP!
FUCKING AMATEURS.
DROP YOUR WEAPONS. NOW.
SURE.
CLACK
DINK DINK DINK
WHAT THE--?
SMOKE PELLETS.
SHOOT THEM!

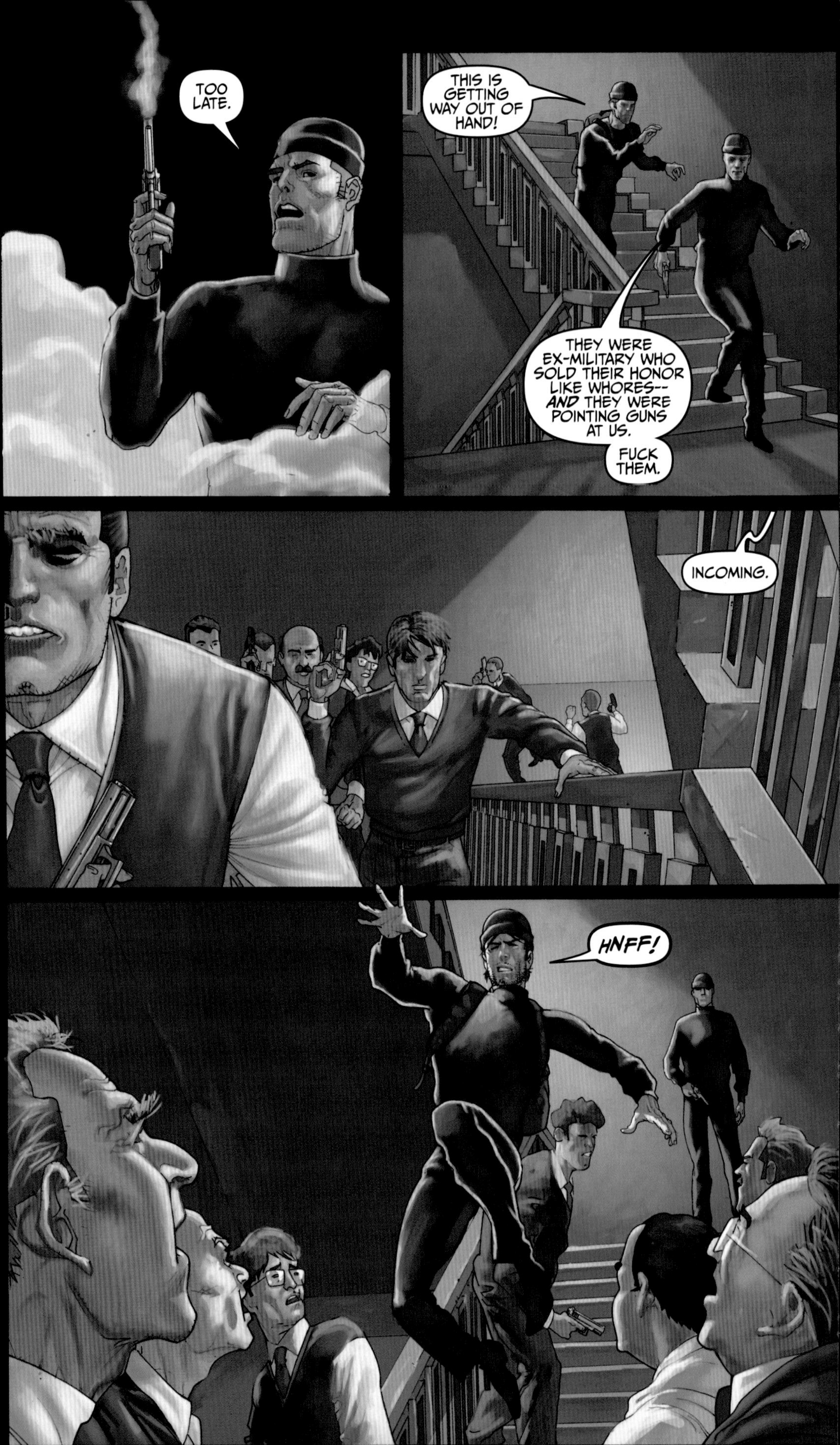
TOO LATE.
THIS IS GETTING WAY OUT OF HAND!
THEY WERE EX-MILITARY WHO SOLD THEIR HONOR LIKE WHORES-- AND THEY WERE POINTING GUNS AT US.
FUCK THEM.
INCOMING.
HNFF!

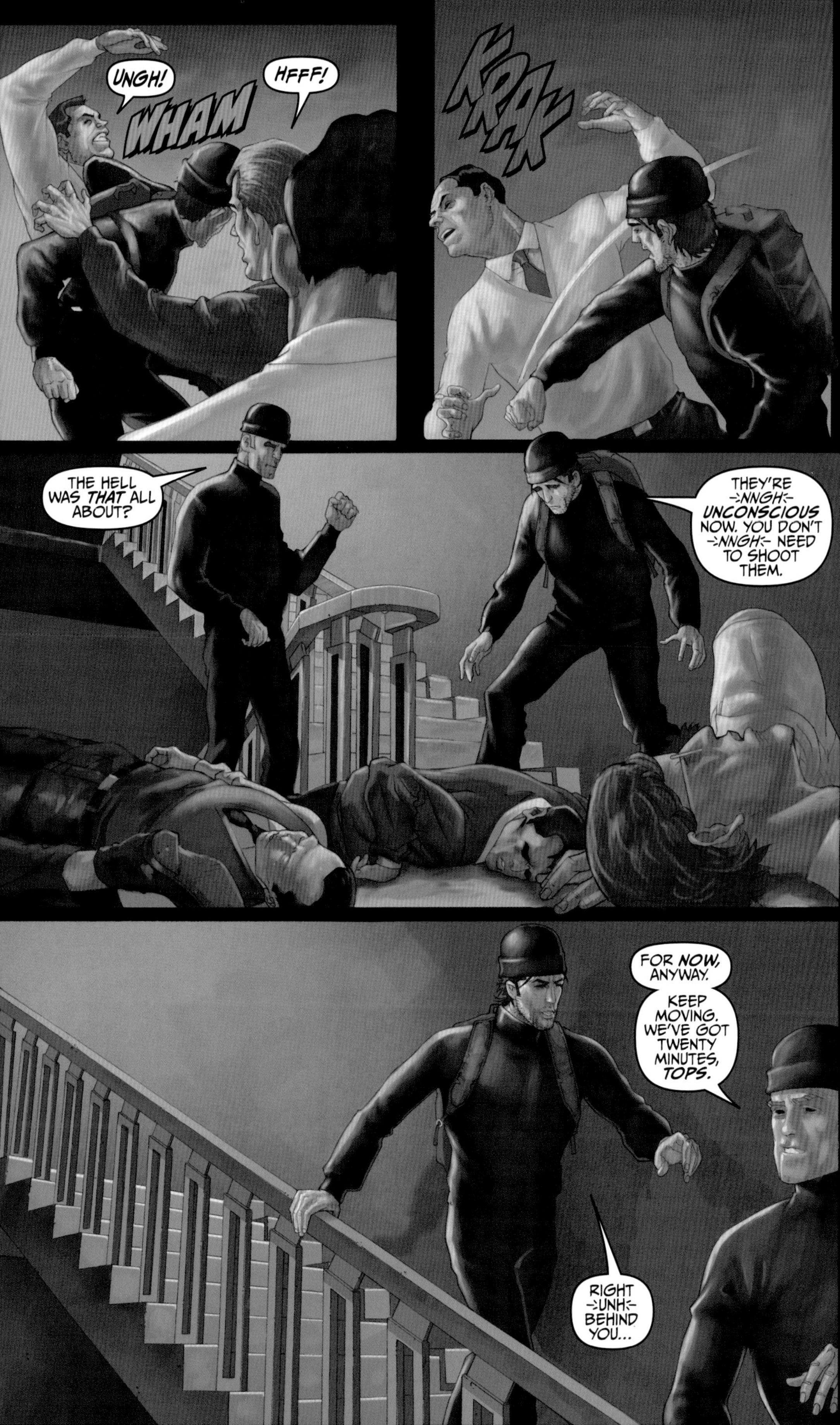
UNGH!
WHAM
HFFF!
KRAK
THE HELL WAS THAT ALL ABOUT?
THEY'RE -NNGH- UNCONSCIOUS NOW. YOU DON'T -NNGH- NEED TO SHOOT THEM.
FOR NOW, ANYWAY.
KEEP MOVING. WE'VE GOT TWENTY MINUTES, TOPS.
RIGHT -UNH- BEHIND YOU...

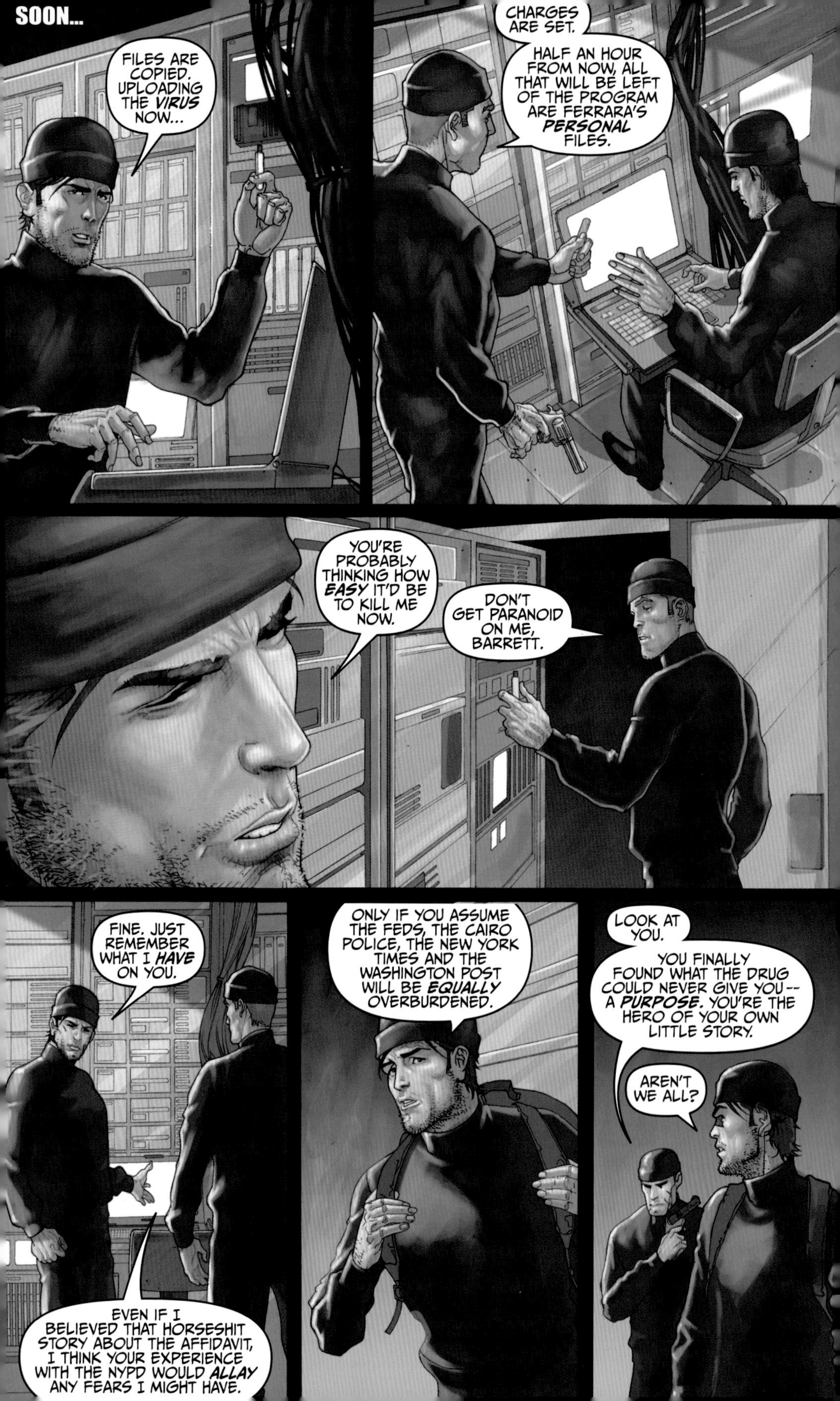
SOON...
FILES ARE COPIED. UPLOADING THE *VIRUS* NOW...
CHARGES ARE SET.
HALF AN HOUR FROM NOW, ALL THAT WILL BE LEFT OF THE PROGRAM ARE FERRARA'S *PERSONAL* FILES.
YOU'RE PROBABLY THINKING HOW *EASY* IT'D BE TO KILL ME NOW.
DON'T GET PARANOID ON ME, BARRETT.
FINE. JUST REMEMBER WHAT I *HAVE* ON YOU.
EVEN IF I BELIEVED THAT HORSESHIT STORY ABOUT THE AFFIDAVIT, I THINK YOUR EXPERIENCE WITH THE NYPD WOULD *ALLAY* ANY FEARS I MIGHT HAVE.
ONLY IF YOU ASSUME THE FEDS, THE CAIRO POLICE, THE NEW YORK TIMES AND THE WASHINGTON POST WILL BE *EQUALLY* OVERBURDENED.
LOOK AT YOU.
YOU FINALLY FOUND WHAT THE DRUG COULD NEVER GIVE YOU-- A *PURPOSE.* YOU'RE THE HERO OF YOUR OWN LITTLE STORY.
AREN'T WE ALL?

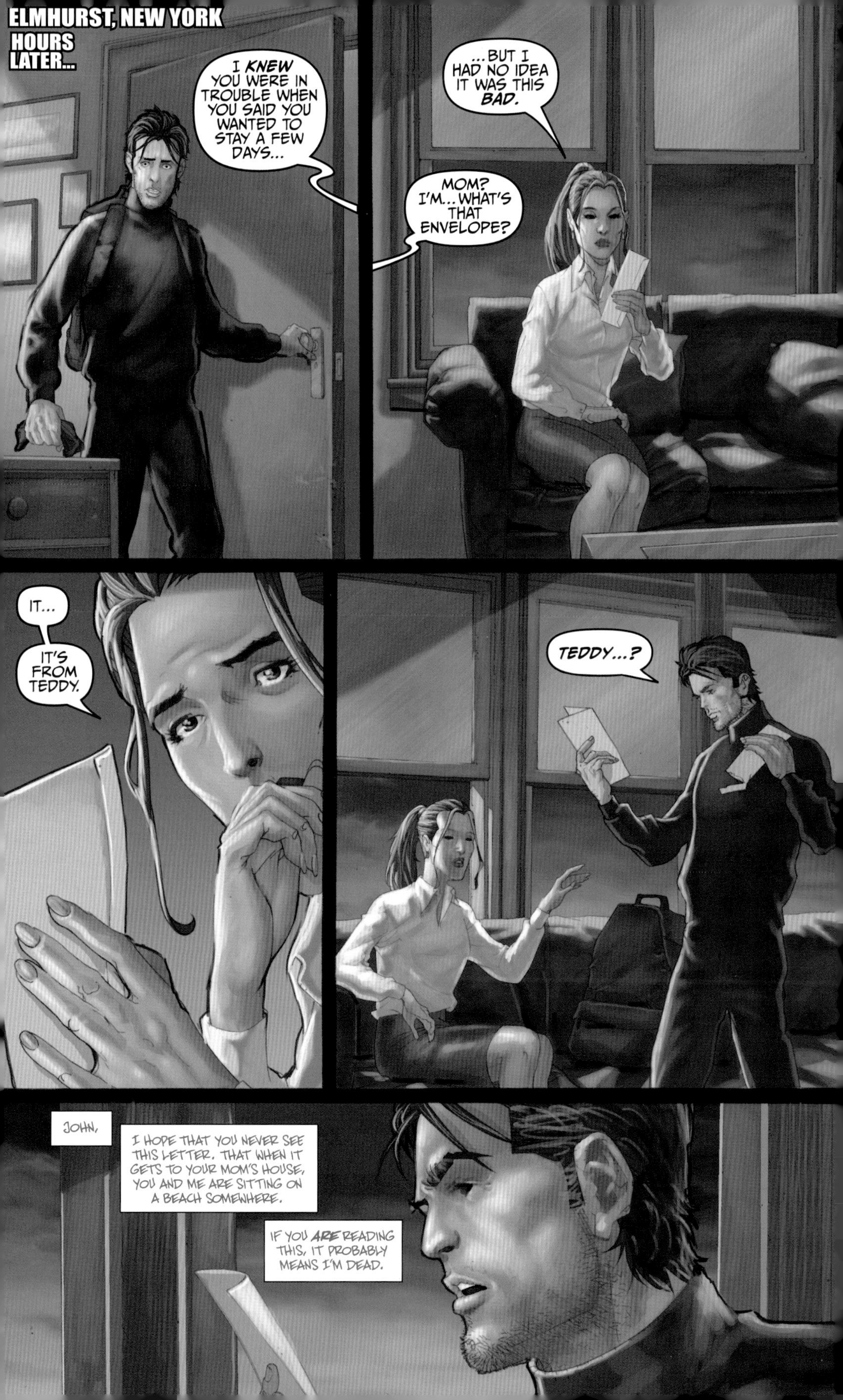
ELMHURST, NEW YORK
HOURS LATER...
I KNEW YOU WERE IN TROUBLE WHEN YOU SAID YOU WANTED TO STAY A FEW DAYS...
...BUT I HAD NO IDEA IT WAS THIS BAD.
MOM? I'M... WHAT'S THAT ENVELOPE?
IT...
IT'S FROM TEDDY.
TEDDY...?
JOHN,
I HOPE THAT YOU NEVER SEE THIS LETTER. THAT WHEN IT GETS TO YOUR MOM'S HOUSE, YOU AND ME ARE SITTING ON A BEACH SOMEWHERE.
IF YOU ARE READING THIS, IT PROBABLY MEANS I'M DEAD.

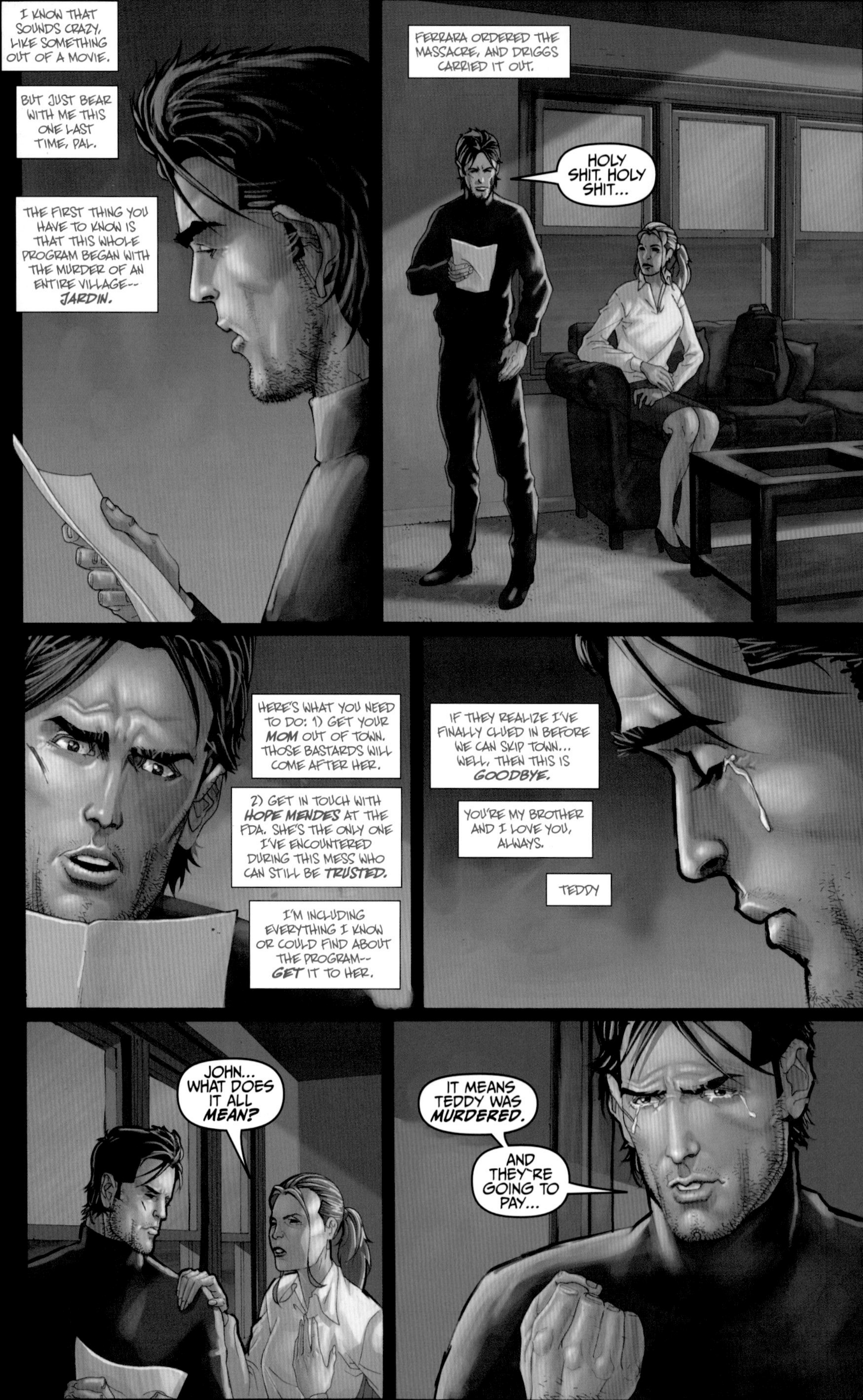
I KNOW THAT SOUNDS CRAZY, LIKE SOMETHING OUT OF A MOVIE.
BUT JUST BEAR WITH ME THIS ONE LAST TIME, PAL.
THE FIRST THING YOU HAVE TO KNOW IS THAT THIS WHOLE PROGRAM BEGAN WITH THE MURDER OF AN ENTIRE VILLAGE-- JARDIN.
FERRARA ORDERED THE MASSACRE, AND DRIGGS CARRIED IT OUT.
HOLY SHIT. HOLY SHIT...
HERE'S WHAT YOU NEED TO DO: 1) GET YOUR MOM OUT OF TOWN. THOSE BASTARDS WILL COME AFTER HER.
2) GET IN TOUCH WITH HOPE MENDES AT THE FDA. SHE'S THE ONLY ONE I'VE ENCOUNTERED DURING THIS MESS WHO CAN STILL BE TRUSTED.
I'M INCLUDING EVERYTHING I KNOW OR COULD FIND ABOUT THE PROGRAM-- GET IT TO HER.
IF THEY REALIZE I'VE FINALLY CLUED IN BEFORE WE CAN SKIP TOWN... WELL, THEN THIS IS GOODBYE.
YOU'RE MY BROTHER AND I LOVE YOU, ALWAYS.
TEDDY
JOHN... WHAT DOES IT ALL MEAN?
IT MEANS TEDDY WAS MURDERED.
AND THEY'RE GOING TO PAY...

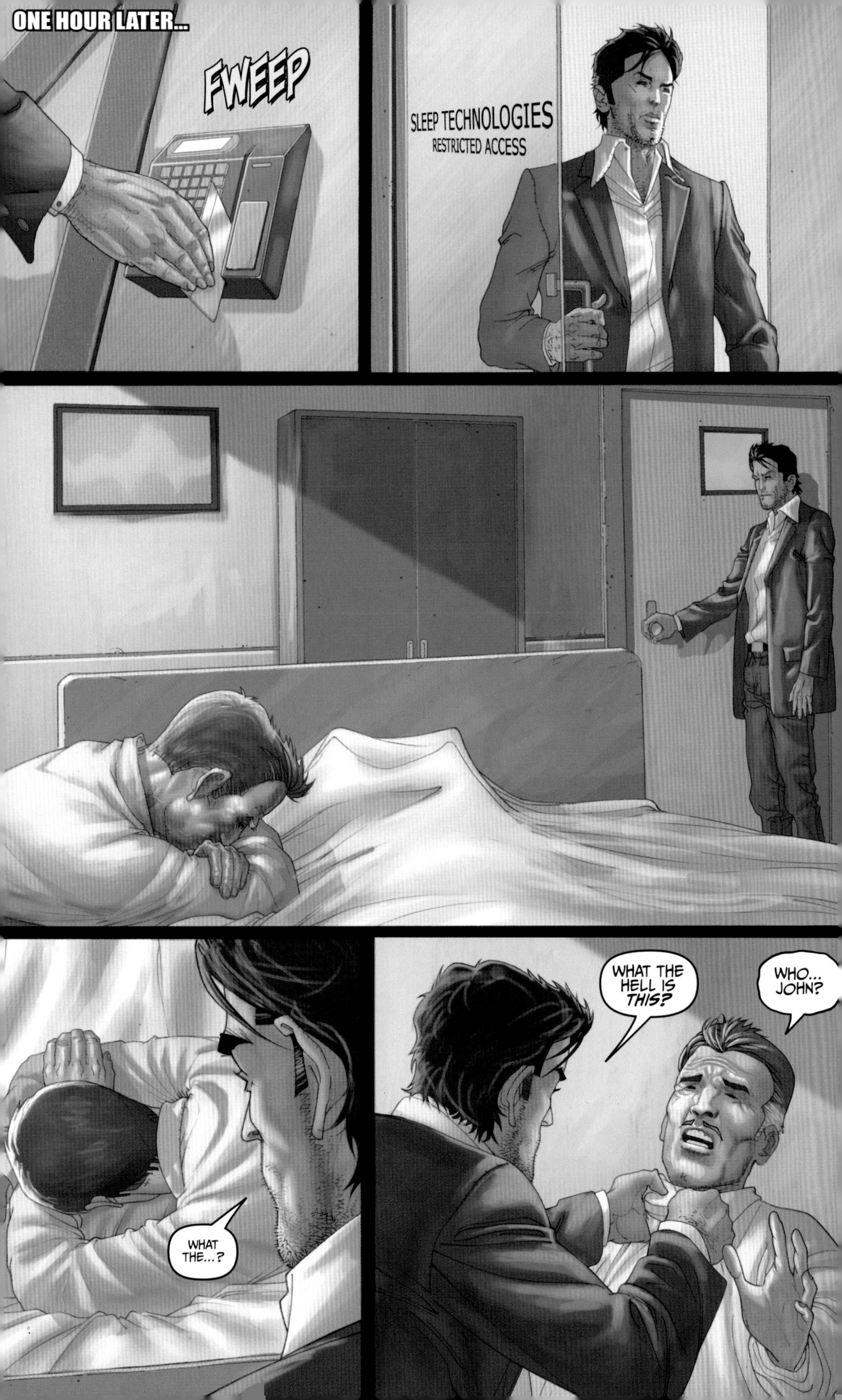
ONE HOUR LATER...
FWEEP
SLEEP TECHNOLOGIES
RESTRICTED ACCESS
WHAT THE...?
WHAT THE HELL IS *THIS?*
WHO... JOHN?

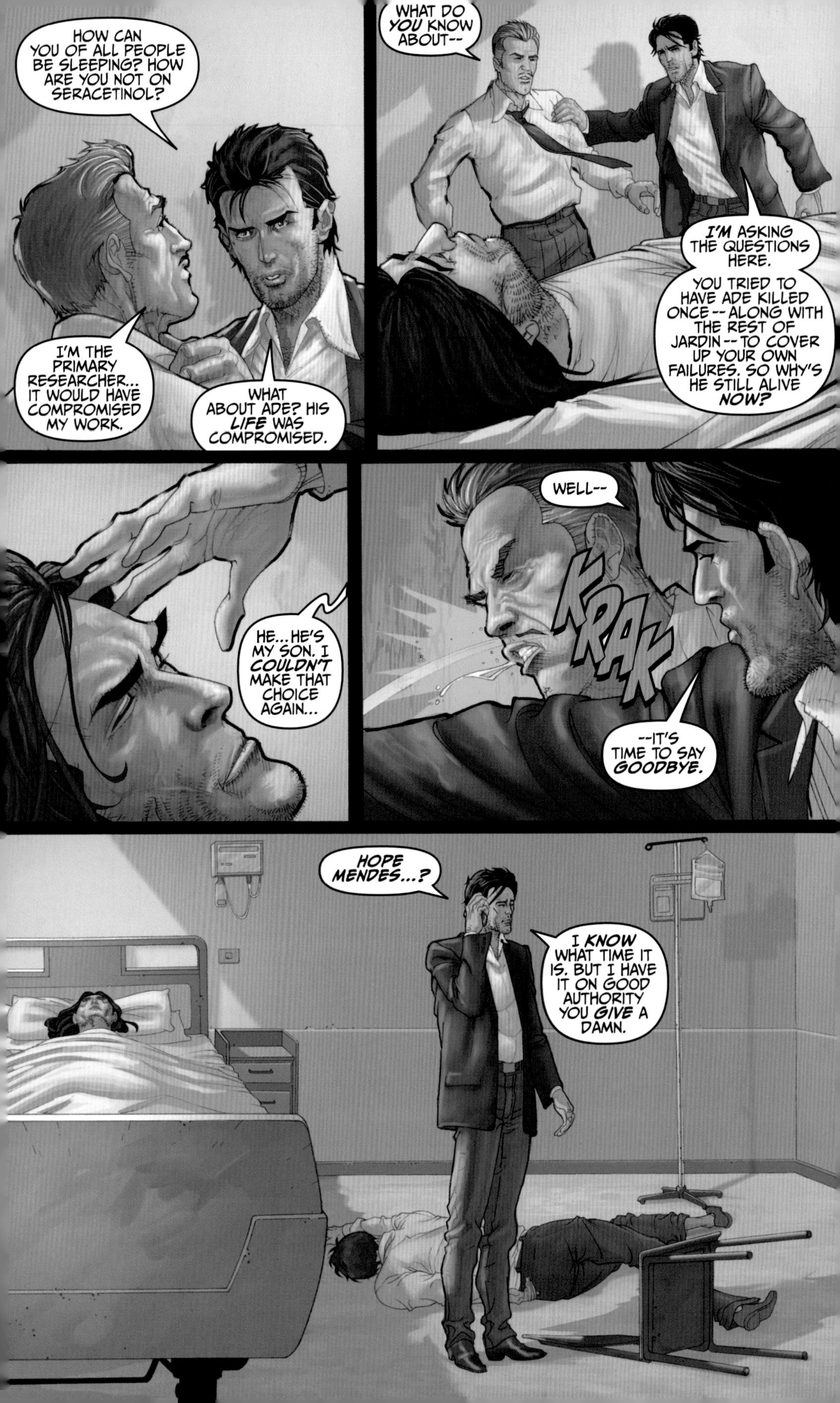
HOW CAN YOU OF ALL PEOPLE BE SLEEPING? HOW ARE YOU NOT ON SERACETINOL?
I'M THE PRIMARY RESEARCHER... IT WOULD HAVE COMPROMISED MY WORK.
WHAT ABOUT ADE? HIS *LIFE* WAS COMPROMISED.
WHAT DO *YOU* KNOW ABOUT--
I'M ASKING THE QUESTIONS HERE.
YOU TRIED TO HAVE ADE KILLED ONCE--ALONG WITH THE REST OF JARDIN--TO COVER UP YOUR OWN FAILURES. SO WHY'S HE STILL ALIVE *NOW?*
HE...HE'S MY SON. I *COULDN'T* MAKE THAT CHOICE AGAIN...
WELL--
KRAK
--IT'S TIME TO SAY *GOODBYE.*
HOPE MENDES...?
I *KNOW* WHAT TIME IT IS. BUT I HAVE IT ON GOOD AUTHORITY YOU *GIVE* A DAMN.

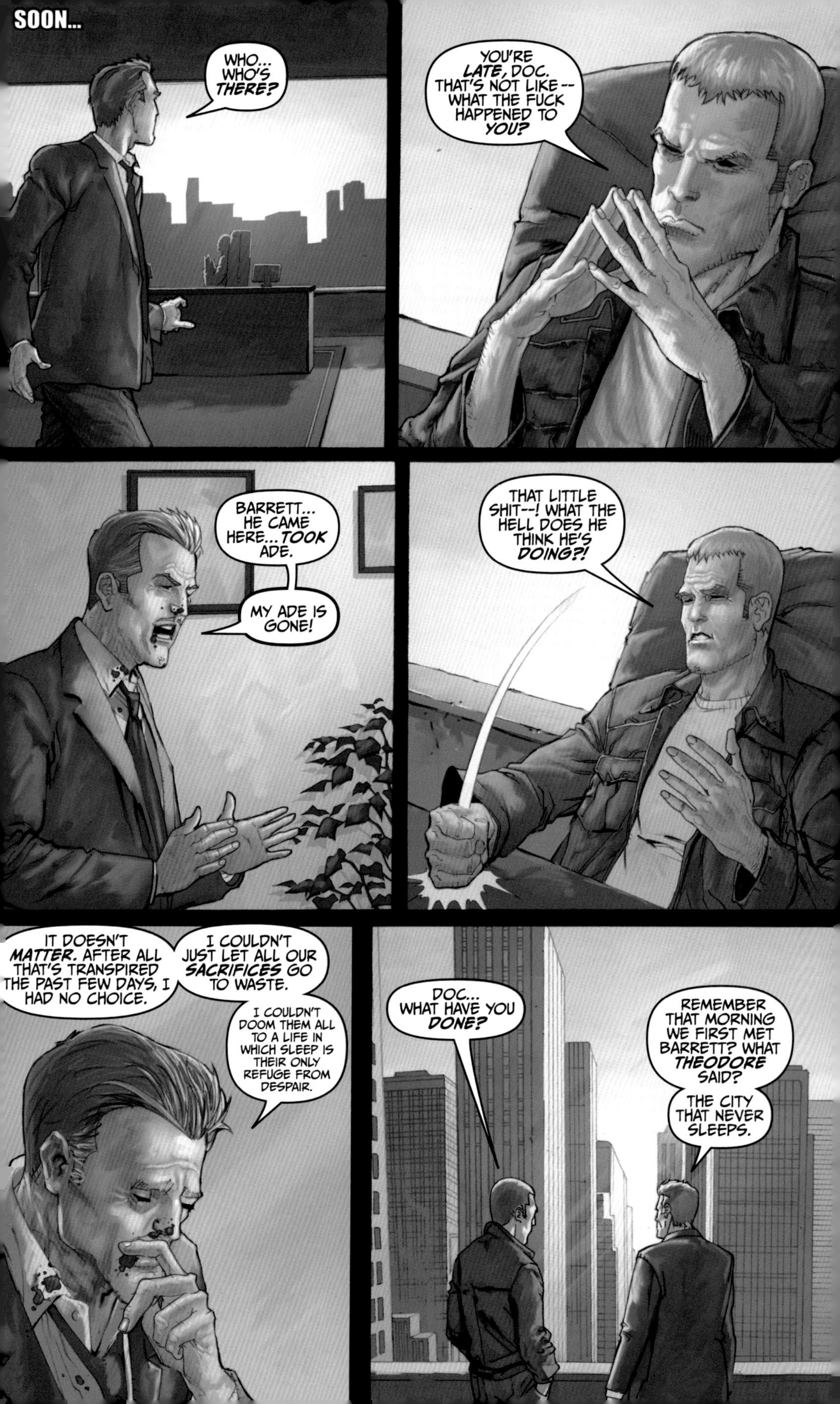
SOON...
WHO... WHO'S THERE?
YOU'RE LATE, DOC. THAT'S NOT LIKE-- WHAT THE FUCK HAPPENED TO YOU?
BARRETT... HE CAME HERE...TOOK ADE.
MY ADE IS GONE!
THAT LITTLE SHIT--! WHAT THE HELL DOES HE THINK HE'S DOING?!
IT DOESN'T MATTER. AFTER ALL THAT'S TRANSPIRED THE PAST FEW DAYS, I HAD NO CHOICE.
I COULDN'T JUST LET ALL OUR SACRIFICES GO TO WASTE.
I COULDN'T DOOM THEM ALL TO A LIFE IN WHICH SLEEP IS THEIR ONLY REFUGE FROM DESPAIR.
DOC... WHAT HAVE YOU DONE?
REMEMBER THAT MORNING WE FIRST MET BARRETT? WHAT THEODORE SAID?
THE CITY THAT NEVER SLEEPS.

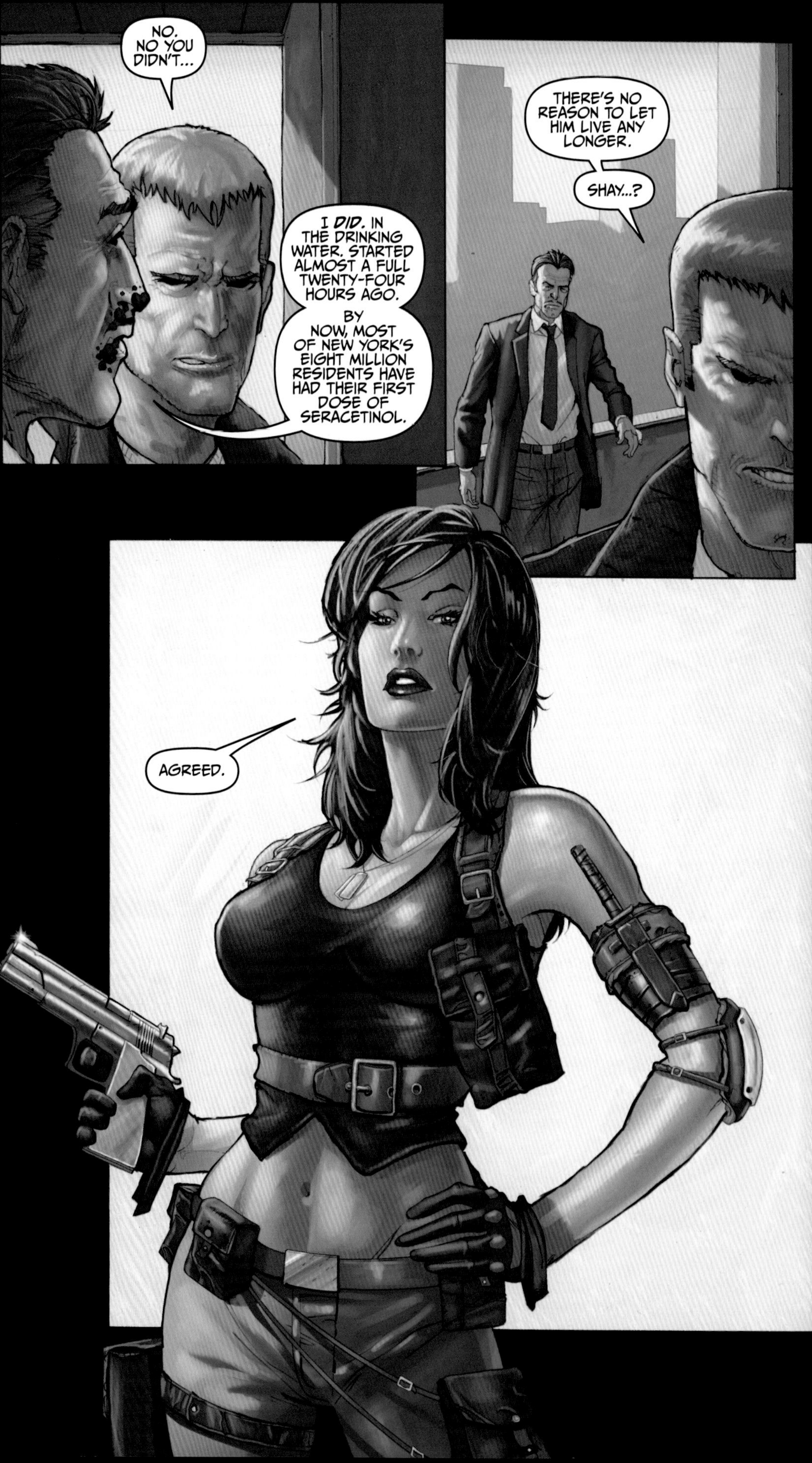
NO. NO YOU DIDN'T...
I DID. IN THE DRINKING WATER. STARTED ALMOST A FULL TWENTY-FOUR HOURS AGO.
BY NOW, MOST OF NEW YORK'S EIGHT MILLION RESIDENTS HAVE HAD THEIR FIRST DOSE OF SERACETINOL.
THERE'S NO REASON TO LET HIM LIVE ANY LONGER.
SHAY...?
AGREED.

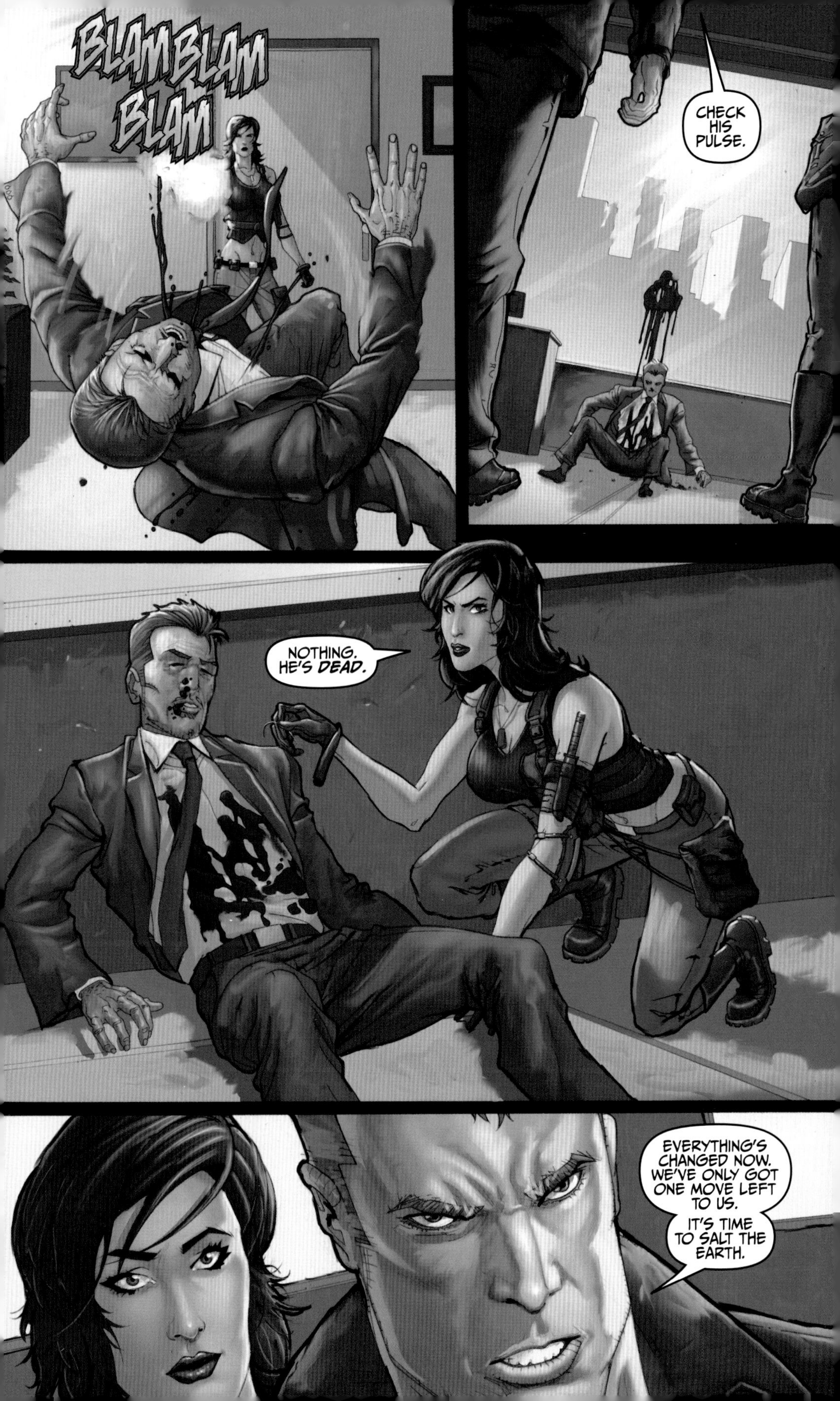
BLAMBLAM BLAM
CHECK HIS PULSE.
NOTHING. HE'S *DEAD*.
EVERYTHING'S CHANGED NOW. WE'VE ONLY GOT ONE MOVE LEFT TO US.
IT'S TIME TO SALT THE EARTH.

Rest #5

written by: **Mark Powers**
line art by: **Marco Castiello**
& **Abhishek Malsuni**
colors by: **Michael Atieyh**
letters by: **Troy Peteri**
• • • • •

original edition edited by: **Filip Sablik**
& **Phil Smith**

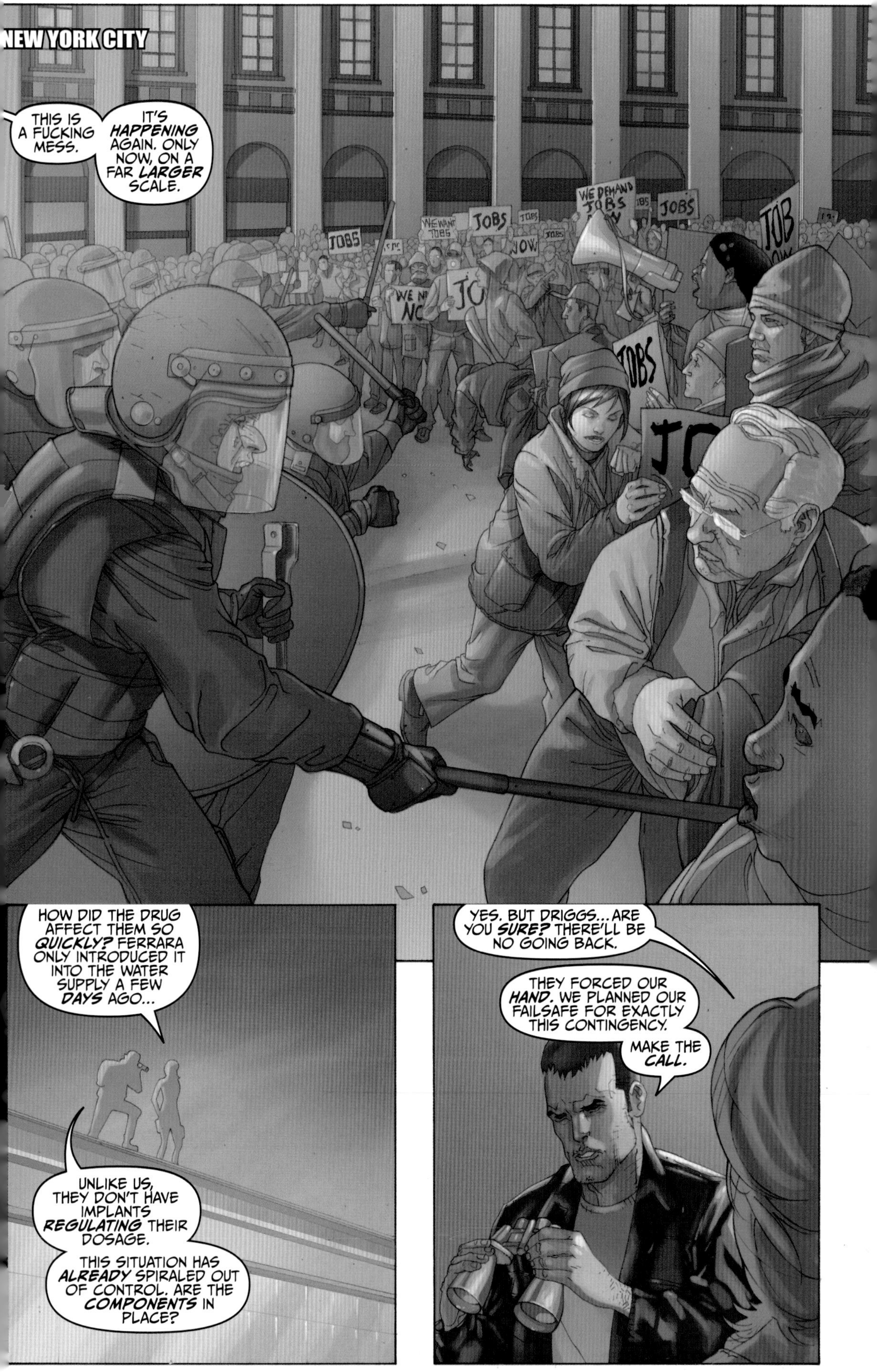
NEW YORK CITY
THIS IS A FUCKING MESS.
IT'S HAPPENING AGAIN. ONLY NOW, ON A FAR LARGER SCALE.
HOW DID THE DRUG AFFECT THEM SO QUICKLY? FERRARA ONLY INTRODUCED IT INTO THE WATER SUPPLY A FEW DAYS AGO...
UNLIKE US, THEY DON'T HAVE IMPLANTS REGULATING THEIR DOSAGE.
THIS SITUATION HAS ALREADY SPIRALED OUT OF CONTROL. ARE THE COMPONENTS IN PLACE?
YES. BUT DRIGGS... ARE YOU SURE? THERE'LL BE NO GOING BACK.
THEY FORCED OUR HAND. WE PLANNED OUR FAILSAFE FOR EXACTLY THIS CONTINGENCY.
MAKE THE CALL.

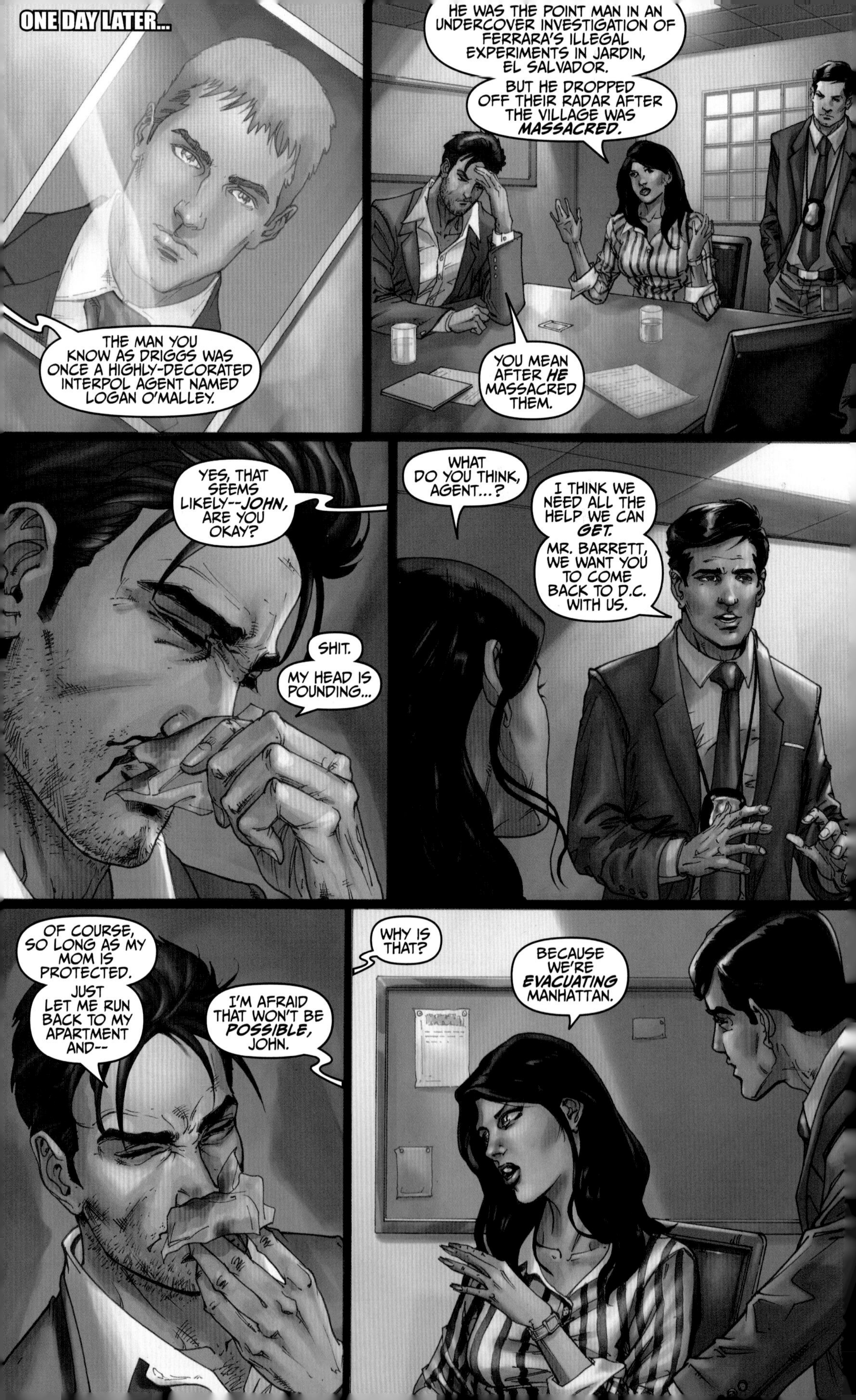
ONE DAY LATER...
THE MAN YOU KNOW AS DRIGGS WAS ONCE A HIGHLY-DECORATED INTERPOL AGENT NAMED LOGAN O'MALLEY.
HE WAS THE POINT MAN IN AN UNDERCOVER INVESTIGATION OF FERRARA'S ILLEGAL EXPERIMENTS IN JARDIN, EL SALVADOR.
BUT HE DROPPED OFF THEIR RADAR AFTER THE VILLAGE WAS MASSACRED.
YOU MEAN AFTER HE MASSACRED THEM.
YES, THAT SEEMS LIKELY--JOHN, ARE YOU OKAY?
SHIT.
MY HEAD IS POUNDING...
WHAT DO YOU THINK, AGENT...?
I THINK WE NEED ALL THE HELP WE CAN GET.
MR. BARRETT, WE WANT YOU TO COME BACK TO D.C. WITH US.
OF COURSE, SO LONG AS MY MOM IS PROTECTED.
JUST LET ME RUN BACK TO MY APARTMENT AND--
I'M AFRAID THAT WON'T BE POSSIBLE, JOHN.
WHY IS THAT?
BECAUSE WE'RE EVACUATING MANHATTAN.

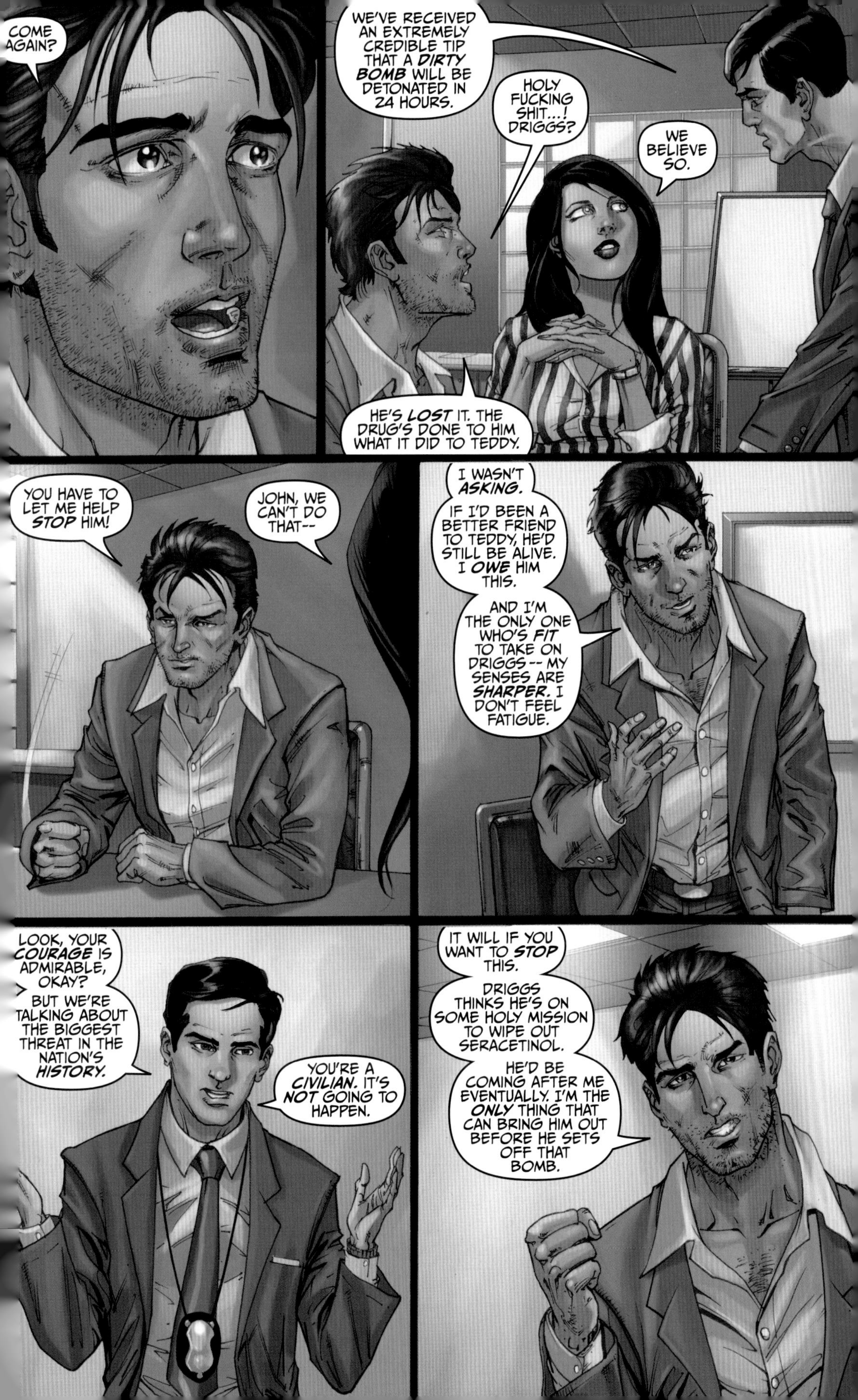
COME AGAIN?
WE'VE RECEIVED AN EXTREMELY CREDIBLE TIP THAT A DIRTY BOMB WILL BE DETONATED IN 24 HOURS.
HOLY FUCKING SHIT...! DRIGGS?
WE BELIEVE SO.
HE'S LOST IT. THE DRUG'S DONE TO HIM WHAT IT DID TO TEDDY.
YOU HAVE TO LET ME HELP STOP HIM!
JOHN, WE CAN'T DO THAT--
I WASN'T ASKING.
IF I'D BEEN A BETTER FRIEND TO TEDDY, HE'D STILL BE ALIVE. I OWE HIM THIS.
AND I'M THE ONLY ONE WHO'S FIT TO TAKE ON DRIGGS-- MY SENSES ARE SHARPER. I DON'T FEEL FATIGUE.
LOOK, YOUR COURAGE IS ADMIRABLE, OKAY?
BUT WE'RE TALKING ABOUT THE BIGGEST THREAT IN THE NATION'S HISTORY.
YOU'RE A CIVILIAN. IT'S NOT GOING TO HAPPEN.
IT WILL IF YOU WANT TO STOP THIS.
DRIGGS THINKS HE'S ON SOME HOLY MISSION TO WIPE OUT SERACETINOL.
HE'D BE COMING AFTER ME EVENTUALLY. I'M THE ONLY THING THAT CAN BRING HIM OUT BEFORE HE SETS OFF THAT BOMB.

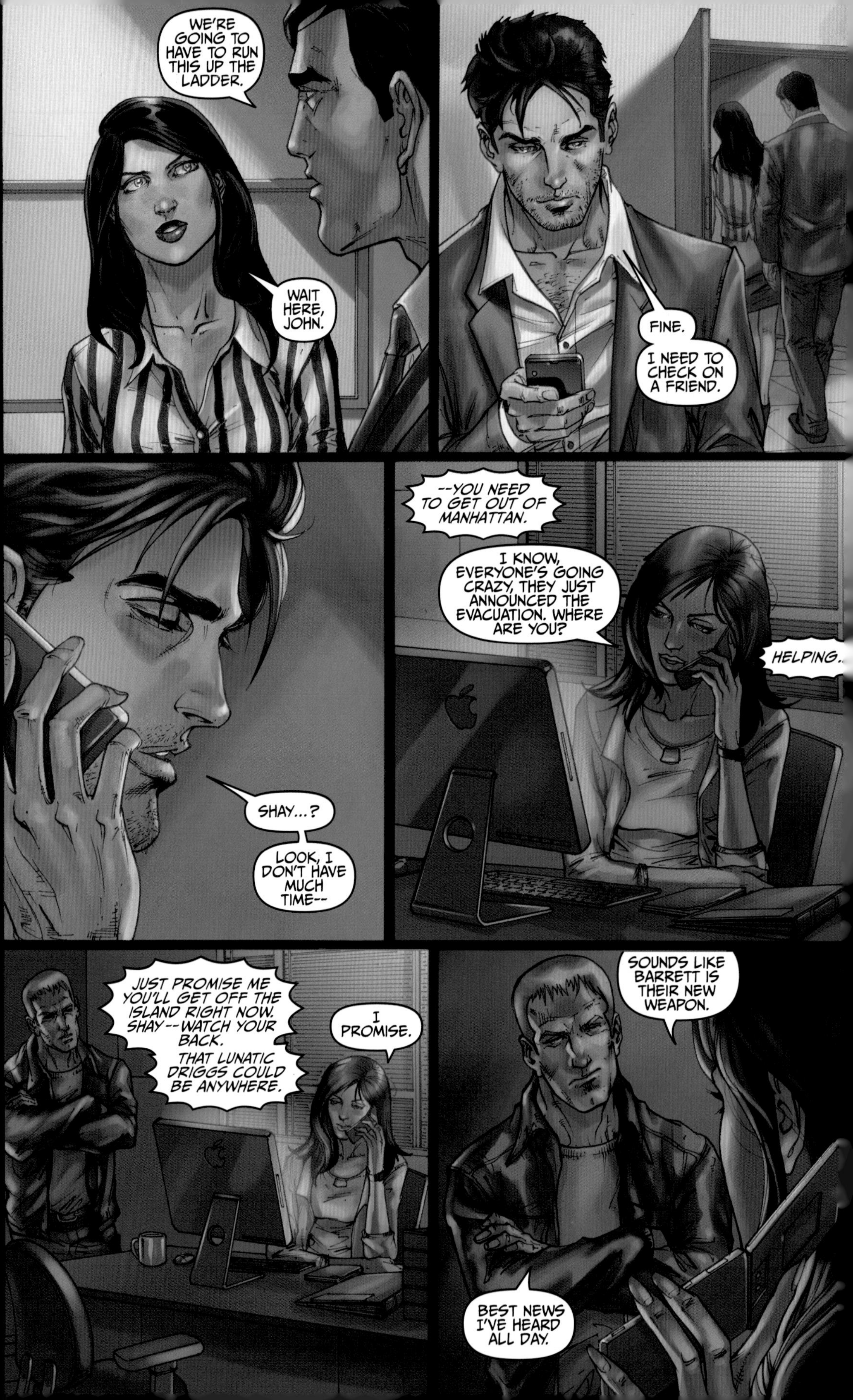
WE'RE GOING TO HAVE TO RUN THIS UP THE LADDER.
WAIT HERE, JOHN.
FINE.
I NEED TO CHECK ON A FRIEND.
SHAY...?
LOOK, I DON'T HAVE MUCH TIME--
--YOU NEED TO GET OUT OF MANHATTAN.
I KNOW, EVERYONE'S GOING CRAZY, THEY JUST ANNOUNCED THE EVACUATION. WHERE ARE YOU?
HELPING...
JUST PROMISE ME YOU'LL GET OFF THE ISLAND RIGHT NOW. SHAY--WATCH YOUR BACK.
THAT LUNATIC DRIGGS COULD BE ANYWHERE.
I PROMISE.
SOUNDS LIKE BARRETT IS THEIR NEW WEAPON.
BEST NEWS I'VE HEARD ALL DAY.

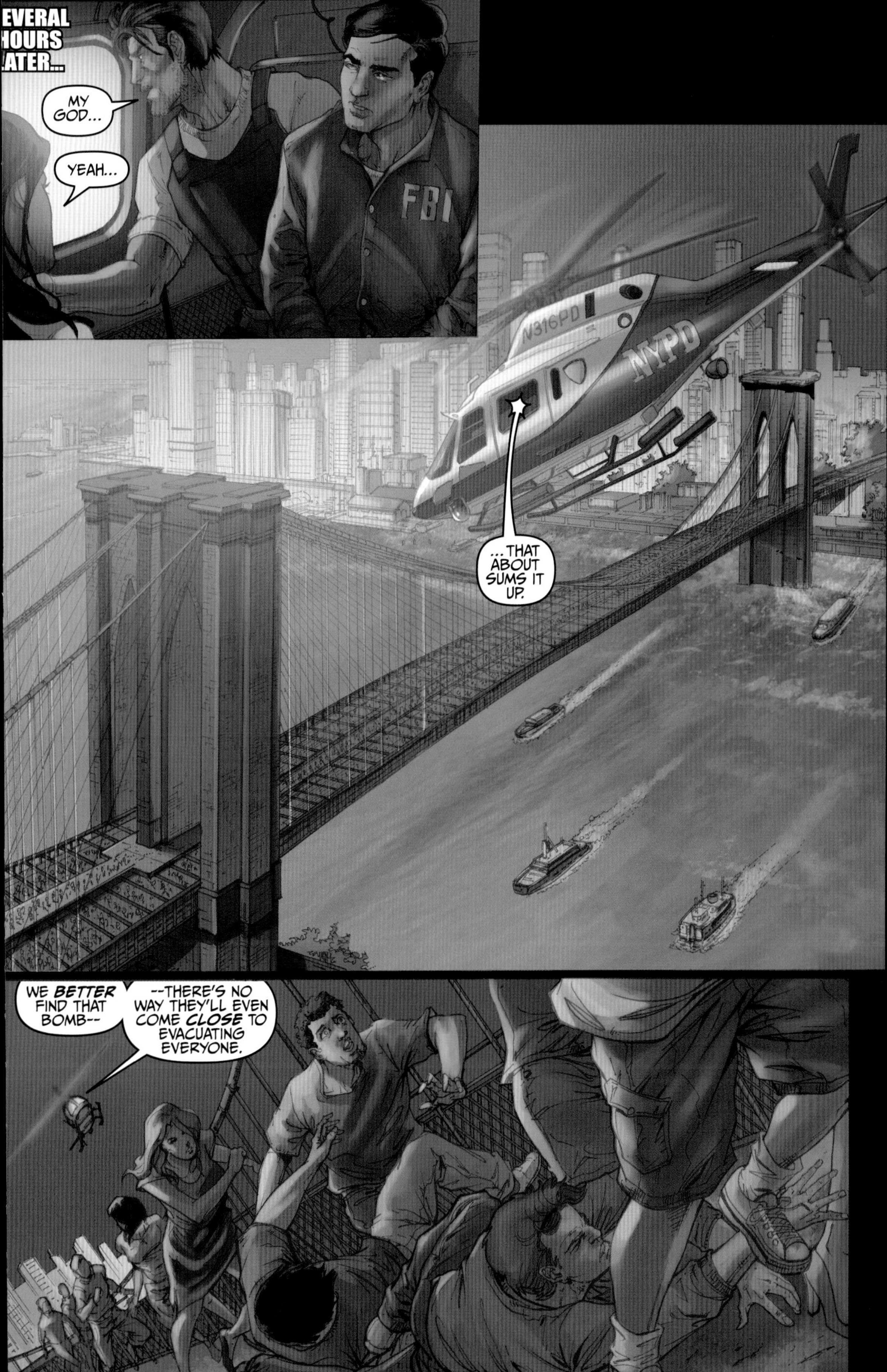
EVERAL HOURS LATER...
MY GOD...
YEAH...
N316PD
NYPD
...THAT ABOUT SUMS IT UP.
WE BETTER FIND THAT BOMB--
--THERE'S NO WAY THEY'LL EVEN COME CLOSE TO EVACUATING EVERYONE.

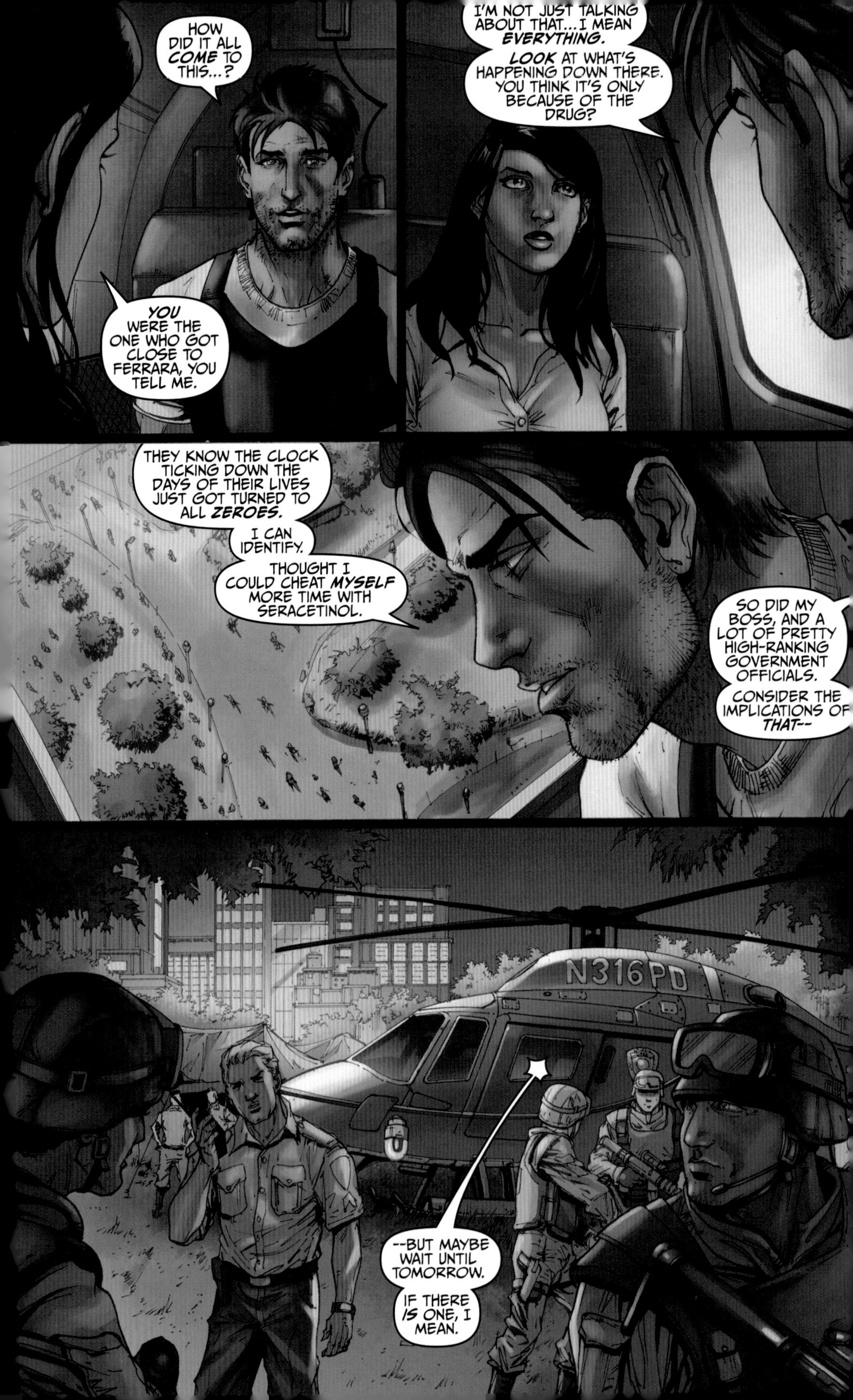
HOW DID IT ALL COME TO THIS...?
YOU WERE THE ONE WHO GOT CLOSE TO FERRARA, YOU TELL ME.
I'M NOT JUST TALKING ABOUT THAT... I MEAN EVERYTHING.
LOOK AT WHAT'S HAPPENING DOWN THERE. YOU THINK IT'S ONLY BECAUSE OF THE DRUG?
THEY KNOW THE CLOCK TICKING DOWN THE DAYS OF THEIR LIVES JUST GOT TURNED TO ALL ZEROES.
I CAN IDENTIFY.
THOUGHT I COULD CHEAT MYSELF MORE TIME WITH SERACETINOL.
SO DID MY BOSS, AND A LOT OF PRETTY HIGH-RANKING GOVERNMENT OFFICIALS.
CONSIDER THE IMPLICATIONS OF THAT--
N316PD
--BUT MAYBE WAIT UNTIL TOMORROW.
IF THERE IS ONE, I MEAN.

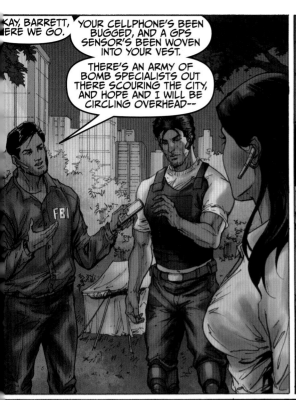

OKAY, BARRETT, HERE WE GO. YOUR CELLPHONE'S BEEN BUGGED, AND A GPS SENSOR'S BEEN WOVEN INTO YOUR VEST.

THERE'S AN ARMY OF BOMB SPECIALISTS OUT THERE SCOURING THE CITY, AND HOPE AND I WILL BE CIRCLING OVERHEAD--

--BUT THERE'S NO WAY WE CAN WATCH YOU *EVERY* SECOND.

THEN IT'S A GOOD THING I'VE HAD SO MUCH EXTRA TIME ON MY HANDS THE PAST YEAR.

I'M PROBABLY MORE QUALIFIED FOR THIS THAN YOU ARE.

-:SIGH:-

THIS IS A 10 MILIMETER GLOCK 20 SEMI-AUTOMATIC--

I GOT IT.

ALL RIGHT THEN, LET'S *DO* THIS.

HELLO, JOHN.

CRAZY DAY, HUH?

FUCK YOU, DRIGGS. WE NEED TO *MEET.*

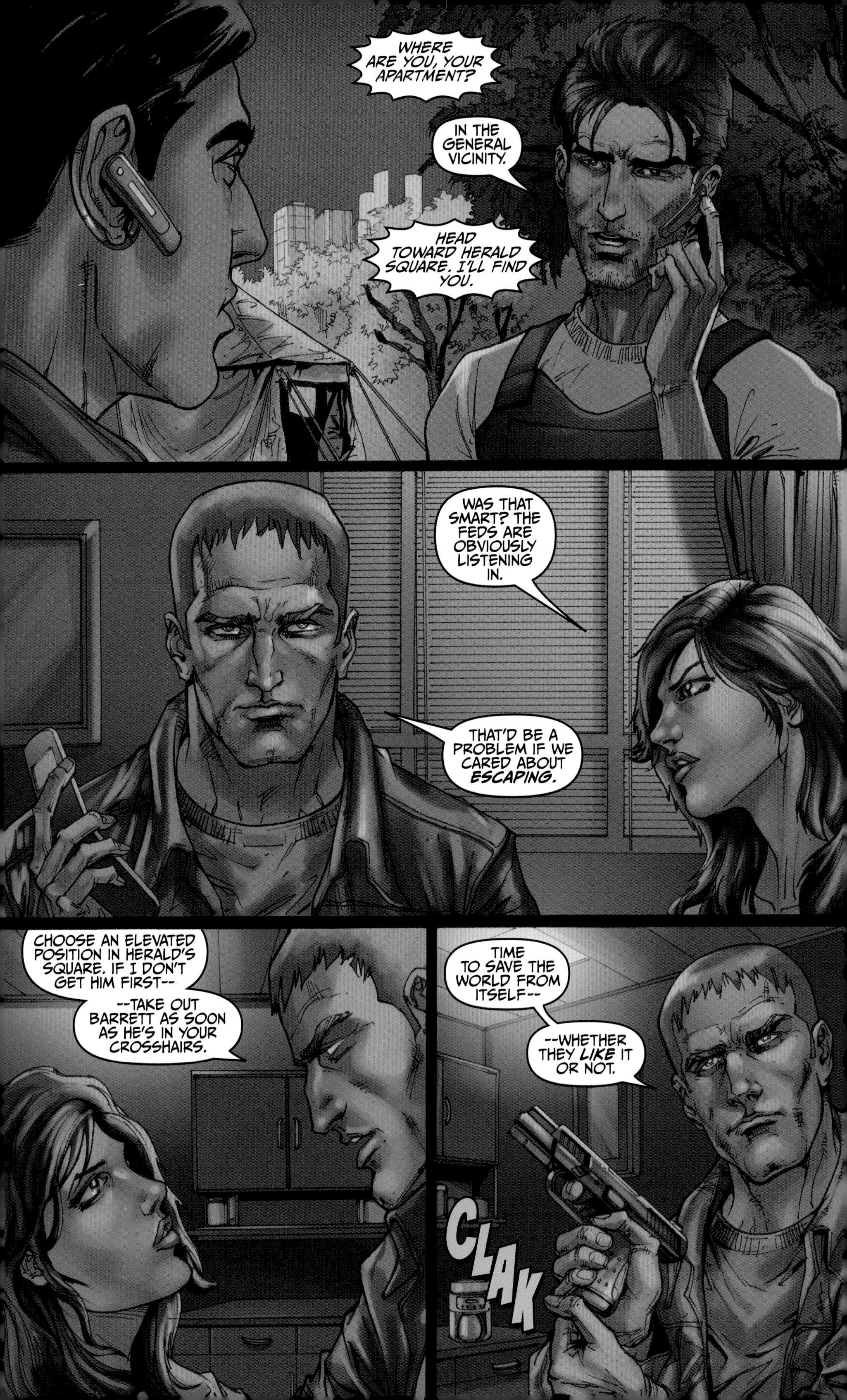
WHERE ARE YOU, YOUR APARTMENT?
IN THE GENERAL VICINITY.
HEAD TOWARD HERALD SQUARE. I'LL FIND YOU.
WAS THAT SMART? THE FEDS ARE OBVIOUSLY LISTENING IN.
THAT'D BE A PROBLEM IF WE CARED ABOUT *ESCAPING.*
CHOOSE AN ELEVATED POSITION IN HERALD'S SQUARE. IF I DON'T GET HIM FIRST--
--TAKE OUT BARRETT AS SOON AS HE'S IN YOUR CROSSHAIRS.
TIME TO SAVE THE WORLD FROM ITSELF--
--WHETHER THEY *LIKE* IT OR NOT.
CLAK

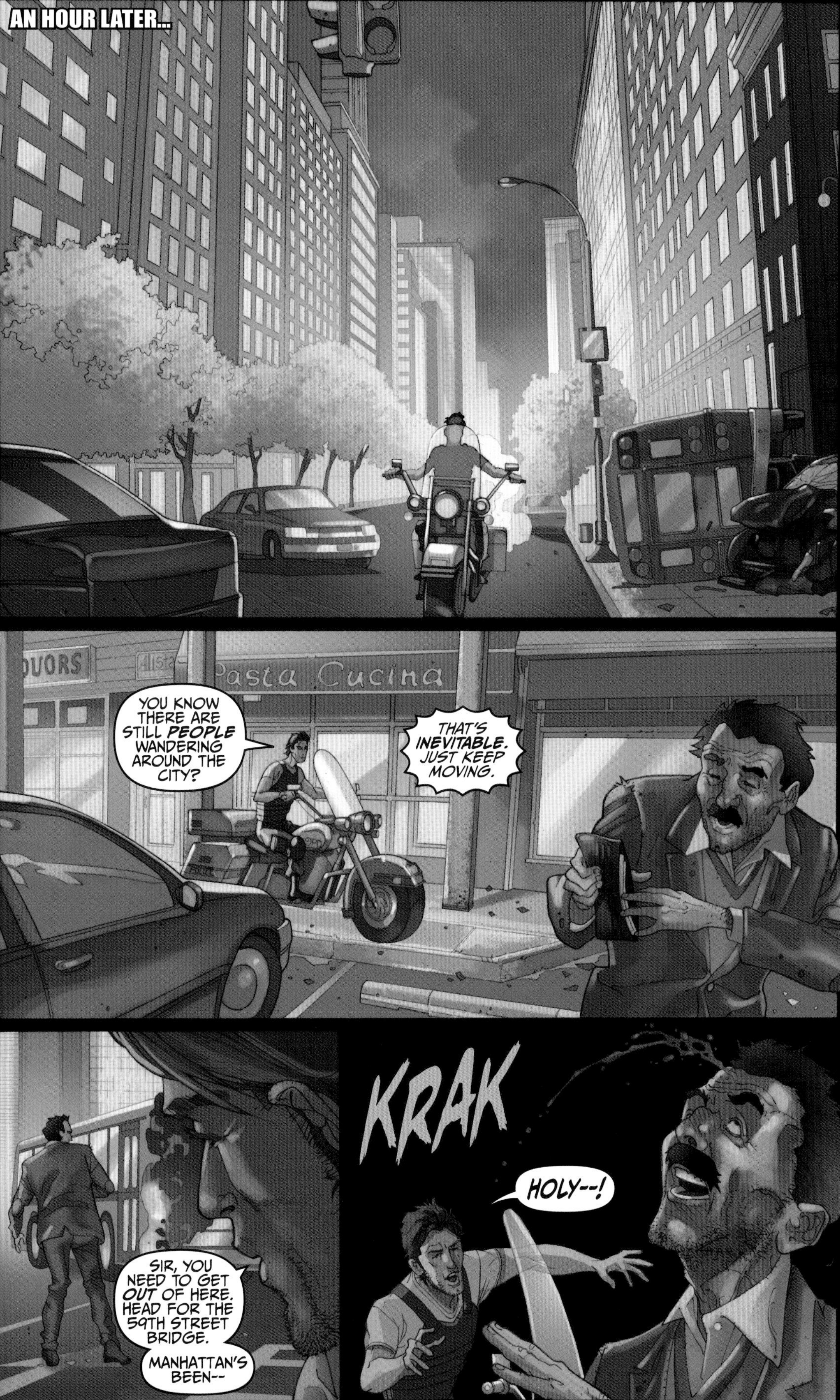
AN HOUR LATER...
OUORS
Pasta Cucina
YOU KNOW THERE ARE STILL *PEOPLE* WANDERING AROUND THE CITY?
THAT'S *INEVITABLE.* JUST KEEP MOVING.
SIR, YOU NEED TO GET *OUT* OF HERE. HEAD FOR THE 59TH STREET BRIDGE.
MANHATTAN'S BEEN--
KRAK
HOLY--!

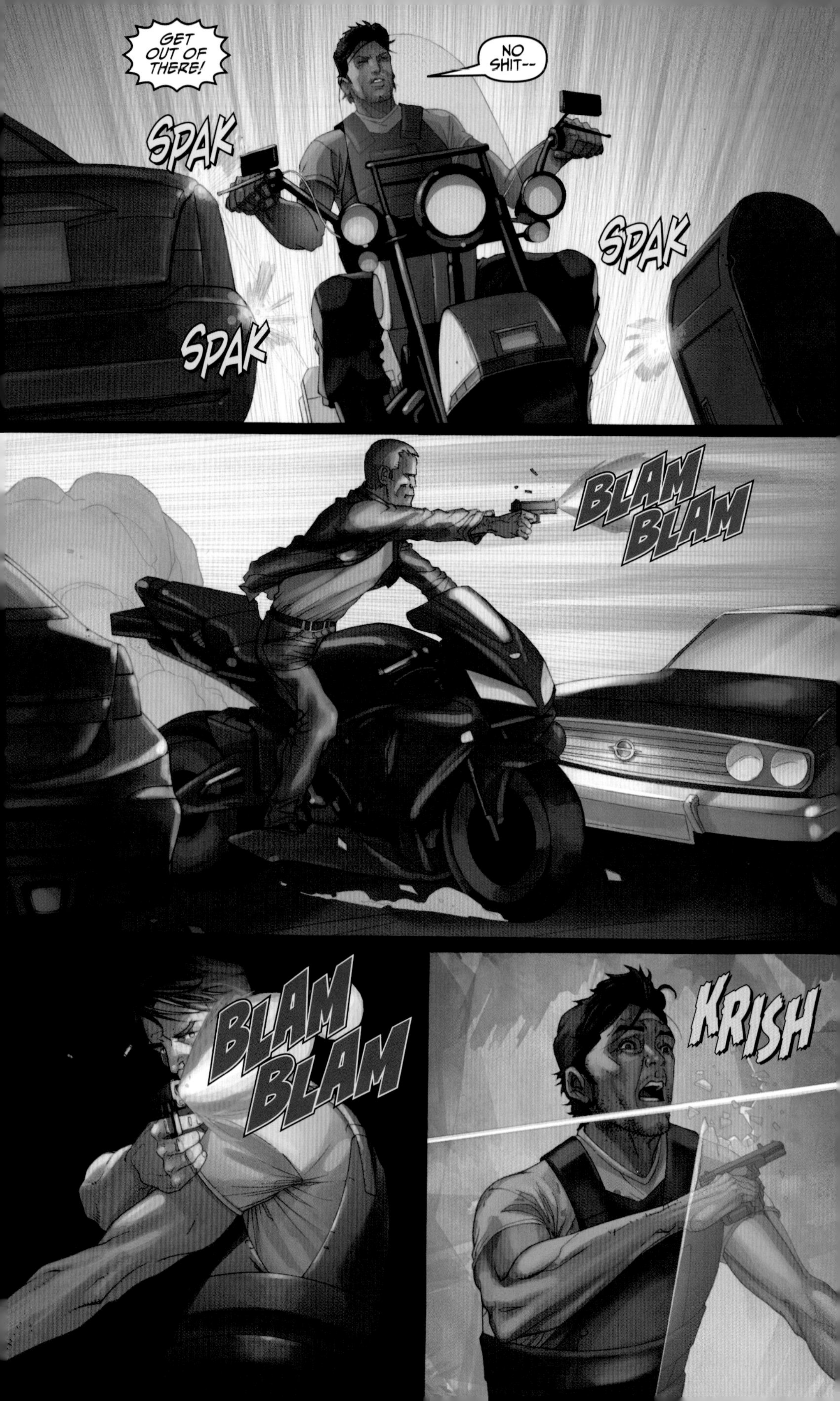
GET OUT OF THERE!
NO SHIT--
SPAK
SPAK
SPAK
BLAM BLAM
BLAM BLAM
KRISH

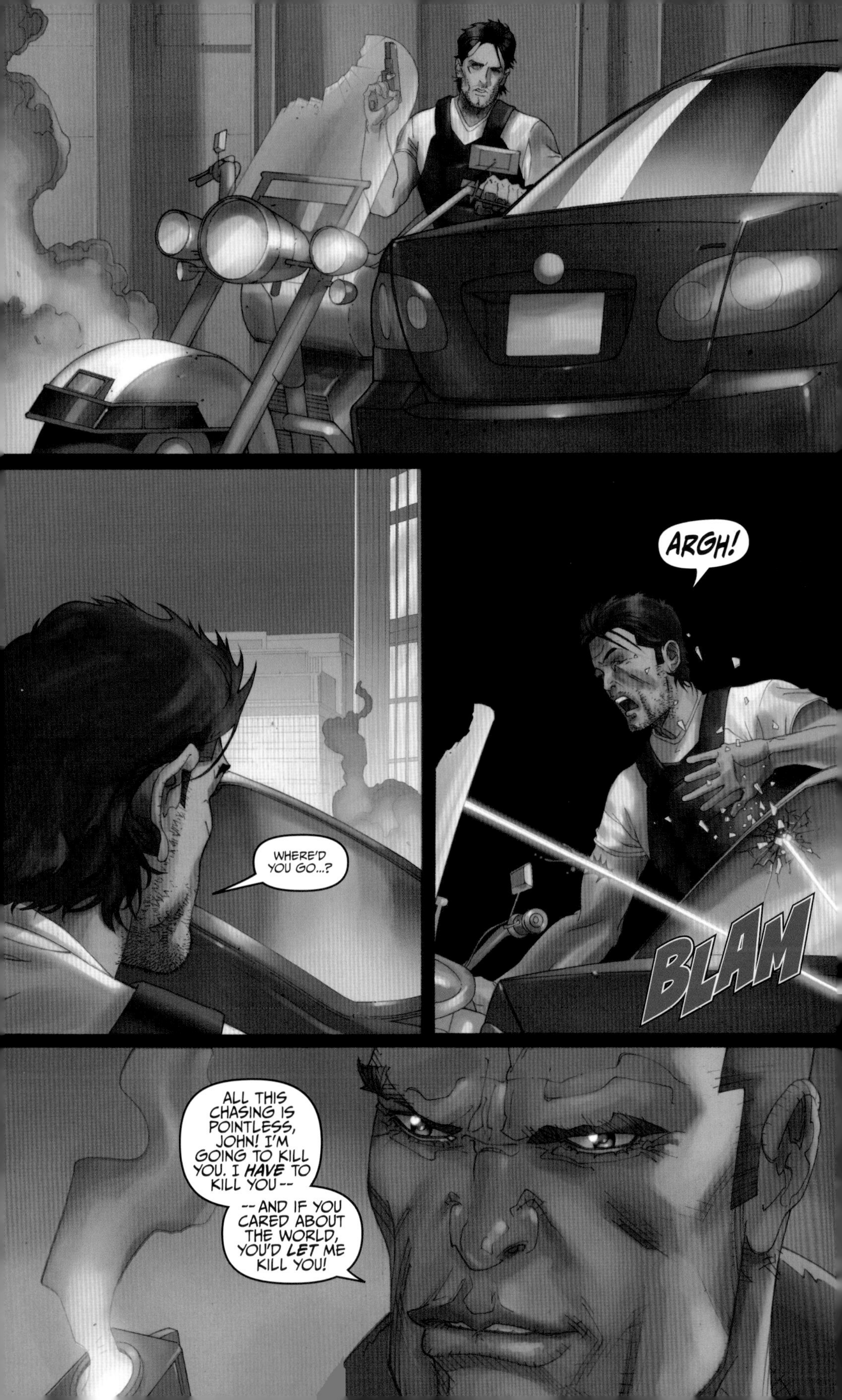
WHERE'D YOU GO...?
ARGH!
BLAM
ALL THIS CHASING IS POINTLESS, JOHN! I'M GOING TO KILL YOU. I HAVE TO KILL YOU--
--AND IF YOU CARED ABOUT THE WORLD, YOU'D LET ME KILL YOU!

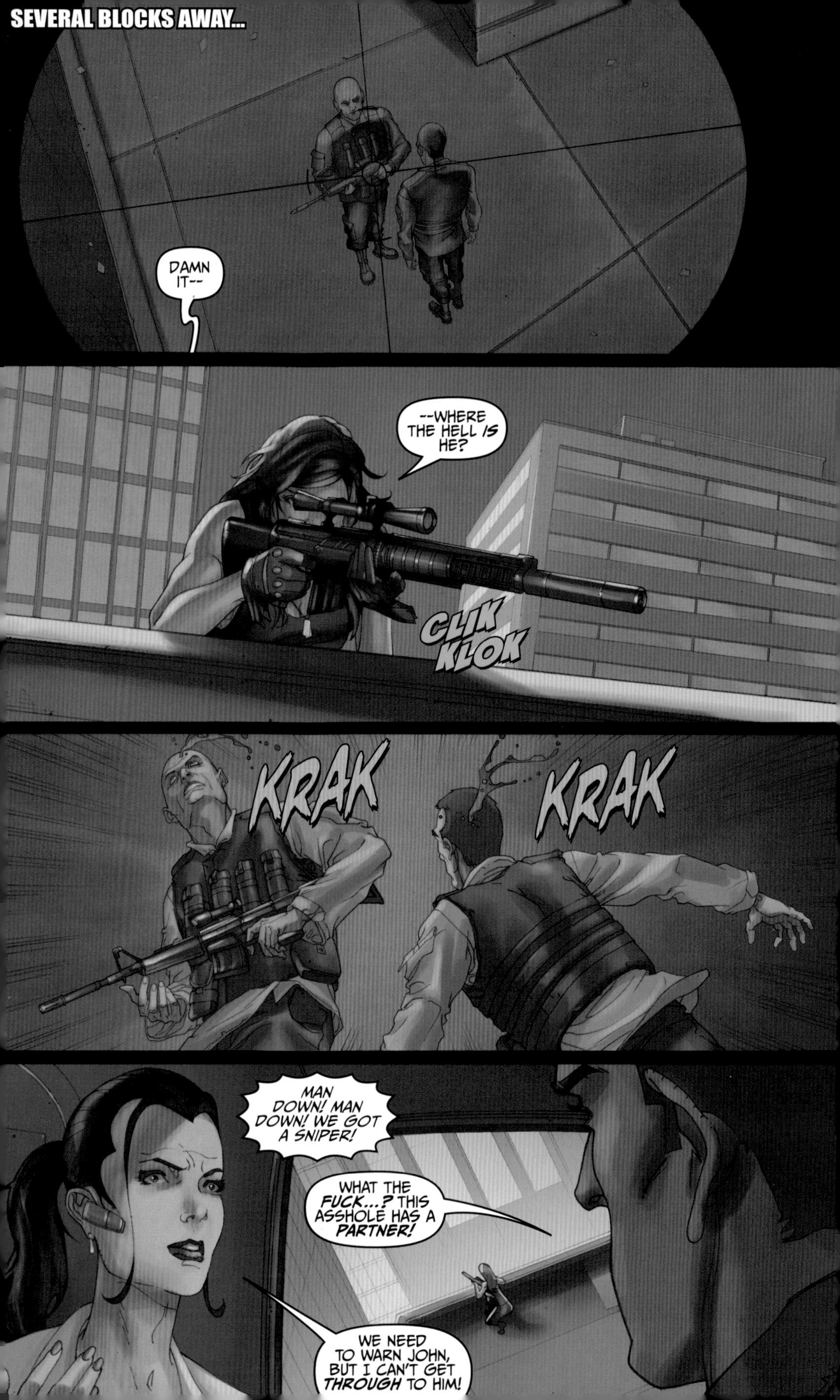
SEVERAL BLOCKS AWAY...
DAMN IT--
--WHERE THE HELL IS HE?
CLIK KLOK
KRAK
KRAK
MAN DOWN! MAN DOWN! WE GOT A SNIPER!
WHAT THE FUCK...? THIS ASSHOLE HAS A PARTNER!
WE NEED TO WARN JOHN, BUT I CAN'T GET THROUGH TO HIM!

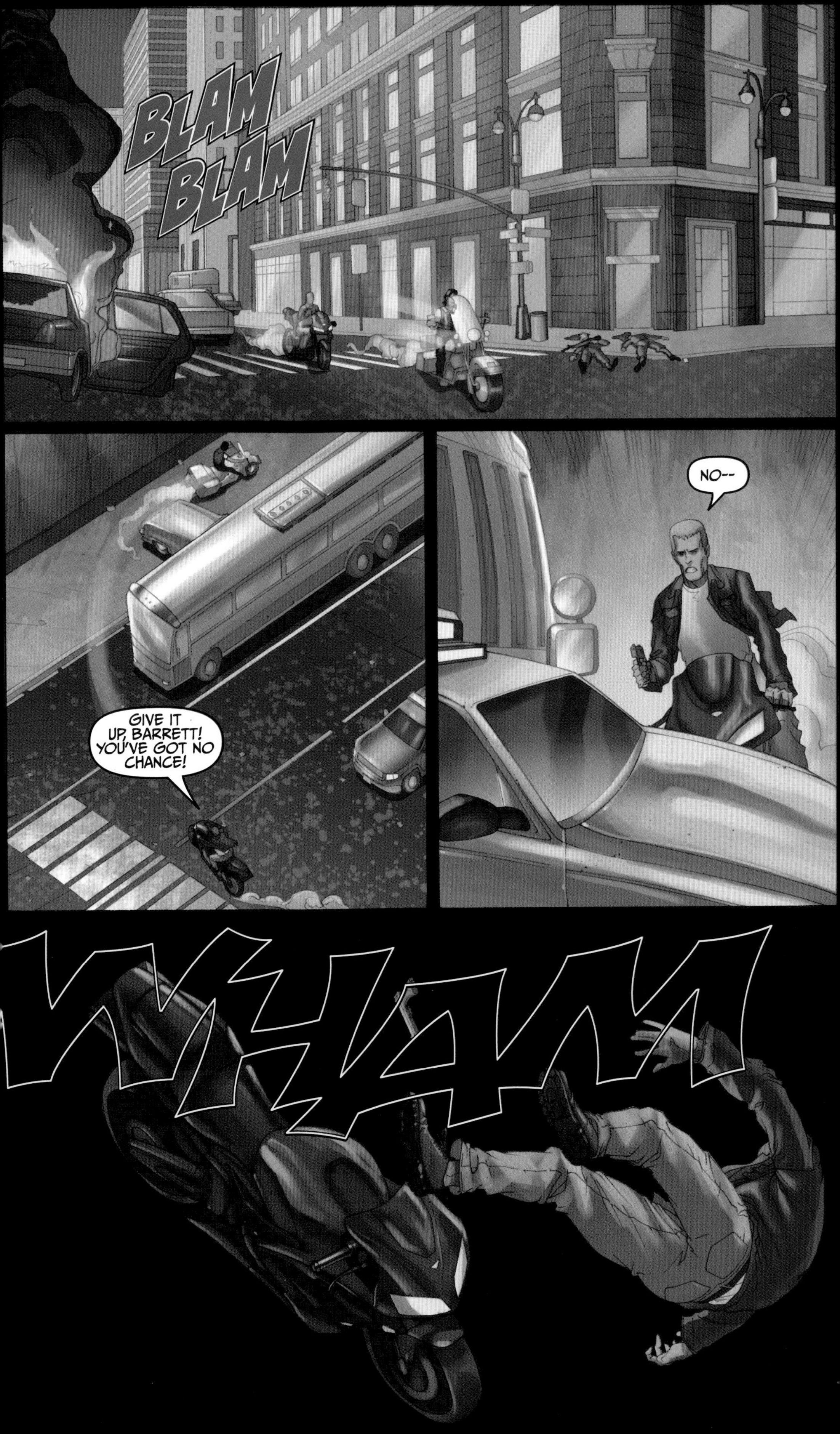
BLAM
BLAM
GIVE IT UP, BARRETT! YOU'VE GOT NO CHANCE!
NO--
WHAM

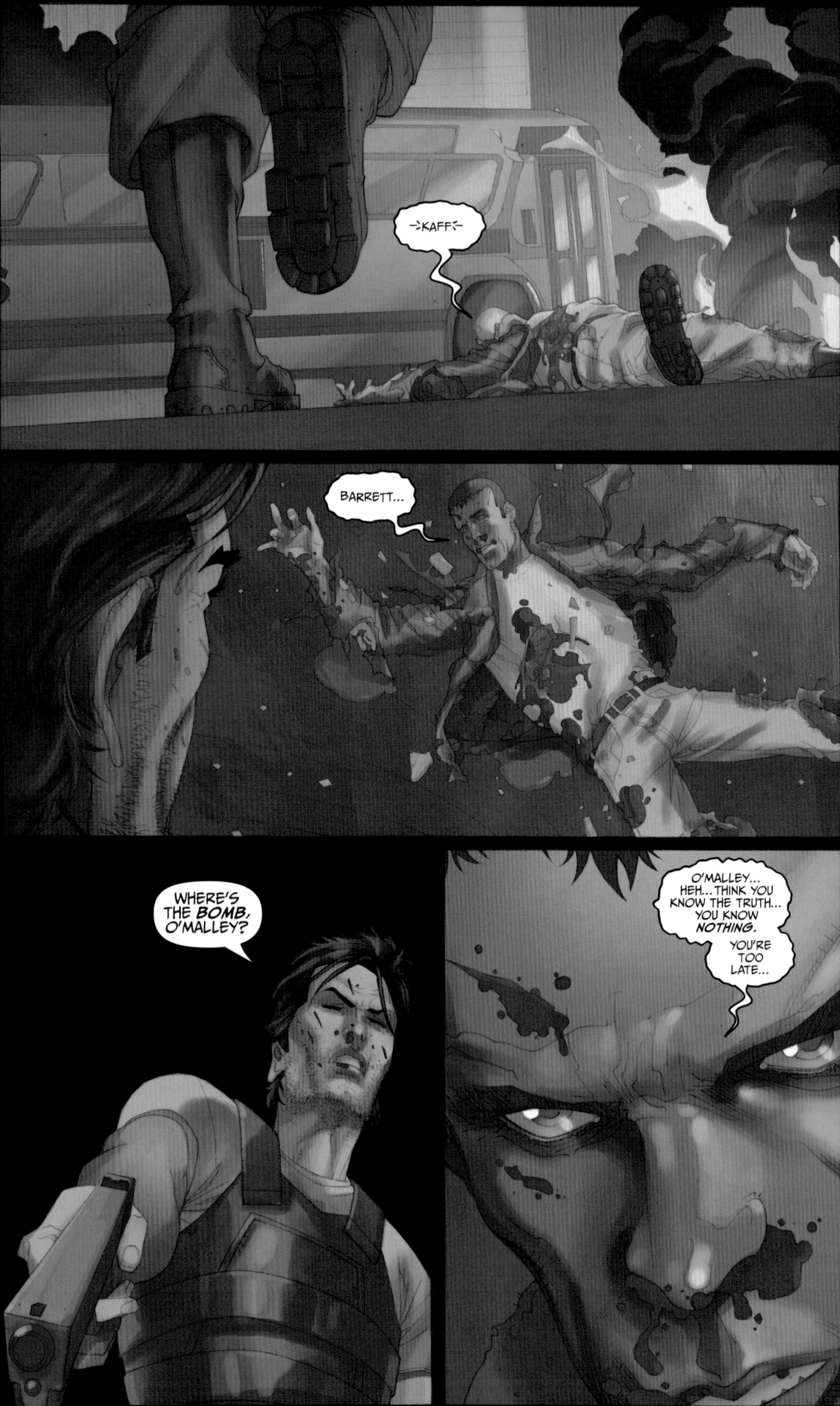
-KAFF-
BARRETT...
WHERE'S THE BOMB, O'MALLEY?
O'MALLEY... HEH...THINK YOU KNOW THE TRUTH... YOU KNOW NOTHING.
YOU'RE TOO LATE...

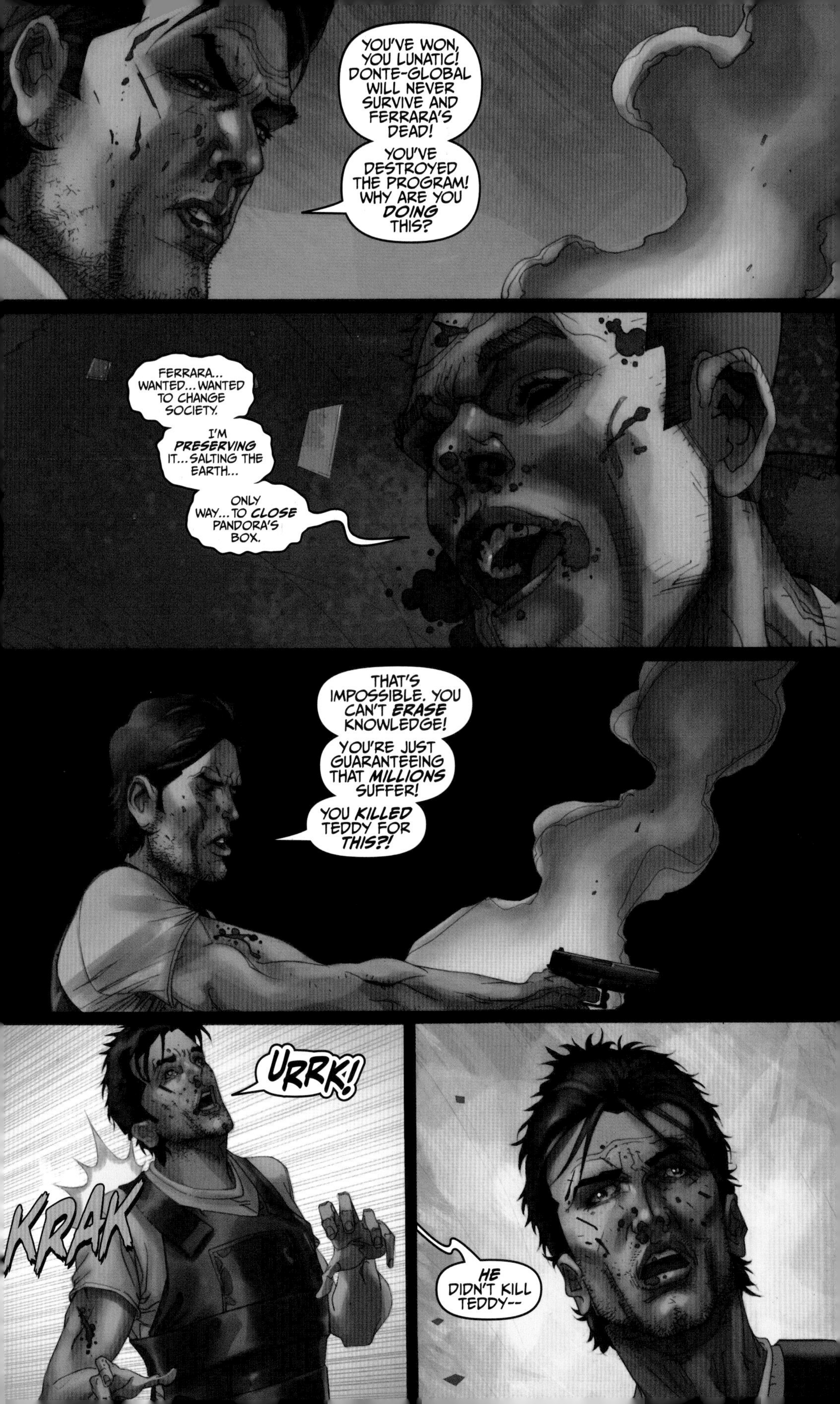
YOU'VE WON, YOU LUNATIC! DONTE-GLOBAL WILL NEVER SURVIVE AND FERRARA'S DEAD!
YOU'VE DESTROYED THE PROGRAM! WHY ARE YOU DOING THIS?
FERRARA... WANTED... WANTED TO CHANGE SOCIETY.
I'M PRESERVING IT... SALTING THE EARTH...
ONLY WAY... TO CLOSE PANDORA'S BOX.
THAT'S IMPOSSIBLE. YOU CAN'T ERASE KNOWLEDGE!
YOU'RE JUST GUARANTEEING THAT MILLIONS SUFFER!
YOU KILLED TEDDY FOR THIS?!
URRK!
KRAK
HE DIDN'T KILL TEDDY--

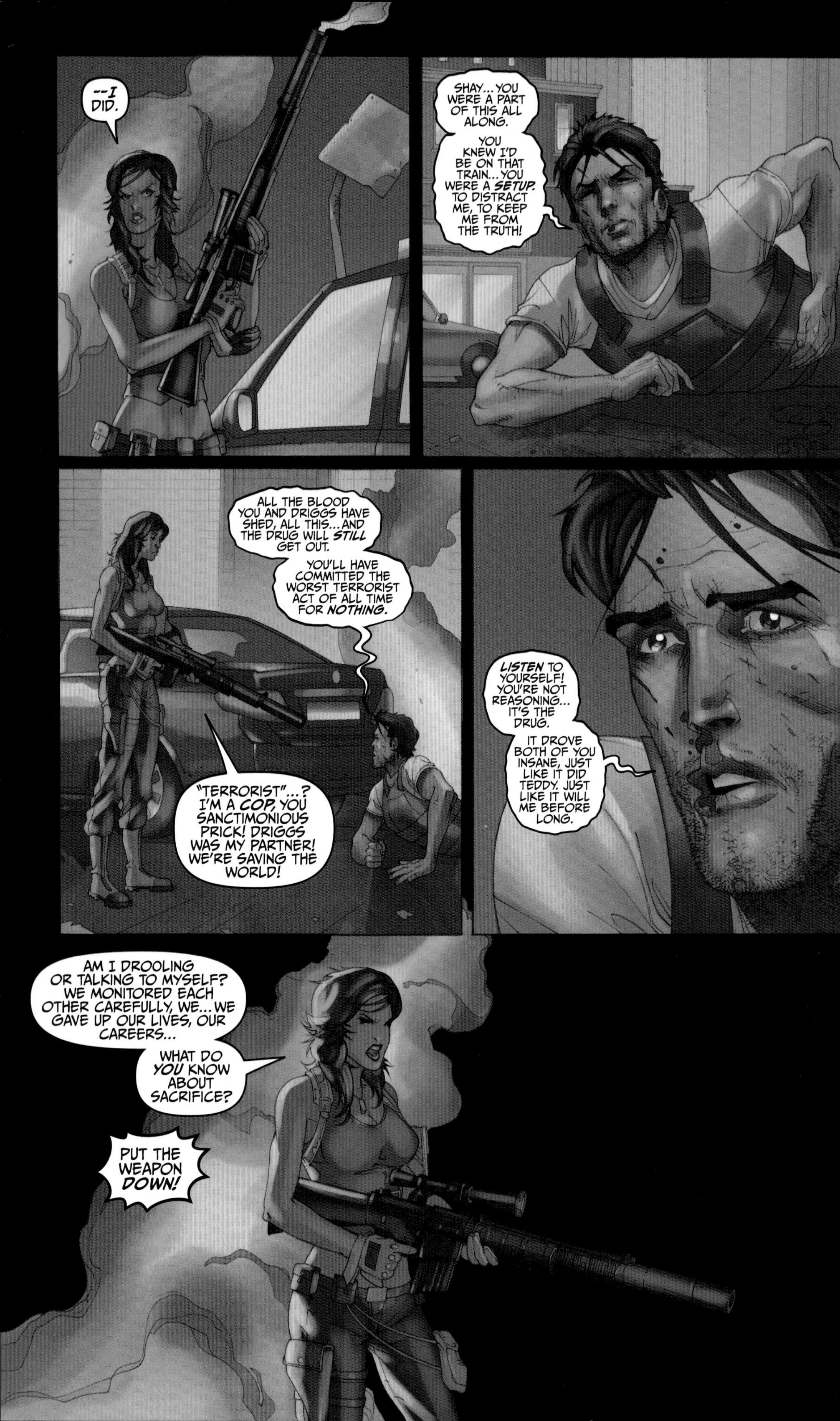
--I DID.
SHAY... YOU WERE A PART OF THIS ALL ALONG.
YOU KNEW I'D BE ON THAT TRAIN... YOU WERE A SETUP. TO DISTRACT ME, TO KEEP ME FROM THE TRUTH!
ALL THE BLOOD YOU AND DRIGGS HAVE SHED, ALL THIS... AND THE DRUG WILL STILL GET OUT.
YOU'LL HAVE COMMITTED THE WORST TERRORIST ACT OF ALL TIME FOR NOTHING.
"TERRORIST"...? I'M A COP, YOU SANCTIMONIOUS PRICK! DRIGGS WAS MY PARTNER! WE'RE SAVING THE WORLD!
LISTEN TO YOURSELF! YOU'RE NOT REASONING... IT'S THE DRUG.
IT DROVE BOTH OF YOU INSANE, JUST LIKE IT DID TEDDY. JUST LIKE IT WILL ME BEFORE LONG.
AM I DROOLING OR TALKING TO MYSELF? WE MONITORED EACH OTHER CAREFULLY, WE... WE GAVE UP OUR LIVES, OUR CAREERS...
WHAT DO YOU KNOW ABOUT SACRIFICE?
PUT THE WEAPON DOWN!

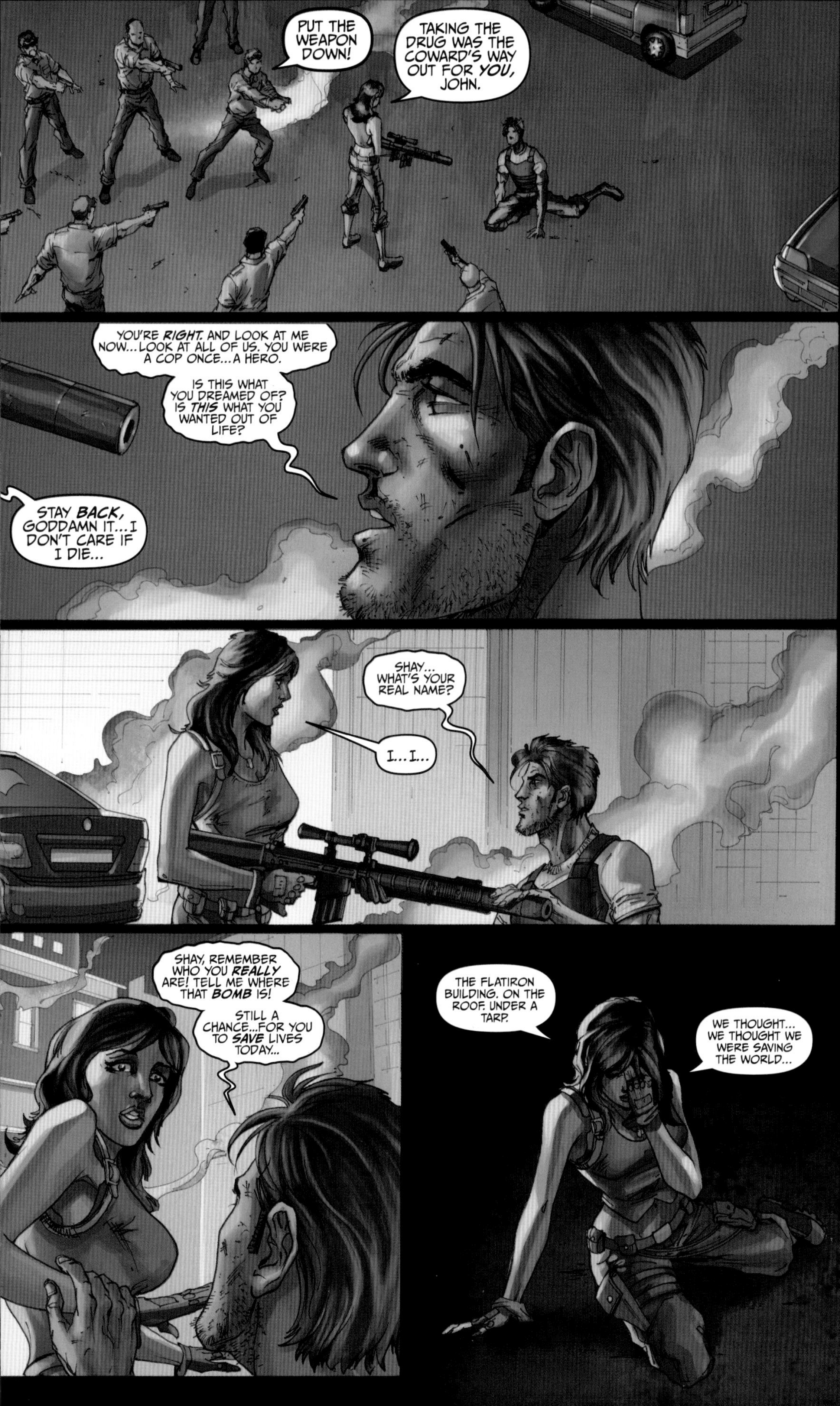
PUT THE WEAPON DOWN!
TAKING THE DRUG WAS THE COWARD'S WAY OUT FOR YOU, JOHN.
YOU'RE RIGHT. AND LOOK AT ME NOW... LOOK AT ALL OF US. YOU WERE A COP ONCE... A HERO.
IS THIS WHAT YOU DREAMED OF? IS THIS WHAT YOU WANTED OUT OF LIFE?
STAY BACK, GODDAMN IT... I DON'T CARE IF I DIE...
SHAY... WHAT'S YOUR REAL NAME?
I... I...
SHAY, REMEMBER WHO YOU REALLY ARE! TELL ME WHERE THAT BOMB IS!
STILL A CHANCE... FOR YOU TO SAVE LIVES TODAY...
THE FLATIRON BUILDING. ON THE ROOF. UNDER A TARP.
WE THOUGHT... WE THOUGHT WE WERE SAVING THE WORLD...

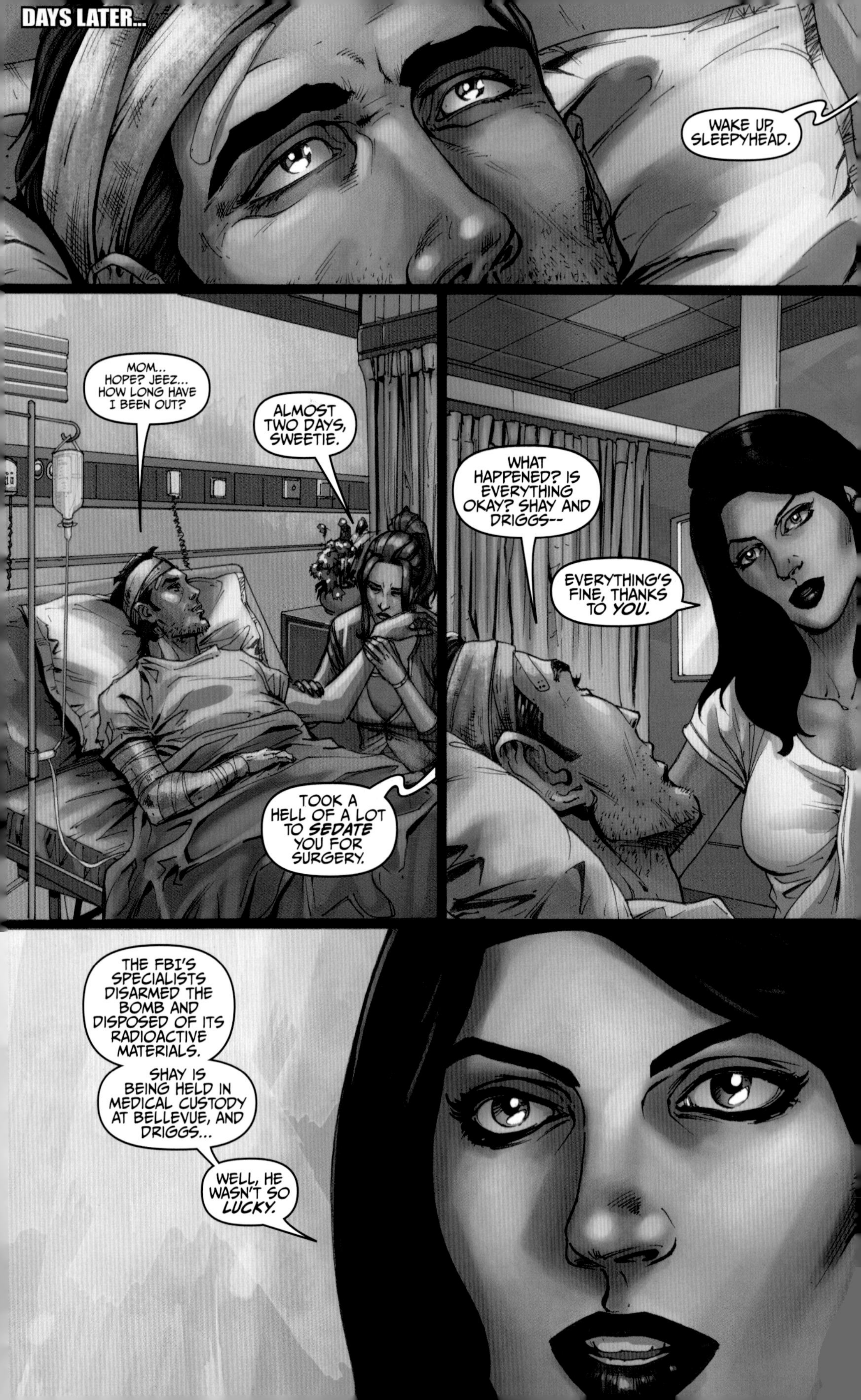
DAYS LATER...
WAKE UP, SLEEPYHEAD.
MOM... HOPE? JEEZ... HOW LONG HAVE I BEEN OUT?
ALMOST TWO DAYS, SWEETIE.
TOOK A HELL OF A LOT TO SEDATE YOU FOR SURGERY.
WHAT HAPPENED? IS EVERYTHING OKAY? SHAY AND DRIGGS--
EVERYTHING'S FINE, THANKS TO YOU.
THE FBI'S SPECIALISTS DISARMED THE BOMB AND DISPOSED OF ITS RADIOACTIVE MATERIALS.
SHAY IS BEING HELD IN MEDICAL CUSTODY AT BELLEVUE, AND DRIGGS...
WELL, HE WASN'T SO LUCKY.

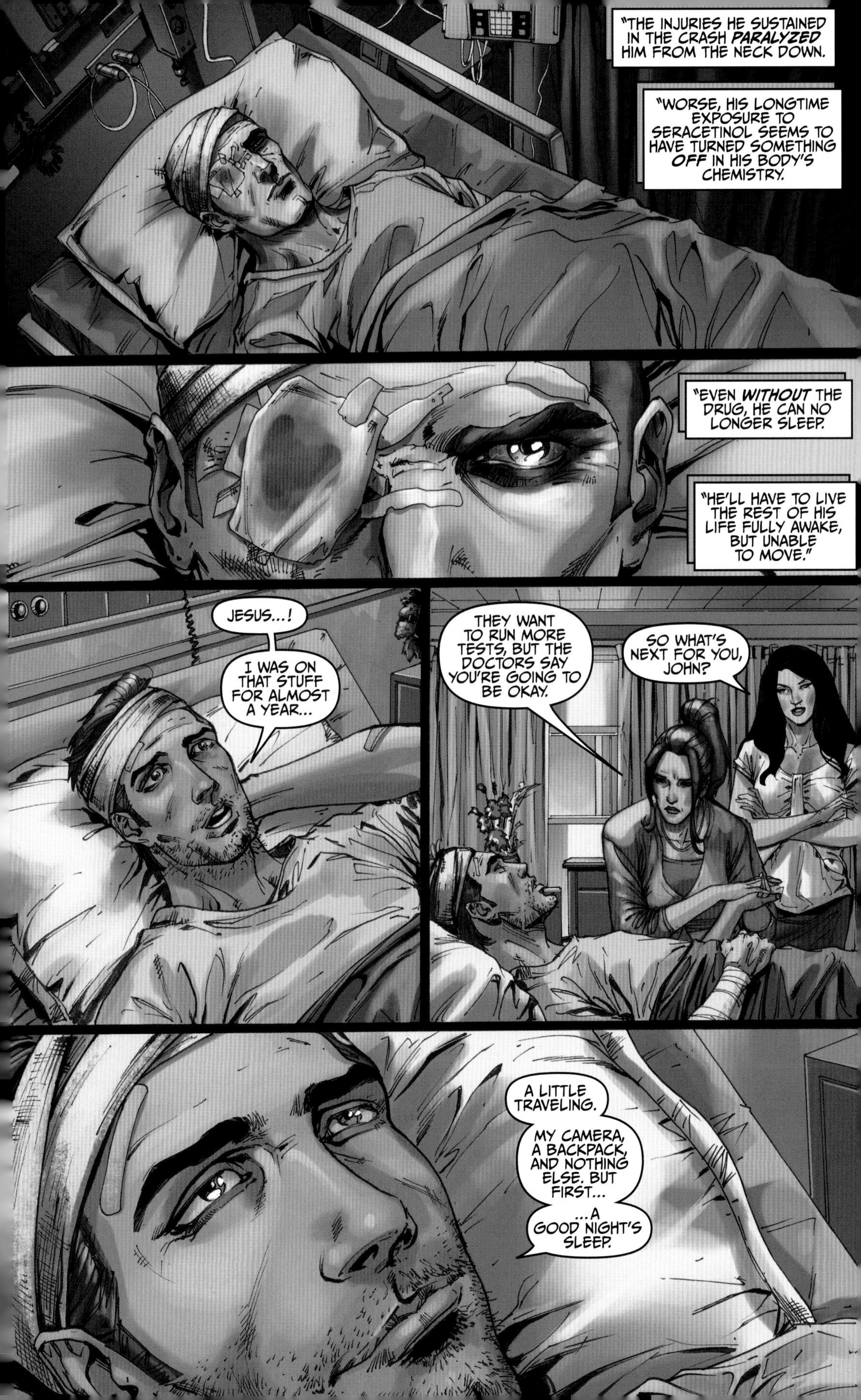
"THE INJURIES HE SUSTAINED IN THE CRASH PARALYZED HIM FROM THE NECK DOWN.
"WORSE, HIS LONGTIME EXPOSURE TO SERACETINOL SEEMS TO HAVE TURNED SOMETHING OFF IN HIS BODY'S CHEMISTRY.
"EVEN WITHOUT THE DRUG, HE CAN NO LONGER SLEEP.
"HE'LL HAVE TO LIVE THE REST OF HIS LIFE FULLY AWAKE, BUT UNABLE TO MOVE."
JESUS...!
I WAS ON THAT STUFF FOR ALMOST A YEAR...
THEY WANT TO RUN MORE TESTS, BUT THE DOCTORS SAY YOU'RE GOING TO BE OKAY.
SO WHAT'S NEXT FOR YOU, JOHN?
A LITTLE TRAVELING.
MY CAMERA, A BACKPACK, AND NOTHING ELSE. BUT FIRST...
...A GOOD NIGHT'S SLEEP.

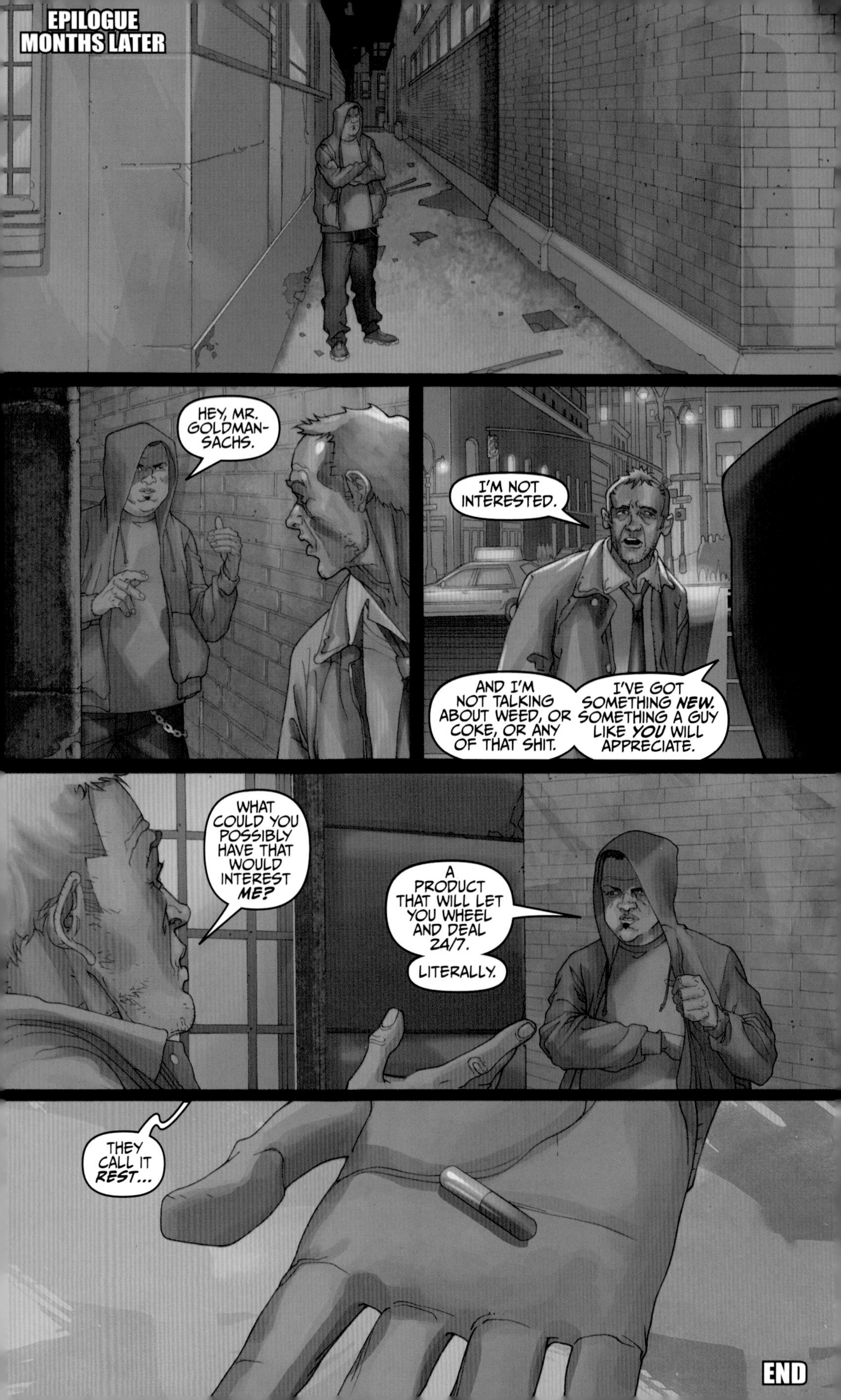
EPILOGUE
MONTHS LATER
HEY, MR. GOLDMAN-SACHS.
I'M NOT INTERESTED.
I'VE GOT SOMETHING NEW. SOMETHING A GUY LIKE YOU WILL APPRECIATE.
AND I'M NOT TALKING ABOUT WEED, OR COKE, OR ANY OF THAT SHIT.
WHAT COULD YOU POSSIBLY HAVE THAT WOULD INTEREST ME?
A PRODUCT THAT WILL LET YOU WHEEL AND DEAL 24/7.
LITERALLY.
THEY CALL IT REST...
END

Rest [RX] (SERACETINOL) BONUS MATERIALS

On the following pages:
-Original Edition covers
-Character Designs by **Marco Castiello**

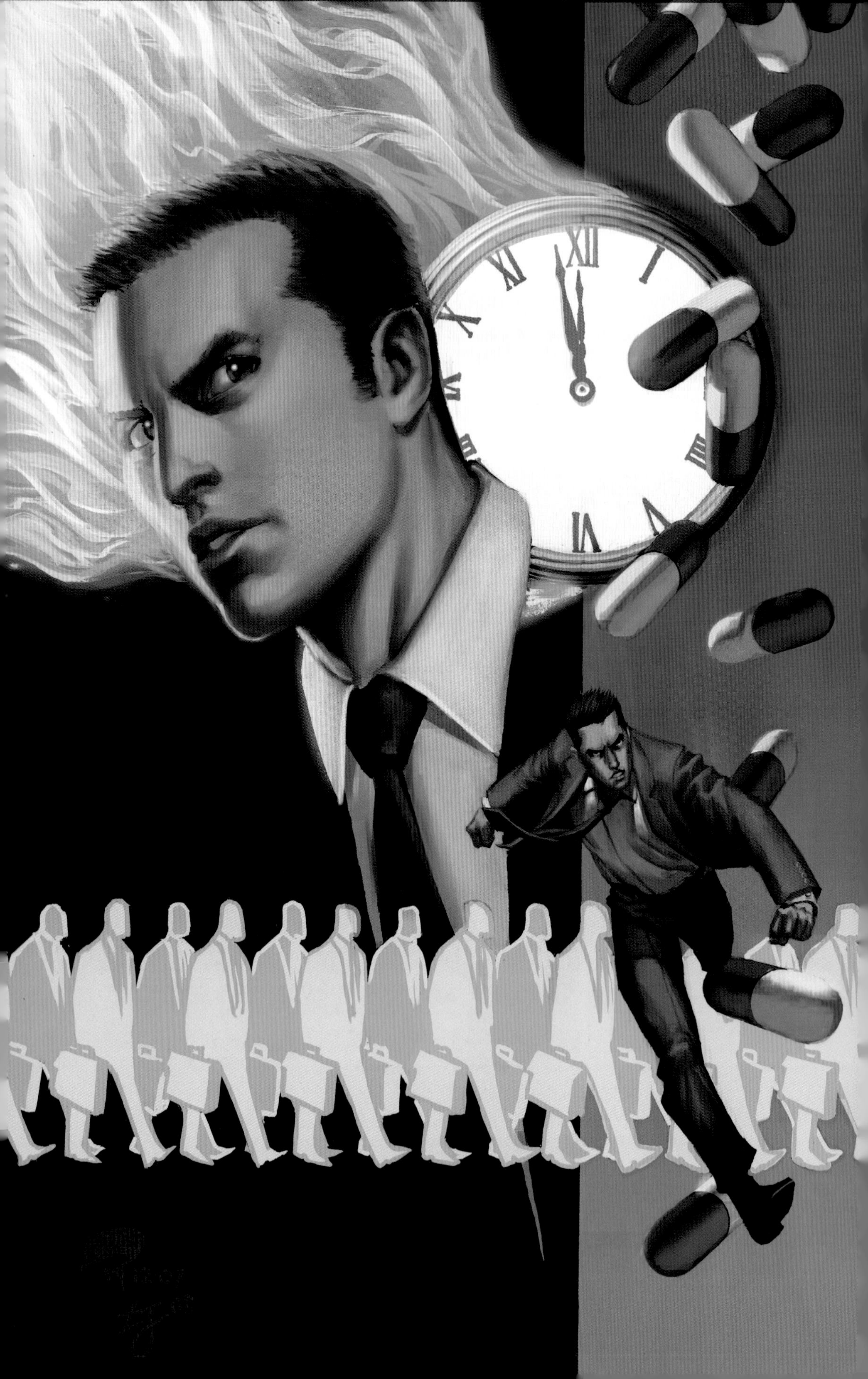

REST issue #0 cover
art by: **Roger Robinson** and **Lizzy John**

REST issue #1 cover A
art by: **Tim Sale** and **Dave Stewart**

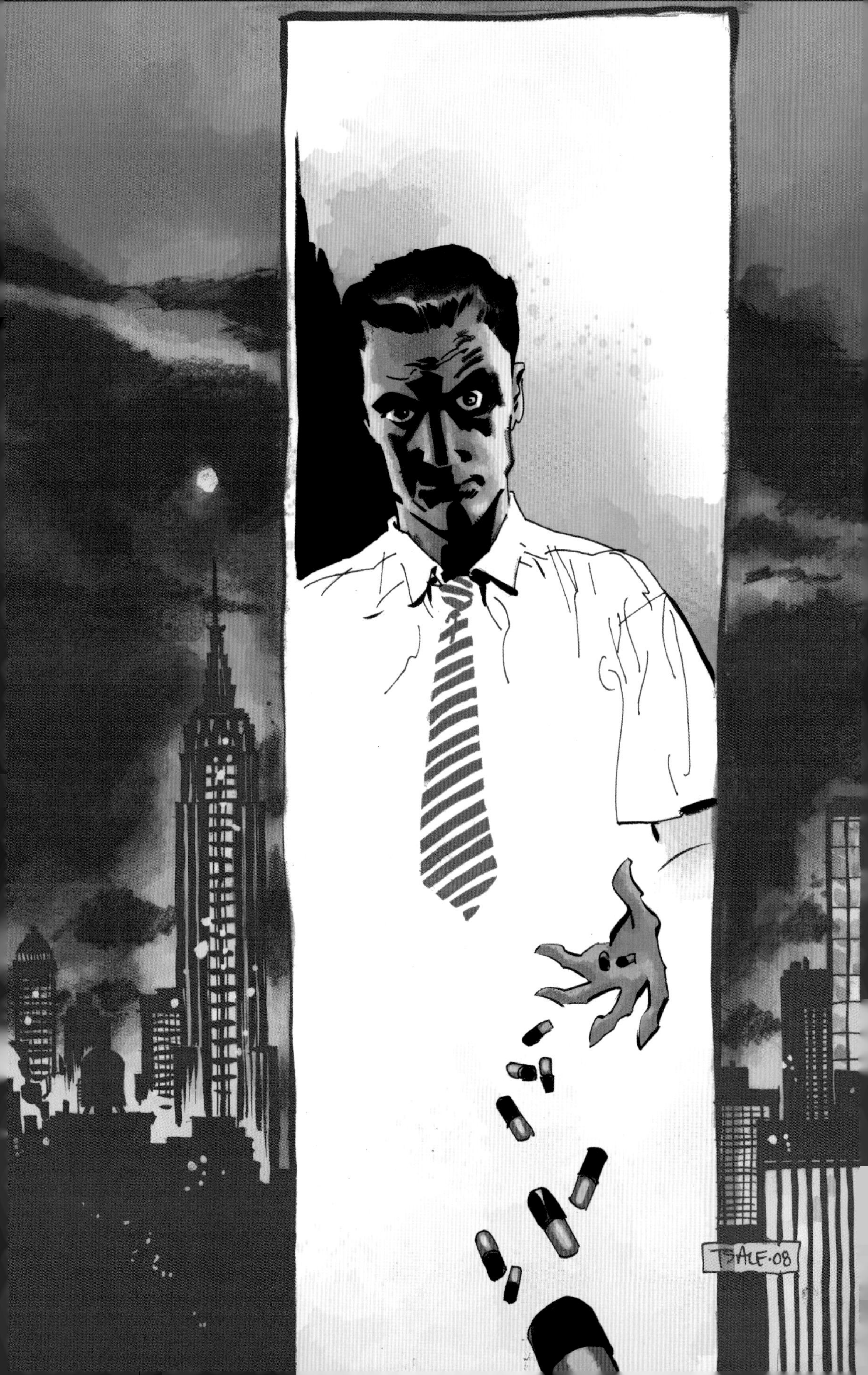

REST issue #1 cover B
art by: **Zac Fisher** and **Charles Bush** with thanks to **Geek Magazine**

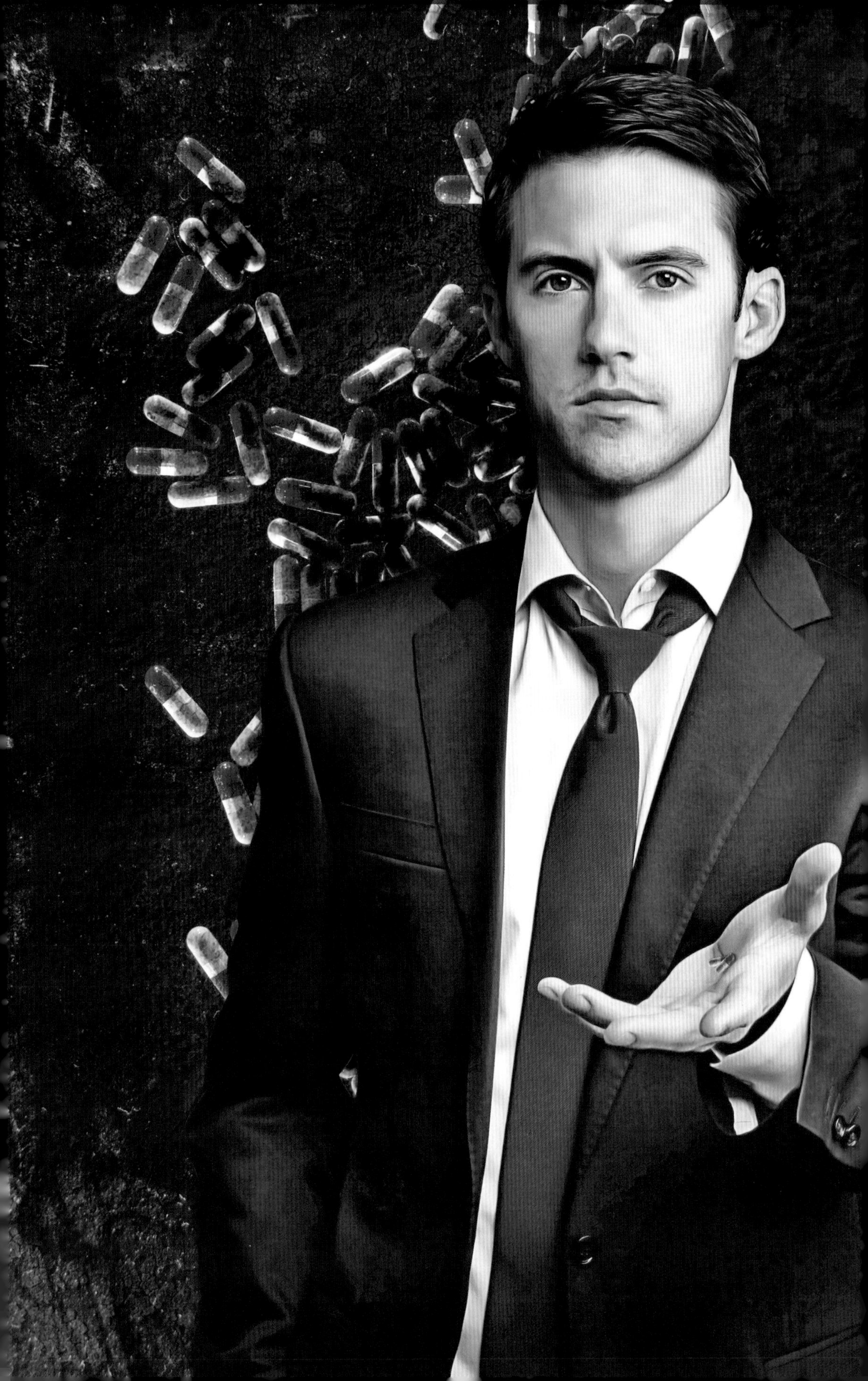

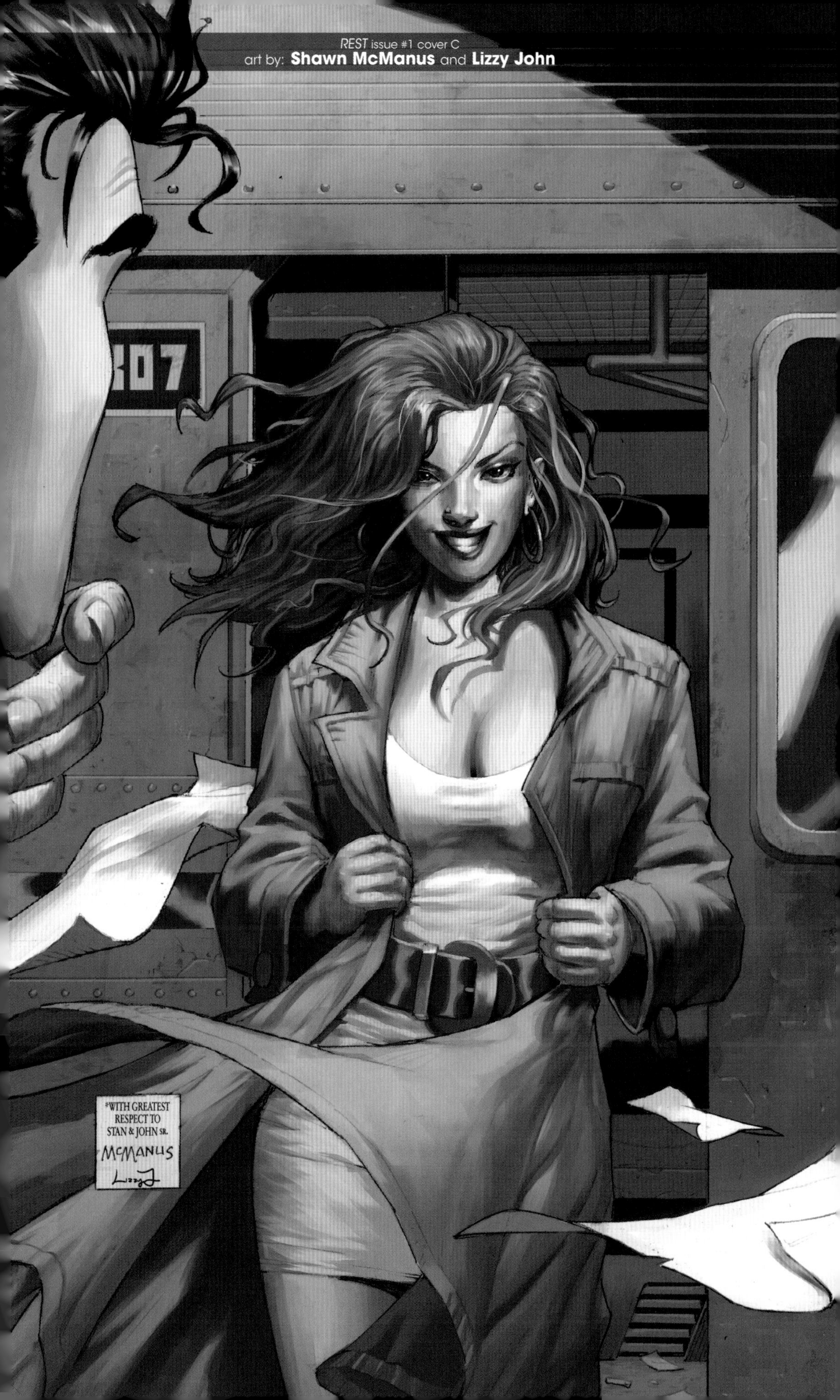
*WITH GREATEST
RESPECT TO
STAN & JOHN SR.
McMANUS

REST issue #1 cover C
art by: **Shawn McManus** and **Lizzy John**

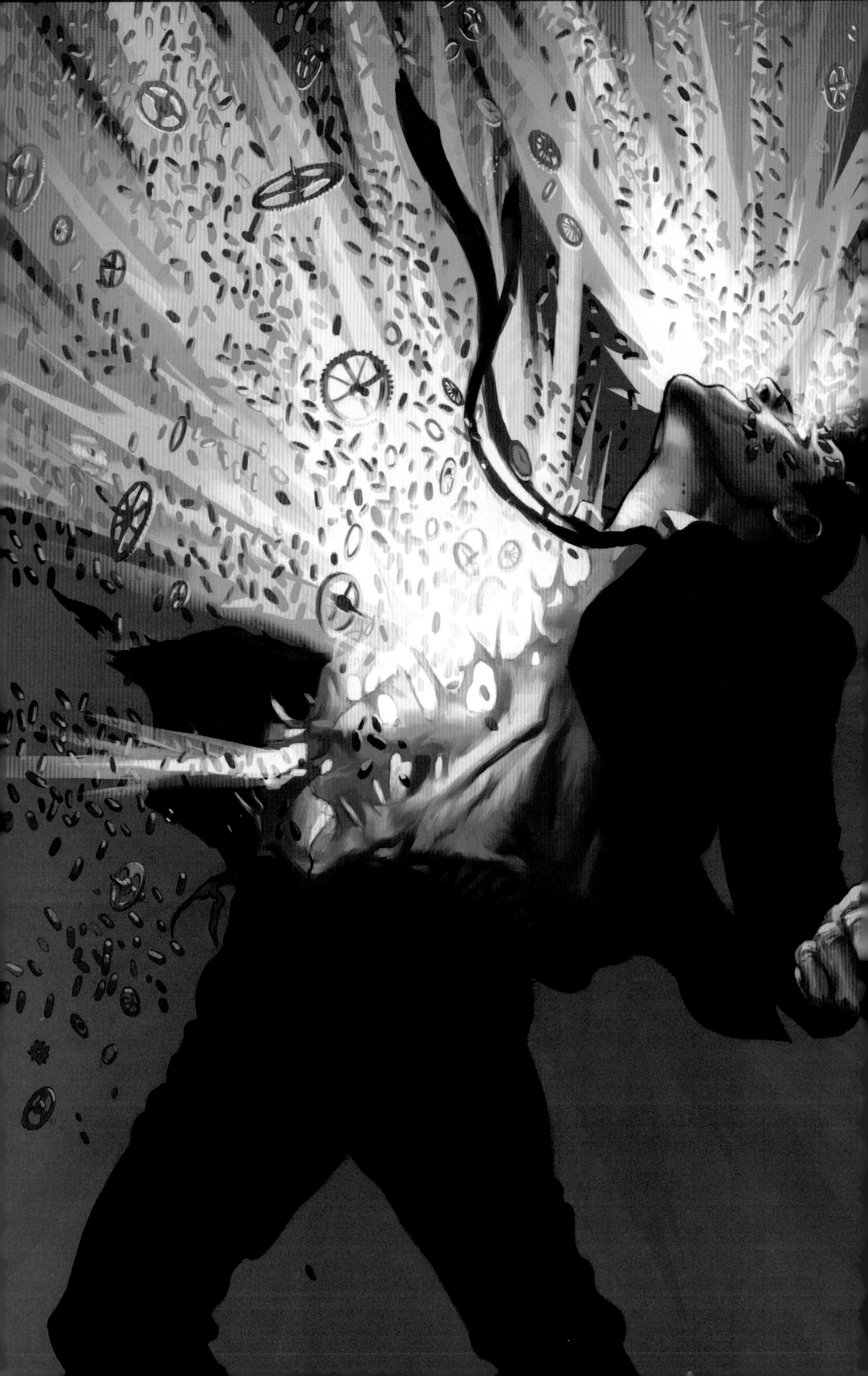

REST issue #2 cover A
art by: **Phil Jimenez** and **Lizzy John**

REST issue #2 cover B
art by: **Zac Fisher** and **Charles Bush** with thanks to **Geek Magazine**

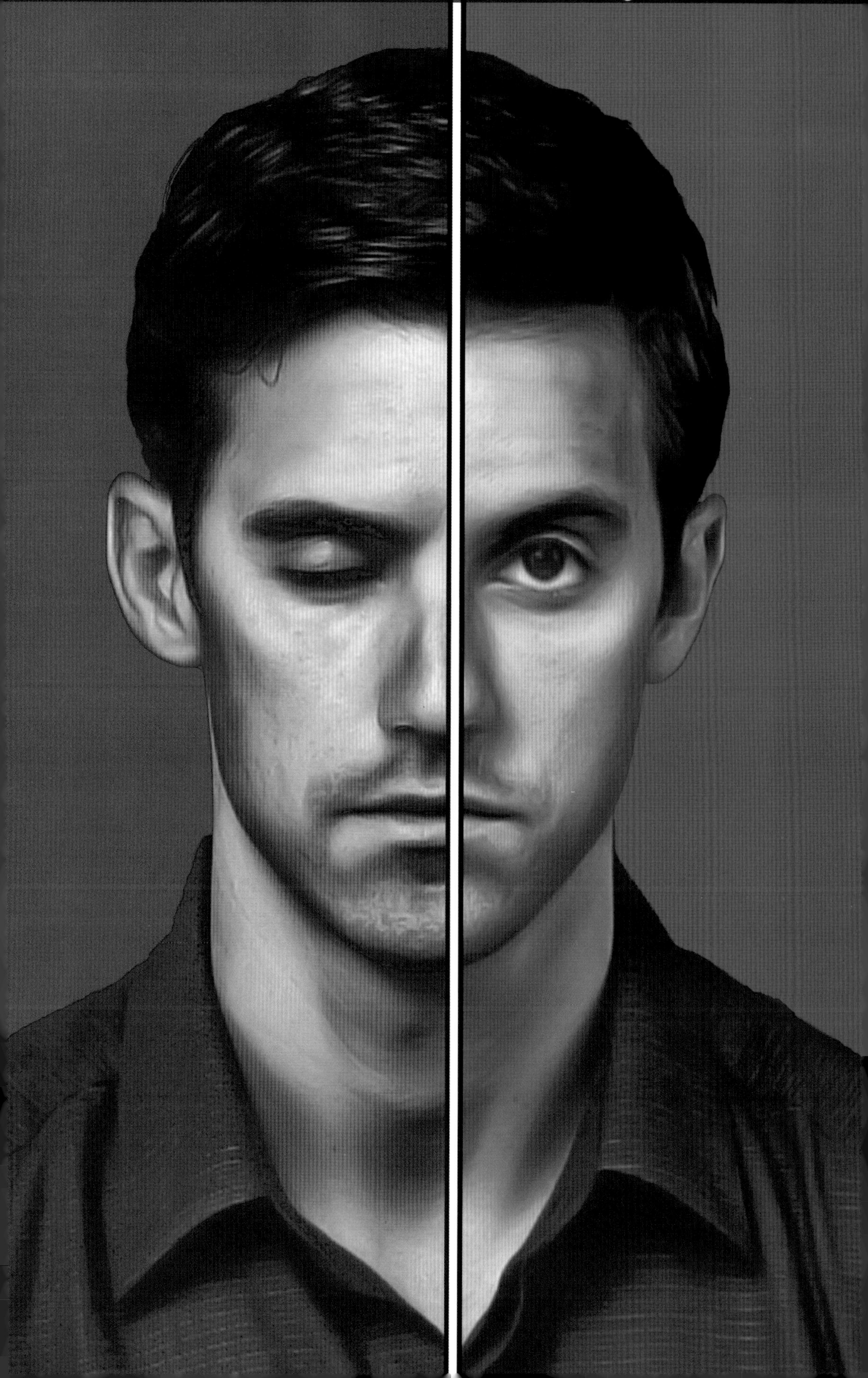

Character Designs by **Marco Castiello**

Check out more from DiVide and Top Cow Productions, Inc.!

RICK LOVERD • JEREMY HAUN
BERSERKER
DIVIDE
FEATURING AN INTRODUCTION BY:
MILO VENTIMIGLIA AND RUSS CUNDIFF
TOP COW

Berserker

vol.1

written by:
Rick Loverd
art by:
Jeremy Haun

The lives of Aaron and Farris, two young and completely different men, are turned upside down when they discover an animalistic and uncontrollable rage living inside them. Meanwhile, two mysterious organizations seek them out for their newfound strength and power for their own purposes. But what good is strength and power when you can't tell friend from foe?

From screenwriter **Rick Loverd** and artist **Jeremy Haun** (*Detective Comics*, *Leading Man*) featuring cover gallery with works by Haun and **Dale Keown**.

(ISBN: 978-1-60706-109-0) $14.99

RON MARZ • STJEPAN SEJIC
WITCHBLADE
REDEMPTION
VOLUME 1
FEATURING AN INTRODUCTION BY: TODD MCFARLANE
TOP COW

Witchblade

Redemption vol.1

written by:
Ron Marz
art by:
Stjepan Sejic

After the tumultuous events of 'War of the Witchblades,' New York City Police Detective Sara Pezzini is once more the sole bearer of the Witchblade, a mysterious artifact that takes the form of a deadly and powerful gauntlet. Now Sara must try reconcile her darker side while controlling the Witchblade, even as she investigates the city's strangest, most supernatural crimes.

In this first volume of the "Redemption" book series, readers are reintroduced to Sara, her boyfriend and partner, Patrick Gleason, and the strange, supernatural world of the Witchblade. Fans are also reintroduced to Aphrodite IV, the fan-favorite emerald-haired cyborg assassin.

This volume collects issues #131-136 by long time writer **Ron Marz** (*Artifacts*) and artistic partner **Stjepan Sejic** (*Angelus*) and is a perfect introductory volume for new readers.

Book Market Edtion
(ISBN: 978-1-60706-193-9) $9.99

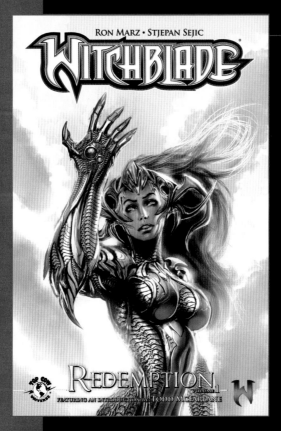

Jump into the Top Cow Universe with The Darkness!

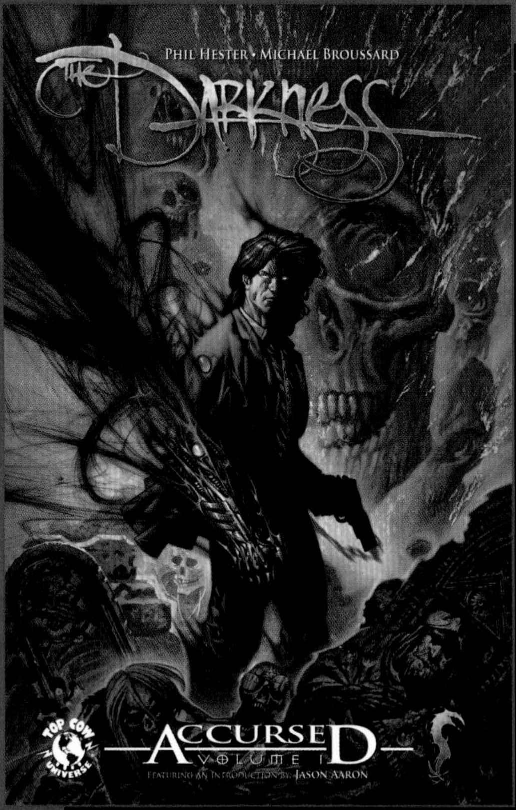
PHIL HESTER • MICHAEL BROUSSARD
The Darkness
ACCURSED
VOLUME I
FEATURING AN INTRODUCTION BY JASON AARON

The Darkness
Accursed vol.1

written by:
Phil Hester

pencils by:
Michael Broussard

Mafia hitman Jackie Estacado was both blessed and cursed on his 21st birthday when he became the bearer of The Darkness, an elemental force that allows those who wield it access to an otherwordly dimension and control over the demons who dwell there. Forces for good in the world rise up to face Jackie and the evil his gift represents, but there is one small problem. In this story...they are the bad guys.

Now's your chance to read "Empire," the first storyline by the new creative team of **Phil Hester** (*Firebreather, Green Arrow*) and **Michael Broussard** (*Unholy Union*) that marked the shocking return of *The Darkness* to the Top Cow Universe!

Book Market Edition
(ISBN: 978-1-58240-958-0) $9.99

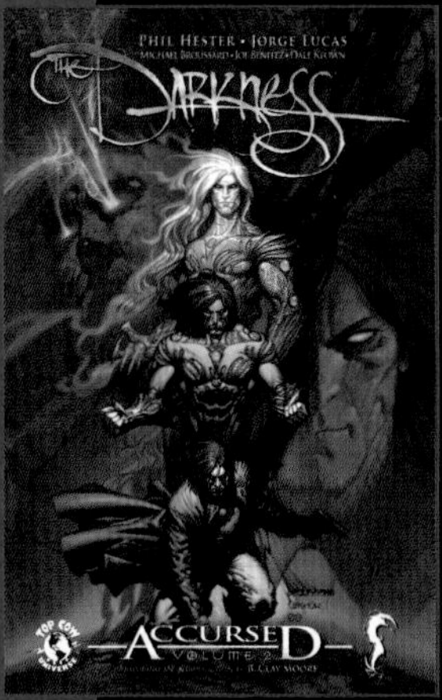
PHIL HESTER • JORGE LUCAS
The Darkness
ACCURSED
VOLUME 2

The Darkness
Accursed vol.2

written by: Phil Hester

pencils by: Jorge Lucas, Michael Broussard, Joe Benitez, Dale Keown and more!

Collects *The Darkness* volume 3 #7-10 and the double-sized *The Darkness* #75 (issue #11 before the Legacy Numbering took effect), plus a cover gallery and behind-the-scenes extras!

(ISBN: 978-1-58240-044-4) $9.99

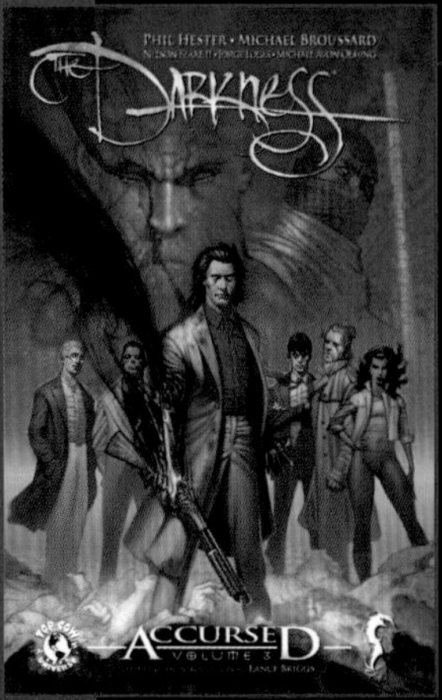
PHIL HESTER • MICHAEL BROUSSARD
The Darkness
ACCURSED
VOLUME 3

The Darkness
Accursed vol.3

written by: Phil Hester

pencils by: Michael Broussard, Jorge Lucas, Nelson Blake II and Michael Avon Oeming.

Collects issues #76-79 plus the stand alone Tales of The Darkness story entitled "Lodbrok's Hand." Features art by regular series artist Michael Broussard (*Unholy Union, Artifacts*), Nelson Blake II (*Magdalena, Broken Trinity: Witchblade*), Jorge Lucas (*Broken Trinity: Aftermath, Wolverine*), and Michael Avon Oeming (*Mice Templar, Powers*).

(ISBN: 978-1-58240-100-7) $12.99

Ready for more? Jump into the Top Cow Universe with *Witchblade*!

RON MARZ • MIKE CHOI
WITCHBLADE
VOLUME 1
FEATURING AN INTRODUCTION BY
RON MARZ

Witchblade

volume 1 - volume 7

written by:
Ron Marz
art by:
Mike Choi, Stephen Sadowski, Keu Cha, Chris Bachalo, Stjepan Sejic and more!

Get in on the ground floor of Top Cow's flagship title with these affordable trade paperback collections from Ron Marz's series-redefining run on Witchblade! Each volume collects a key story arc in the continuing adventures of Sara Pezzini and the Witchblade, culminating in the epic 'War of the Witchblades' storyline!

Book Market Edition, **volume 1**
collects issues #80-#85
(ISBN: 978-1-58240-906-1) $9.99

RON MARZ • MIKE CHOI • CHRIS BACHALO • KEU CHA
WITCHBLADE
VOLUME 2
FEATURING AN INTRODUCTION BY
PHIL HESTER

volume 2
collects issues #86-#92
(ISBN: 978-1-58240-886-6)
U.S.D. $14.99

WITCHBLADE
VOLUME 3

volume 3
collects issues #93-#100
(ISBN: 978-1-58240-887-3)
U.S.D. $14.99

RON MARZ • ADRIANA MELO • STJEPAN SEJIC • SAMI BASRI
WITCHBLADE
VOLUME 4

volume 4
collects issues #101-109
(ISBN: 978-1-58240-898-9)
U.S.D. $17.99

WITCHBLADE
VOLUME 5
FEATURING AN INTRODUCTION BY
ROBERT KIRKMAN

volume 5
collects issues #110-115,
First Born issues #1-3
(ISBN: 978-1-58240-899-6)
U.S.D. $17.99

WITCHBLADE

volume 6
collects issues #116-#120
(ISBN: 978-1-60706-041-3)
U.S.D. $14.99

RON MARZ • STJEPAN SEJIC
WITCHBLADE
VOLUME 7

volume 7
collects issues #121-#124 &
Witchblade Annual #1
(ISBN: 978-1-60706-058-1)
U.S.D. $14.99

RON MARZ • STJEPAN SEJIC
WITCHBLADE

volume 8
collects issues #125-#130
(ISBN: 978-1-60706-102-1)
U.S.D. $14.99

Collected works by J. Michael Straczynski from Top Cow Productions, Inc..

J. MICHAEL STRACZYNSKI'S
MIDNIGHT
NATION

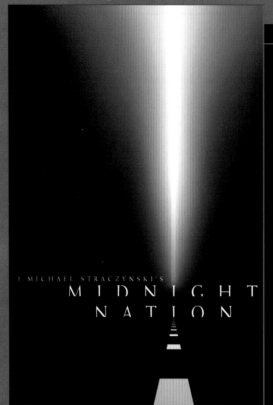

Midnight Nation

written by:
J. MIchael Straczynski
pencils by:
Gary Frank

When homicide detective David Grey's soul is stolen by a mysterious supernatural entity known only as The Other Guy, he falls through the cracks in the world to the place in-between, a shadow-world populated by the lost, the uncared-for and the thrown-away. To confront the entity and reclaim his soul, he must travel on foot from Los Angeles to New York accompanied by Laurel, a beautiful and engimatic woman who may be far more than she appears to be. Together they run a gauntlet of those determined to stop them, and along the way discover wonder, terror, beauty, danger and an unexpected love.

These editions include *Midnight Nation* #1-#12, along with the *Wizard* #1/2 issue and a spectacular cover gallery.

Softcover Edition
(ISBN: 978-1-58240-460-8) $24.99
Oversized Deluxe Edition w/poster & slipcase
(ISBN: 978-1-60706-040-6) $100.00

J. MICHAEL STRACZYNSKI'S
RISING
STARS
COMPENDIUM
VOLUME 1
FROM THE SCREENWRITER OF CHANGELING AND THE CREATOR OF BABYLON 5

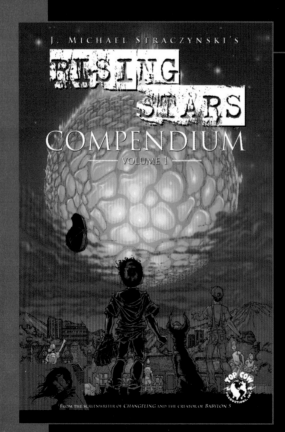

Rising Stars
Compendium vol.1

written by:
J. Michael Straczynski

pencils by:
Keu Cha, Ken Lashley
Gary Frank, Brent Anderson
and more!

The *Rising Stars* Compendium Edition collects the entire saga of the Pederson Specials, including the entire original series written by series creator **J. Michael Straczynski**, (*Supreme Power/Midnight Nation*) as well as the three limited series Bright, Voices of the Dead and Untouchable written by **Fiona Avery**, (*Amazing Fantasy/No Honor*).

Collects *Rising Stars* issues #0, #1/2, #1-24, Prelude, the short story "Initiations", the limited series *Bright* issues #1-3, *Voices of the Dead* issues #1-6 and *Untouchable* issues #1-5

SC (ISBN: 978-1-58240-802-6) $59.99
HC (ISBN: 978-1-58240-032-1) $99.99